GUEST EDITORIAL

Reclaiming the Integrity of Science in Expert Witnessing

Bruce D. Sales
University of Arizona

Daniel W. Shuman
Southern Methodist University

Scientific information is often of substantial importance to the courts in the resolution of disputes. For instance, scientific evidence can be used to assist the decision maker to decide the ultimate issue in the case, even though the science is not itself the ultimate issue. In a murder case, for example, when the defendant claims self-defense, the use of a psychological autopsy to suggest the victim's likely behavior addresses a mediate issue in the case (Shuman, 1986). The jury could believe the usefulness of the psychological autopsy and conclude that the defendant's use of force was justified or disbelieve the usefulness of the psychological autopsy and still conclude based on other evidence that the defendant's use of force was justified. However, because many courtroom observers think that experts who purport to present scientific information have special powers of persuasion, they fear that experts often shape the ultimate decision in the case, even when their testimony addresses only mediate issues. And, indeed, in many civil cases (i.e., professional malpractice, toxic torts, or products liability), the key to reaching the jury is the presentation of expert testimony on a mediate issue.

Scientific evidence can also be the ultimate issue in the case. For example, in a case claiming infringement of a biotechnology patent, the existence and uniqueness of the technology is the central, ultimate issue. The presentation of scientific evidence is critical in aiding the jury to determine if the patent was infringed.

Requests for reprints should be sent to Bruce D. Sales, Department of Psychology, University of Arizona, Tucson, AZ 85721.

Perhaps because of its importance to litigation and its frequent use, it is commonplace to hear complaints about the behavior of expert witnesses. Critics complain that many experts who testify abandon their scientific integrity and that the legal system stimulates this result. The intensity of these complaints can be traced to the importance of expert testimony to the law and to science. In regard to the former, the legal system's decision makers—judges and juries—are not chosen because they have any particular expertise in science in general or in the specific scientific questions presented in a specific case. Juries are composed of people who are thought to represent community values. However, they are asked to determine the facts, which requires assessing the credibility of an expert witness's scientific testimony. Judges are chosen because of their legal expertise. Yet, like juries, they also must always evaluate the expert and the proffered scientific testimony. Specifically, they must judge the admissibility of expert testimony in all trials and the credibility of experts and their testimony in bench trials. In addition, they are called on to determine if the proffered information rises to such a level that the court should take judicial notice of it, rather than requiring the parties to prove or disprove its value by traditional methods of proof; judicial notice may be taken whenever information is not subject to reasonable dispute. Thus, although numerous disputes come before the courts that require scientific information for their resolution, the courts (judges and juries) are not well suited to resolve them without specialized assistance.

In regard to science and to the extent that expert witnesses do not maintain the same rigorous standards that apply to their work outside of the courtroom, a slippery slope is presented justifying less than competent work in differentiated settings. Science is predicated on rigorous attention to theory building, hypothesis generation, operationalization of hypothetical constructs, research methodology, statistical analyses, and interpretation of the data. If scientists assume that less rigor is acceptable for tasks performed in the courtroom, it opens the door to similar compromises in other settings. At what point might it generalize to the scientific enterprise outside of the judicial context, for example, in interpreting the data and drawing conclusions?

Expert testimony can affect science in other ways as well. The citation to and discussion of science in the courtroom can influence public perception of the state and quality of science and its appropriate use. For example, consumer choices to use mental health services may be influenced by the portrayal of mental health professionals' expertise in the courtroom. These perceptions also filter through the political process and can influence funding availability and, concomitantly, the direction of scientific research and practice.

Independent of influencing perceptions and their consequences, incorporation of bad science into law can directly influence the course of science. For example, when an insufficiency or inadequacy of current scientific research to address a legal issue is identified in a case, there are numerous scientists ready to seek the answers that the court wanted (Sales & Simon, this issue).

Given the importance of expert testimony and the pool of competent attorneys and scientists, what explains the perceived problems with expert witnessing? An important reason lies in the inherent conflicts between the goals of attorneys and the goals of scientists/experts (Champagne, Shuman, & Whitaker, 1991; Sales & Simon, this issue). Because the legal system is an adversarial system and science is not, the goals of the attorneys and the goals of the scientist/experts differ. Attorneys need partisan experts to persuade the trier of fact (judge or jury), which weighs in favor of the selection of the most articulate, understandable, presentable, and persuasive expert rather than the best scientist. Even when there are good scientists who fit the bill, attorneys have a strong incentive to choose the person whose presentation and interpretation of the data is most sympathetic to the attorney's cause. As Champagne et al. (1991) noted in their empirical study of the use of experts, "lawyers seemingly want articulate, partisan experts with integrity" (p. 387).

Science, on the other hand, demands that scientists focus only on scientific knowledge without the influence—whether subtle or explicit—of the attorney's goals. Of equal concern is that the attorneys respond to current cases, which causes them to pressure experts to reach firm conclusions on the witness stand, even if the science on the issue and the scientific enterprise is tentative and iterative in nature or if the scientific information is unavailable (see Sales & Simon, this issue, for further explication of the causes of expert-witnessing problems).

Although the law has attempted to address some of these problems (e.g., through the rules of evidence and the cases interpreting them), its solutions have neither quieted the legal debate nor provided helpful guidance to the dilemmas scientists experience as expert witnesses (Sales & Simon, this issue). Thus, to the extent that scientists have placed their hopes for a resolution of this dilemma on the legal system, they have been disappointed. Perhaps the law should not be expected to be overly concerned about the needs of science given that it is not the law's focus; the law focuses on the resolution of disputes between parties.

Prior discussions of these problems by scientists are not terribly helpful. In the main, when those writings have focused on what scientists can do to address these problems, they have reflected the values of the individual author, rather than on a rule or principled analysis. The intervention of a rule or principled analysis could provide a systematic approach to generating insights and guidelines for solutions. To the extent that ethics governs all scientific and professional behavior—which it does—it is only appropriate that it become the first metric against which to judge the expert witnessing of scientists and professionals.

Although the problems of expert witnessing transcend the presentation of a particular type of scientific expert, focusing on the use of psychologists and other mental health professionals as expert witnesses provides important insights on this issue. The usefulness of their information is debated within and without the legal system, and they have not been spared criticism in the debate over the lost integrity of scientists as expert witnesses. In addition, because psychologists have a well-developed system of ethics that bears on their activities (see, e.g., Section 8.01 of the "Ethical Principles of Psychologists and Code of Conduct," American Psychological Association [APA], 1992, referred to hereafter as ethics code), an ethical analysis of expert testimony by psychologists is informative.

Perhaps the most obvious case of the applicability of the ethics code (APA, 1992) to expert witnessing is the obligation to be competent. Section 7.02(b) notes that ". . . psychologists provide . . . testimony of the psychological characteristics of an individual only after they have conducted an examination of the individual adequate to support their statements or conclusions." Section 7.02(c) notes: "When, despite reasonable efforts, such an examination is not feasible, psychologists clarify the impact of their limited information on the reliability and validity of their . . . testimony, and they appropriately limit the nature and extent of their conclusions." As Haas (this issue) notes, in the area of child custody evaluations and testimony, adherence to the ethics code would obviate some of the shoddy testimony introduced in child custody hearings. Too many cases are reported in which the psychologist did not evaluate one of the parties, but felt free to testify about both parties' qualifications to receive custody, without noting the limitations of the bases for their conclusions.

One area in which competence is particularly specified in the ethics code (APA, 1992) is testing (Butcher & Pope, this issue). The ethics code has numerous standards directly relevant to evaluation, assessment, or intervention that also must be considered when testifying about the results of such professional activity (e.g., Section 2). For example, the expert's time pressure to appear in court and the attorney's financial incentive to the expert to sway his or her testimony in favor of the hiring attorney/party may come into direct conflict with the admonitions to perform one's services competently (Section 2.02). In addition, this pressure and incentive may conflict with the ethics code's standard that the psychologist use techniques that are "appropriate [for the task] in light of the research on or evidence of the usefulness and proper application of the techniques" (Section 2.02[a]).

In some cases, the ethical standards do not directly speak to an issue, although they provide guidance in resolving the dilemma. Shuman (this issue), for example, considers the circumstance in which a court-ordered examiner provides a warning to the examinee about the purpose and potential use of the examination but then engages in therapeutic relationship building (i.e., incorporating the use of reflective empathy—the communication by the examiner to the examinee that they share the "quality of felt awareness" of the examinee's experiences) to obtain information during the assessment that could be inimicable to the examinee's legal interests. He argues that the use of reflective empathy, rather than receptive empathy (i.e., the perception and understanding of the experiences of another person), unethically manipulates and jeopardizes the rights of the examinee. Principle E of the ethics code (APA, 1992) states:

> Psychologists . . . perform their roles in a responsible fashion that avoids or minimizes harm. Psychologists are sensitive to real and ascribed differences in power between themselves and others, and they do not exploit or mislead other people during or after professional relationships.

How this duty compares with the duty to the community to provide full and accurate information in a forensic assessment is, however, unclear. If an ethical analysis is to be maximally useful in guiding the behavior of expert witnesses, future scholarship will need to attend to the following: (a) identify those difficult issues that defy a simple application of the current ethical mandates, (b) provide ethical analyses of these issues, and (c) provide to the scientist/professional specific behavioral guidance, perhaps in the form of commentary to the ethics code.

If a profession's ethical standards are not always clear, a person's interpretation of what is ethical may vary. Perhaps this is nowhere more likely to occur than when a psychologist's sense of social responsibility comes into play. Principle F of the ethics code (APA, 1992) facilitates this ambiguity by directing psychologists to be "aware of their professional and scientific responsibilities to the community and the society in which they work and live," but does not specify or enumerate these responsibilities. Nevertheless, some actions are clearly unethical in this domain, notwithstanding an individual conclusion to the contrary. The psychologist who testifies that an individual meets the state's commitment standard, knowing that this is not the case, is violating his or her social responsibility obligation, despite the psychologist's best intention to help the mentally ill person receive needed mental health services (Clark, this issue). As Principle F notes: "Psychologists try to avoid misuse of their work." In this case, the psychologist's concern for the individual's need for mental health services overshadowed the validity of his or her clinical judgment. In addition, the individual's actions thwarted the law's goal of protecting the right to be free from unwarranted government intrusion, despite Principle F's admonition that "psychologists comply with the law." If the psychologist believes that the law is inappropriate, the solution is not to act incompetently professionally, but to seek change in the law, "Psychologists encourage the development of law and policy that serve the interests of their patients and clients and the public" (Principle F).

Although we demonstrated how adherence to ethical guidelines can both improve the quality of testimony and reduce the ambiguity and frustration that psychologists feel when faced with working in the legal arena, there are still some issues that need to be addressed. For example, do researchers face the same or similar dilemmas that perplex or bedevil clinicians, and do they solve those dilemmas in similar ways? Pfeifer and Brigham's (this issue) article, although based on an informal survey of only researchers, suggests that the range of concerns and responses is similar. For example, researchers faced concerns about whether sufficient knowledge exists to testify about an issue and whether their testimony would be misused by the attorneys. The concerns of different types of experts and the decision making that they engage in when deciding to participate as expert witnesses are important issues that warrant further elaboration.

Finally, if expert witnesses rely on their respective ethics codes to guide their work, to what extent should society be satisfied with a professional organization or learned society's choice of ethical standards? How should its appropriateness or adequacy be judged? Clearly, some of these codes, and perhaps many, reflect political compromises rather than enlightened judgments about the public interest. One way to address this issue is to determine the rationale or principled basis that was used to construct these documents. Bersoff and Koeppl (this issue) show how an ethics code may exemplify fundamental moral principles, such as nonmalfeasance. Although agreement about and utilization of moral principles in the creation of ethics codes is likely to decrease inappropriate code provisions, it is a complex task to implement such a process. Scientists/professionals must agree on what are the appropriate moral principles, how they should be weighted in any given dilemma, how they should translate into ethical principles and standards, and how these standards should be weighted when applied to a particular dilemma.

Ethics codes, even if well developed, cannot address all professional actions, just as laws cannot anticipate all public and private behaviors that may warrant legal scrutiny. Professional guidelines and standards, beyond an ethics code, are needed to flesh out the open texturism of the codes. The "Specialty Guidelines for Forensic Psychologists" (Committee on Ethical Guidelines for Forensic Psychologists, 1991) was created to address this goal for forensic psychologists. Future scholarship will need to evaluate how well it conforms to and derives from the ethics code (APA, 1992), and how well it has succeeded in guiding professional behavior.

Finally, because membership in scientific/professional organizations is voluntary, a professional can avoid compliance with its ethics code by opting out of membership. In addition, for some types of expert witnesses, ethical codes do not yet exist, or if they exist, they are aspirational guidelines rather than mandatory standards or some combination of both, like the APA (1992) ethics code. In these situations, expert witnesses are left to use their own internal standards (Faust, this issue). The result is further exacerbation of the probability that expert testimony will be shoddy and reflect personal values and biases. Once again, the law and science suffer.

REFERENCES

American Psychological Association. (1992). *Ethical principles of psychologists and code of conduct.* Washington, DC: Author.

Champagne, A., Shuman, D. W., & Whitaker, E. (1991). The use of expert witnesses in American courts. *Judicature, 31,* 375–392.

Committee on Ethical Guidelines for Forensic Psychologists. (1991). Specialty guidelines for forensic psychologists. *Law and Human Behavior, 15,* 655–665.

Shuman, D. W. (1986). *Psychiatric and psychological evidence.* Colorado Springs: Shepard's/McGraw-Hill.

Institutional Constraints on the Ethics of Expert Testimony

Bruce D. Sales
University of Arizona

Leonore Simon
Temple University

We examined the dilemmas posed by the involvement of expert witnesses in court cases and the institutional constraints on the ethics of expert testimony. The causes for the incorporation of bad science into legal decisions, potential solutions to this dilemma, and the limitations of these solutions are considered. We concluded that law, science, and experts must respond to the problems posed by expert witnessing.

Key words: ethics, expert testimony, expert witness

A *Wall Street Journal* article chronicles how, for 40 years, the tobacco industry has used scientists to conduct studies for it establishing the absence of a link between cancer and the use of tobacco (Freedman & Cohen, 1993). These same scientists have also testified in court on behalf of tobacco companies defending against civil suits brought against them by smokers and tobacco users who have developed cancer. The authors describe these scientists as follows:

> In relying on such research, the tobacco industry is "exploiting the margins of science," contends Anthony Colucci, a former top researcher and later director of scientific litigation support at R.J. Reynolds. He offers an analogy: "There's a forest full of data that says tobacco kills people, and sitting on one tree is a lizard with a different biochemical and physiological makeup. The industry focuses on that lizard—that tiny bit of marginal evidence." (p. A6)

This story is only one of many that highlights the ethical dilemmas posed by the involvement of scientists and mental health professionals (referred to

---

Requests for reprints should be sent to Bruce D. Sales, Department of Psychology, University of Arizona, Tucson, AZ 85721.

hereinafter as scientists) in the legal system (see, e.g., "Brief," 1993). Yet, there is a long history of cases in which the courts seek scientific information to aid their decision making, make judgments as to what are the true scientific facts for the purpose of that case, and then create law partially based on these facts (e.g., Anderson & Winfree, 1987; Black, 1988; *Brown v. Board of Education,* 1954; Ennis & Litwack, 1974; Faigman, 1989; Gianelli, 1980; Loftus, 1986; Loftus & Monahan, 1980; Moenssens, 1984; Munsterberg, 1908; Osborne, 1990). If the proffered scientific evidence is invalid and/or unreliable, erroneous rulings and bad law can result (e.g., Christian, 1990; Faigman, 1986, 1989; Faust & Ziskin, 1988; Gianelli, 1980; Huber, 1991a, 1991b; Osborne, 1990; Saks, 1989, 1991).

This is a significant problem for the fields of law and science. To the extent that legal opinions must be based on facts, including scientific facts, and to the extent that the conclusions made about scientific matters may be invalid due to the misuse of science by scientists and lawyers (e.g., Champagne, Shuman, & Whitaker, 1991; Faust & Ziskin, 1988; Saks, 1991; Shuman, Whitaker, & Champagne, in press), the law will be compromised.[1] This problem is compounded by the fact that scientifically compromised judgments presented in legal proceedings can be used by lawyers and judges who look to prior appellate court decisions to support their conclusions about the validity and reliability of certain scientific testimony. Thus, a particular form of scientific testimony could gain legal acceptance without ever undergoing independent rigorous scientific or legal scrutiny. Indeed, once scientific judgments become part of the court's holding in a case, they take on precedential value and can be applied in analogous situations.[2] For example, consider the case of the admissibility of expert witness testimony on battered woman syndrome to establish self-defense in criminal cases in which women have killed their partners after a history of physical abuse. Most courts accept the admissibility of battered woman syndrome testimony in such cases (Ewing, 1987, cited in Faigman, 1987) with little scientific or legal scrutiny of its supporting research.

---

[1] One may argue that promoting desired policies or values is more important to the law than rendering decisions based on scientific facts. For example, in *Price Waterhouse v. Hopkins* (1989), the court admitted expert testimony about the nature of sexual stereotyping in sex discrimination litigation involving a woman denied partnership in a leading accounting firm. In cases such as these, it may be more important to increase the number of woman partners in large accounting firms than to ensure that the psychological findings about sexual stereotyping are validly applied to such real-life cases. It is not clear to what extent courts engage in this kind of legal politics. We expect, however, that it describes only a small percentage of the total number of cases.

[2] The holding typically consists of the application of the law to a particular set of facts. Once a fact is included in the court's holding, it becomes the law to be followed in similar future cases. This is in contrast to facts that may appear in the body of the opinion and are not included in the actual holding itself. These latter facts would possess no precedential value under the doctrine of *stare decisis.*

Faigman (1986, 1987) criticized the logic and methodology of the research on which such testimony is based, and he suggested that such expert witnesses may bias their research to comport with their testimony and theories.

Indeed, the law, including bad law, can affect the future course of science. For example, consider the history of the admissibility of expert witness testimony on the existence of rape trauma syndrome to show that a complainant did not consent to sexual behavior with an accused rape defendant. Such testimony was first held to be admissible in a 1982 Kansas Supreme Court case (*State v. Marks,* 1982). The *State v. Marks* decision was rationalized on the basis of a small number of studies that were methodologically flawed. Not surprising, at about the same time, the Minnesota Supreme Court decided that, except possibly in extraordinary cases in which the complainant is a child or mentally retarded, the rape trauma syndrome is inadmissible (*State v. Saldana,* 1982). Such disparity in judicial acceptance, combined with the visibility of the scientific issue, encouraged mental health researchers to conduct more studies to document the existence and breadth of rape trauma syndrome as a clinical entity. Thus, the goals of science and the direction and course of ensuing research in some cases can be influenced and subtly biased by the needs of litigants. The frequency of research being initiated at the request of litigants or potential litigants is significant enough that the Carnegie Commission on Science, Technology, and Government argued in an amicus brief before the U.S. Supreme Court that the lack of peer review of research should not be a barrier to its introduction into litigation ("Brief," 1992).

Given that scientific judgments can be and are being made by the law and that the development and use of scientific information will be affected by the law in the future, the rest of this article focuses on the causes of the incorporation of bad science in the law, the potential solutions to this dilemma, and the limitations of these solutions.

CAUSES FOR CONCERN

When scientists disagree in their daily work, it is typically for legitimate reasons. Scholars may have different theoretical and methodological orientations, existing research may not provide definitive answers, the same data can be interpreted in a variety of ways, the appropriateness of the sampling techniques may be disputed, the appropriateness of the statistics chosen may be open to question, and so forth. When scientists are acting as experts in litigation, however, the question is whether the disagreements among them, when they have been hired by opposing sides in the case, are legitimately based or if there are other reasons driving the divergence in their opinions (e.g., Epstein & Klein, 1987; Faigman, 1986; Graham, 1986; Shuman et al., in press). Consequently, scientists, lawyers, and policy makers need to concern themselves with the way the law seeks out and uses scientific information. In fact, as is discussed next, there are numerous problems with the use of scientific evidence presented by experts that are caused by characteristics of the legal process and the scientific enterprise.

To begin with, it is important to recognize that, in the majority of legal cases, the attorneys do not care about the discovery of scientific truth (or, arguably, any other type of truth or justice). Instead, they are concerned only with winning the case for their client. This means that they maximize the data and testimony that support their case and minimize those data and facts that conflict with their theory of the facts (e.g., Holden, 1989; Saks, 1990, 1993). If scientific information will help them achieve this goal, they will use it (Shuman et al., in press). They will also bend it, however, or selectively present the parts of it that suit their needs, even if the partial representation distorts the scientific truth.

This activity is neither illegal nor immoral for attorneys.

> The advocate's duty is to advance the most persuasive evidence and arguments on behalf of a client that can be done without perpetrating a fraud on the court. Presenting "biased" arguments and evidence in this endeavor not only is permitted, it generally is ethically required. This is part of what it means to be an advocate. (Saks, 1993, p. 5)

Although they cannot knowingly lie, lawyers are not required to present the whole truth. Rather, truth is supposed to emerge from the adversarial process, with each side presenting the strongest, biased case for their client. Even though in most cases the science is ancillary to the litigation, the scenario would not differ if the scientific issues were the focal point. Each side would still be obligated to present the best case in order to win for the client, even if the scientific truths became half truths in the process.

Given the lawyer's alliance with the client's interests, it should not be surprising that many lawyers actively seek an expert who will present evidence that supports the client's cause, not someone who may be the best advocate for the science (Shuman et al., in press). Indeed, lawyers go expert shopping until they find the right expert for their needs (e.g., Champagne et al., 1991; Shuman et al., in press). If an expert disagrees with the lawyer's view of the facts, he or she will not be hired to testify.

Finding the right experts often means indoctrinating them at the outset. As Saks and Van Duizend (1983, p. 73) aptly put it, "it is probably not correct to say that experts can be bought, but proper to say they can be sold—by the same professional advocates who will have to sell the case to judges and juries." Although lawyers often do not tell the experts what to say for fear that this information can be revealed during cross examination, the lawyers manage to convey the message to the experts by giving them briefs and motions to read and by sharing with them their theories of the facts of case. Empirical studies suggest that lawyers and experts are not always so discreet. For example, there is evidence that lawyers frequently coach experts and that experts are generally receptive to being coached (Champagne et al., 1991; Shuman et al., in press). This process can, and in many cases probably does, lead experts to present something less than scientific truth (e.g., Shuman et al., in press). Indeed lawyers' interests in winning for their respective clients can lead to the hiring of experts whose sole job is to help the retaining lawyer discredit the opposing expert and the expert's testimony. Consequently, it is not uncommon for litigation to deteriorate into a battle of the experts (where experts can become adversaries) instead of remaining neutral and propounding truly scientific ideas.

Perhaps a larger problem is the lack of a scientifically appropriate definition of an expert in the law. For example, according to Rule 702 of the Federal Rules of Evidence (1974),

> If scientific, technical, of other specialized knowledge will assist the trier of fact to understand the evidence or to determine a fact in issue, a witness qualified as an expert by knowledge, skill, experience, training, or education may testify thereto in the form of a opinion or otherwise. (p. 91)

In addition, Rule 104 of the Federal Rules of Evidence requires the court to make a preliminary determination of the expert's qualifications and an analysis of whether such testimony aids the trier of fact.

The threshold for what constitutes the requisite specialized knowledge or skills and the consequent threshold for admitting expert testimony is so low that virtually anyone with some knowledge beyond that of the average juror might qualify (e.g., Brief of the Group of American Law Professors, 1992). And this determination of an expert witness's competency is discretionary with the court (e.g., *Shipp v. General Motors Corp.,* 1985). Some commentators suggested that judges applying the admissibility standards merely check the credentials of the experts, confusing experts with expertise (e.g., Sales, Shuman, & O'Connor, in press), thereby increasing the probability of misrepresenting untested biases as science. This has been partially corroborated empirically by a study finding that judges do not use criteria measuring expertise in the scientific community to qualify expert witnesses (Shuman et al., in press). Thus, the first-year PhD's testimony could be admitted in the same trial in opposition to the seasoned senior scholar's testimony, or the young scholar who is truly an expert on a particular topic could be challenged by a senior person who stopped being productive 20 years earlier. There is also nothing in the rules to prevent the PhD with training in one area from becoming the lawyer's expert on an entirely different matter, despite the fact that one of the characteristics of expertise is that it is task specific, with very little transfer from high-level proficiency in one area to proficiency in another area (Bedard & Chi, 1992). Conversely, the lack of operational standards for defining experts that judges follow can lead to true experts not being admitted to testify. In a case involving the use of excessive force by police officers, an expert on police administration and field procedures was deemed by the judge to possess no expertise beyond matters of common sense (J. Fyfe, personal communication, February 23, 1993).

Even with a definition of expert that scientists would find more appropriate, the problem with the law's use of experts would still be substantial. For instance, how does the lawyer find an appropriate expert? A seemingly simple problem can pose an enormous obstacle for the uninitiated. It is relatively easy for scientists to call a few colleagues and identify 6 experts on a topic, but the typical lawyer would not know who to start calling. This should not be surprising. Can the typical scientist identify the 6 best lawyers in any of the numerous subareas of law?

Finally, although the lawyer will find some scientist to act as the expert, most lawyers are simply not knowledgeable about who is a true expert on a particular topic—at least from the scientists' point of view. When you combine this fact with the lawyer's obligation to present the best case for winning his or her client's cause, it is easy to see why lawyers would choose as experts those individuals who would support the position of their clients and be maximally persuasive to the judge or jury—and not necessarily choose the most knowledgeable or ethical scientists on the matter.

Scientists are not innocent parties in this scenario. Part of the reason for this lies in the distinction between the type of and sophistication of the expertise needed. The law may ask for two types of information from the expert: *adjudicative facts*—facts that are used in determining whether an event relevant to a specific case occurred; and *legislative facts*—facts that transcend the particular dispute, are used to create or modify a rule of law, and establish the factual assumptions on which fundamental questions of law are decided (Davis, 1942). For instance, in a child custody dispute, psychological testimony that Parent A was more fit to rear the child than Parent B would constitute evidence of an adjudicative fact. In the same type of case, expert testimony opining that the presence of mothers are considered by psychologists to be more important than fathers to the healthy psychological development of a child would be evidence of a legislative fact. Clearly, the level of scientific sophistication required to address each type of knowledge can vary from the relatively mundane to state of the art. Yet, experts typically are not rigorously prequalified by the attorney for their ability to handle these types of problems or for their ability to engage in various levels of sophistication in analysis.

What will stop a scientist from being honest with the lawyer and the factfinder about the limits of his or her expertise? Obviously, some scientists are poor monitors of their own inadequacies. These scientists would assume that they are doing a competent job for science when they are not. As for other scientists, there is no justifiable reason why their limitations are not made clear to the attorneys and why they play a compromised role. Unfortunately, most scientists do not apply the same rigor in the decision-making process when deciding to be experts and when acting as experts as they do when deciding to engage in or when conducting research.[3] In addition, when conducting research, the scientist has to prove every assertion; when in a legal setting, scientists can earn quick money with opinion testimony rather than established fact. One can see how the witness can wind up advocating for values and biases rather than empirical fact. Indeed, some experts want this to happen because they rely on their ideological commitments as the basis for their testimony rather than premising it on scientific fact.

Yet, the adversarial nature of the litigation should make the scientist want to be a real expert if he or she hopes to survive the rigors of cross examination and be a persuasive advocate for the scientific facts (e.g., *Daubert v. Merrell Dow Pharmaceuticals, Inc.,* 1991). Unfortunately, the scientist may not realize the significance of legal testimony to the parties involved and society, appreciate the rigors of the adversarial process, or have the time or motivation to prepare for the task in a way that would ensure expert testimony.

The fact that many experts may not make the same commitment to a lawsuit as they do to their research is not surprising. Testifying is a burden that almost always supplements the existing workload, not supplants it. For research scientists, there is typically no reward from their university or comparable employer for testifying. If anything, it is looked down on or simply tolerated. And even if there is the time, the consultant's salary typically does not justify expending significant effort in preparation to ensure that the scientific information is state of the art. When the fee is lucrative, scientists are subtly and sometimes not so subtly pressured to bias testimony to conform to the needs of the attorney—that is, if they wish to maintain their consulting role and fees in the case and build a reputation that will bring in other similar consultantships. In some cases, it may not be the lack of time or money that is the difficulty. Instead, it may be the attorney's fault for not impressing on the expert the need for meticulous preparation and exacting accuracy. Nevertheless, this fact does not excuse the scientist from performing their services in a slipshod manner.

Unfortunately, the genuine concern of some scientists with the inadequacies of the adversarial process and their inability, for whatever reason, to cope with it lead them not to become experts. To them, the lack of preparation time, the

---

[3]It is possible that the rigor is similar, which might partially explain why our journals are not filled with brilliant scholarship.

lack of money to justify their time for preparing, the apparent lack of concern of the lawyers for the whole scientific truth, and/or the potential for manipulation on the witness stand by attorneys on both sides make opting out a rational choice. Yet, that decision weakens the quality of the expert pool and negatively influences the overall quality of expert information presented when we look across all cases.

The decision not to participate also may be stimulated by concern that the science has not progressed far enough to provide information that should guide policy decisions or be used in settling disputes (Sechrest, 1985). Opting out in this case seems sensible. Yet, for every scientist who chooses this path, there are several others waiting to jump in—whether it be ego related, for money, or due to a genuine misguided belief that they have something to contribute. As some lawyers are likely to note, the scientific community has its share of "whores." The result, once again, is that the legal system tends toward accepting bad science and making bad law in those cases in which scientific information is at issue.

Finally, we need to spend a moment focusing on the finder of fact (i.e., the judge, or jury if there is one). If the opposing side is not appropriately prepared, the factfinder could be easily swayed by one side's expert testimony—no matter how poorly it may represent scientific facts (Osborne, 1990). For example, many of the police experts in this country make a living by testifying in isolated, small town courts, where scholarly or professional expertise does not exist (J. Fyfe, personal communication, February 23, 1993). Even if both sides are prepared, how is the judge or jury to decide what are the true scientific facts when a battle between diametrically opposed experts ensues? Moreover, the factfinder's power to discern the truth is seriously hampered whenever scientific information is being presented. These individuals are not required to have scientific training and, thus, cannot be judging the scientific evidence on its technical merits. Rather, they must be relying on their (mis)perceptions of its scientific accuracy and/or on extraneous grounds such as the impressiveness of an expert's credentials or demeanor (Brodsky, 1991) and the ability of an expert to communicate their opinions in a nontechnical fashion and reach firm conclusions (Champagne et al., 1991).

ARE THERE REMEDIES?

The potential causes for concern in the way the law often seeks and uses scientific input and in the way scientists often provide such information create a disturbing portrait—one that should not be ignored. What are the potential remedies?

Revising the Law and Restructuring the Legal Process

An obvious approach to minimizing current concerns would be to revise the law relating to expert witnesses. Changing the definition of expert and the standard for the admissibility of scientific information (Sales et al., in press) are logical places to begin. Unfortunately, changing these dimensions is difficult because by tightening the requirements for the admissibility of an expert, for example, we would be tampering with the factfinder's need for access to information. The law has traditionally favored freer access while relying on the factfinder's prerogative to assess the credibility of the witness and the presented information. This is particularly appropriate for cases that require less sophisticated analysis by the expert, but it is inappropriate for cases involving more sophisticated scientific issues. Future scholarship should reconsider the rules of admissibility for expert witnesses by focusing the distinction between clinical and actuarially based expert testimony (Sales et al., in press) and by evaluating the expert in light of the issue and sophistication of the analysis relating to the issue, which will be the focus of the expert's testimony.

Changing standards for the admissibility of the scientific information also is problematic partly because scientists do not always agree on what is acceptable science. Editors of scientific journals know how frequently reviewers disagree on the merits of a manuscript! One approach that should be considered, however, is to focus on the pragmatic considerations that the court would use when implementing the admissibility standard. For example, the U.S. Supreme Court in *Daubert v. Merrell Dow Pharmaceutical, Inc.* (1993) suggested a number of these considerations (e.g., determining whether the proffered scientific information has been subjected to peer review) for implementing the admissibility standard in federal cases. Although it is beyond the scope of this article to explore the decision (see, e.g., Sales et al., in press), suffice it to say that tightening the implementation of pragmatic considerations can go a long way toward gaining precision in the broad legal standard. Scientists could be helpful in the process of specifying these pragmatic considerations.

Another logical focus for change would be on improving the factfinder's ability to adequately assess the credibility of experts and the validity of the assertions they utter on the witness stand. One innovation that warrants attention would be to use a Special Master (a representative of the court, e.g., Rule 53 of the Federal Rules of Civil Procedure) to make findings regarding the scientific facts. Special Masters are often used in complex litigation, which pose some similarities to the cases that involve complex scientific matters. These Special Masters could be selected for their knowledge of the scientific matters under controversy, or they might be a panel of such people rather than an individual. An obvious practical limitation of this innovation is that it would limit the lawyer's opportunity to influence a jury directly through the experts. Thus, some and perhaps many lawyers who rely on experts to successfully conduct their cases might oppose such a change. Using a panel of Special Masters might also raise the issue of improperly usurping the jury's function as factfinder. Despite the potential obstacles, who is better to judge the quality and value of science than scientists?

There are ways to provide expertise to the judge if he or she is the factfinder in the case. Encouraging judges to use independent, neutral, nonwitness, expert consultants to advise them directly is a possibility worth exploring (e.g., *Reilly v. United States,* 1988; Spencer, 1991; also see the next subsection). The limitations of this approach are the restricted circumstances under which the law allows the use of these experts, the reluctance of many judges to use them, and the difficulty courts might have in selecting appropriate individuals to be such experts.

In addition to providing judges with independent experts, special protocols could be developed that spell out in detail the substance and sequence of questions a judge should ask lawyers and experts when faced with particularly complex or arcane scientific evidence. For example, the Federal Judicial Center is developing such a protocol to assist judges with the use of specific types of scientific evidence such as DNA evidence. Such an approach has merit, but questions alone are unlikely to solve the problems of poor science in the courtroom unless the protocols are detailed, available for all scientific issues, and used by the judiciary and bar on a regular basis.

Finally, judges could provide cautionary instructions to jurors about the content and limits of the scientific knowledge. These instructions have already been accepted by some courts (see, e.g., *State v. Long,* 1986; *United States v. Telfaire,* 1972). This is another area in which ethical scientists can aid the court (i.e., by aiding in the development of the content of these instructions).

A Role for Scientific Organizations

Whatever the effects of changing the law and legal process, solving problems of bad science being introduced through expert testimony is not likely to occur without the efforts of the scientific community. One action that should be considered is having professional scientific organizations (e.g., the American Psychological Association [APA], the American Psychological Society, and the American Association for the Advancement of Science) take an active role by providing experts to the legal system, reviewing for accuracy the scientific information that is presented, and evaluating the validity of the scientific assumptions that courts make when reaching their decisions. Although it sounds like a sensible beginning to solving a major problem, the solution is fraught with problems.

Scientific organizations would have difficulty designating who are the true experts on any given topic. For instance, who defines the level of expertise that is needed for each case? Lawyers are typically unsophisticated in the given scientific topic unless they have been handling cases in the area for several years. Scientists in the professional organization would have difficulty with successfully taking on this role because they are not familiar with the law or the nuances of the questions that the law would be asking. In many cases, it would take a scientist working with a lawyer to help define how much expertise is truly needed for each case—a time-consuming, cumbersome, and costly procedure. If this procedure was not followed, however, the criteria for inclusion on a list might remain vague or "loose," and this may result in as wide a disparity in the qualifications of the included experts, as is currently the case with the experts lawyers choose. Even if the impossible happened and such a list could be created for each case, there are practical difficulties that would need to be surmounted. For instance, a large number of talented people cannot translate scientific information in ways that are clear to jurors or deal aptly with cross-examination. It would be very difficult for a professional association to determine in advance whether someone it recommended was up to this task. Without making such an assessment, the expert could damage a lawyer's case.

If these problems do not kill the enterprise, political infighting about who should be included would likely paralyze the selection process. In fact, given the proliferation of scientific and professional organizations, it seems reasonable to conclude that competing scientific groups would try to offer the service with different individuals and different standards of practice. It is important to address the issue of value neutrality in science when allowing scientific organizations to provide experts for the legal system. In addition, some professional experts form professional organizations precisely for this purpose—to sell services rather than ensure expertise.

Conversely, the adversarial nature of lawyers and the legal system would encourage and indeed compel lawyers to seek experts who were willing to present information favorable to their cause. If such experts were not on the organization's list, lawyers would seek them elsewhere. Although a jury might hear about the approved list during the qualification of the expert, it is not at all clear that they would be substantially influenced by this fact. There also would be horrendous logistical problems in matching experts to legal cases. For instance, if the experts are all on the east coast and the case is in South Dakota, what will induce the lawyer to pay the additional cost of securing the services of the out-of-state expert? Extra lead time also may be required to select and match experts to a case. In some cases, the timeframe could be prohibitive. Finally, even if these problems could be solved, antitrust law might prohibit some forms of the activity. A private entity would create a restrictive list of people who provide services and encourage the consumers of those services to contract only with those people. There are ways around creating a legal monopoly that would need to be carefully explored.

Perhaps the scientific organization could play a role in reviewing for accuracy the scientific information that is to be presented in cases. At the trial level, there would be significant barriers to implementing this service. Although both parties might want the service if they could afford it and if it could be used to discredit the other side's expert and expert testimony, they would not want the service if it would be used to discredit their own witnesses. Because they could not be sure of the organization's stance until they hired it to look at the facts, the attorneys might be leery of hiring the organization for fear that this decision could backfire on them.

Even if the lawyers did not fear this possibility, for whom would the organization work—the plaintiff/prosecutor, the defense, or the court? The attorneys are not likely to accept a situation in which the organization worked for both sides. Assuming both sides asked for its services, should the organization work for the side with the best experts and help them discredit the opposing side or work with the side with the weaker experts and educate them about what are the scientific facts? The choice is not an obvious one.

There is also the possibility that such an organization could work for a neutral body such as the court. By having the court employ the experts (e.g., Rule 706 of the Federal Rules of Evidence, 1974; *Students of California School for the Blind v. Honig,* 1984) recommended by the organization, the argument that experts are advocates could be weakened; but this presumes that the organization and its recommended experts are truly unbiased, which may not be accurate. In addition, as already noted, courts infrequently use such neutral experts.

Assuming the service was made available, there are three important limitations of its impact. First, the organization could not force its service on parties that did not solicit its help. As a result, many will not use the service—at least for years to come. Second, for those cases that do come to the organization, there could be too many for the organization to handle competently without compromising the quality of its work or encouraging scientists to give up science and become professional experts. This option is self-defeating because once the scientists become the expert–entrepreneurs, they may compromise their scientific ethics to keep clients happy and to ensure a steady flow of business. Hence, the service's quality may deteriorate over time. Third, there may not be a definitive scientific answer for the issues in the case. Rather, scientists may legitimately disagree. Yet, the judge or jury must find for one side. The legal system will not accommodate the postponement of a decision until more research on the matter is conducted.

Scientific organizations might become involved at the appellate court level as well (e.g., through the drafting and submission of amicus briefs). We do not discuss this possibility because it raises similar issues to those just discussed. In addition, this type of activity is already occurring, and experience has shown that such briefs are submitted in a minuscule number of cases.

Finally, the scientific organization might research the way experts and scientific information are selected and used in litigation. Research needs to shed light on (a) the decisions lawyers make when selecting experts and the decisions scientists make when agreeing to be an expert; (b) the communications that transpire between the lawyer and the scientist and the effect that these interactions have on the scientist's behaviors when acting as an expert; and (c) the match between the scientist chosen to be the expert, the type of social fact question being addressed, the level of sophistication in scientific analysis that would be required to address the issue accurately, the type of preparation that the scientist undertakes in preparing for the task, and the resultant expert testimony that the scientist provides. Such data is essential if we are to document the extent and contours of the problem, develop scientifically sound causal explanations for the observed behaviors, and propose reasonable approaches for remediating the difficulties. The findings of such work will provide the foundation for legal change and for convincing the legal system of its necessity. Although this activity can stimulate long-term solutions, it does not address the dilemma of bad science being introduced into current cases.

Public Scrutiny of Testimony

In science, it is typically assumed that the pressure peers exert when they scrutinize and offer criticism of another's scholarly work helps ensure appropriate scientific behavior. If true, this suggests that we should try to make scientific testimony in litigation readily available for peer review (e.g., M. Cataldo, personal communication, August 16, 1986). Perhaps a journal devoted to such testimony—which publishes information on the issue addressed, the testimony given by the experts, the court's conclusions, and critical peer commentary—would encourage more expert behaviors by scientists when testifying. Traditional specialty journals also might consider publishing such material when the topic of a case warrants it. And professional scientific organizations might become involved in this work (American Psychiatric Association's Council on Psychiatry and Law, 1992).

Although this proposal has merit, the scientific testimony and court's conclusions would be prohibitively long in some cases for a traditional-size journal to publish. A possible solution would be to go to a larger but less costly publishing format, but these formats may drive down what may already be a small readership, making the venture financially unfeasible. In addition, the resources necessary to monitor effectively and evaluate the work of even a majority of expert witnesses would be prohibitive, and there are many more relevant cases than a journal could economically publish. On the other hand, even if this approach is used selectively, it might still have a sobering effect on future expert witnesses and testimony, and such reviews could provide the basis for inquiries into members' ethical violations.

Ethical Principles

Any solution that focuses purely on external controls of the expert is unlikely to be fully successful. Attention must be drawn to modifying the expert's behavior such that the concerns addressed in this article do not occur. A dramatic improvement in the quality of expert testimony could occur if experts reflected on their ethical obligations prior to becoming experts witnesses.

For example, Principle A of the *Ethical Principles of Psychologists and Code of Conduct* (APA, 1992) admonishes psychologists to recognize the boundaries of their competencies and the limitations of their expertise. If an expert witness has not kept up with the literature and testifies using out-of-date information, he or she would be violating the responsibility to be competent. And what of clinical psychologists who testify on a topic without training in the area? The issue of competence becomes salient once again.

Principle B of the ethical principles (APA, 1992) suggests that psychologists should promote integrity in psychology. Is the integrity benefitted or harmed by psychologists who assume the hired gun role or advocate their personal values, rather than presenting scientific knowledge? Advocacy that is one sided and intentionally presented to aid the client rather than present accurate scientific information runs afoul of this principle.

Manipulating testimony to achieve a personal goal might also run afoul of Principle F of the ethical principles (APA, 1992). It admonishes psychologists to apply their knowledge to contribute to and improve the society in which they live and work. For example, some testimony on the battered woman syndrome that passes for expertise involves expert witnesses who misuse their profession by failing to raise the existence of professional criticism about the accuracy of the diagnostic classification (e.g., Vidmar & Schuller, 1989). Such expert testimony would thus constitute a violation of the social responsibility ethic.

Similar examples can be found in the ethical standards that set down enforceable rules for conduct. For example, Ethical Standard 1.04 (APA, 1992) mandates that psychologists perform only within their area of competence, whereas Ethical Standard 1.05 requires psychologists to keep abreast of current scientific information to maintain their competence.

Clearly, ethical principles and standards are important to proscribe certain behaviors. But perhaps most important, if studied and applied regularly and consistently in the normal course of activities, ethical principles and standards provide the impetus for potential expert witnesses to evaluate (a) their decision to participate, (b) the way in which they will prepare for participation, and (c) the way in which they will participate. This self-reflection can improve the quality of expert witnessing.

The use of ethical principles and standards is not without its limits however. By their very nature, ethics documents do not specifically address all issues and conundrums that experts will face in the courtroom. Indeed, ethical principles are typically broadly drawn so that they can be applied to a wide variety of behaviors. For example, Ethical Standard 1.16 (APA, 1992) prohibits psychologists from participating in activities in which their skills or knowledge are misused by others unless corrective mechanisms are available. Does this standard place a duty on psychologists to take reasonable steps to ensure that their testimony is not distorted even by the side that hired them? A potential solution is for the ethical principles to be supplemented by practice standards, such as the "Specialty Guidelines for Forensic Psychologists" (Committee on Ethical Guidelines for Forensic Psychologists, 1991). But whether this document or other practice standards comprehensively address the issues of concern will have to await further analysis (see Sales & Shuman, this issue). In addition, if not adopted by the entire organization, such standards will have limited applicability. For example, the specialty guidelines was adopted by the American Psychology–Law Society/a Division of the APA. As such, it is applicable to the approximately 1,500 members of this division but not the remaining members of the APA.

There are other limitations as well. Standards of practice, including ethical principles and standards, do not guarantee excellence. They only institutionalize the minimum level of acceptable performance—competence. Competence in some court cases may not be sufficient when people's lives and/or property are at stake, particularly if we take our social responsibility ethic seriously. How then would ethical principles specify the expertise needed for different types of cases? A uniform standard may be too low in some cases and too high in others. The ethical principles should focus on the necessity of having requisite skills and engaging in a process of competent preparation to meet the demands of a task. But future writings will need to explore the mechanics of implementing such an approach.

Finally, even if someone's behavior violated the ethical principles and standards, sanctioning the scientist would be a problem. Although the scientific organization that promulgated the ethical principles could enforce them, it could only do so against members. If scientists chose to drop out of the organization, the organization cannot force its rules on them. Even if violators maintained membership, sanctioning the majority of them is unlikely. It takes significant resources to identify and investigate potential violations, hold hearings to give potential violators an opportunity to present their side of the facts, and implement corrective interventions.

Another solution would be to enforce ethical principles and standards through malpractice actions; the principles could be used to designate the acceptable level of practice to which the scientist–consultant would have to adhere. However, expert witness immunity might prevent potential malpractice claims (e.g., *Bruce v. Byrne-Stevens & Associates Engineers, Inc.,* 1989). Even if permissible, the difficulty of this approach is that there would not be a party who would be likely to sue the scientist and have legal standing to do so. The scientist's employer—the lawyer and the client—would not sue if the scientist's testimony included what they hoped to hear; if the scientist was not going to support the lawyer and client's cause, he or she would not have been retained after the initial interview or would not appear in court. The other side would be unlikely to sue because malpractice actions require that the wrongdoer owe the complaining party a duty to adhere to a certain standard. Because the scientist was hired by the opposing side, the duty would be owed to that side. Some creative lawyering might get the courts to make certain that experts understand that they have a duty to both parties to perform competently on the argument that not to do so would hamper the factfinding process in trials or perhaps perpetrate a fraud on the court. We know of no cases that have considered this issue, however, and would not be optimistic that it would be a winning argument.

The truly injured party is an amorphous one—science, most likely as embodied in one of its scientific organizations. Yet, the scientific organization would not have standing to sue. And even if one did, it is unlikely that an organization would use this approach in any but the most flagrant cases because to do so might open up to question and public scrutiny the competence of the professional behaviors of all members.

CONCLUSION

Clearly, from the foregoing discussion, there are numerous avenues in both law and science that can be pursued to ameliorate the problems posed by the law's use of expert witnesses. The most successful approach probably best lies in a multifaceted attack—one that focuses on the institutional structures of law and science, as well as on modifying the behavior of scientists. In this article, we posited and explored many of the options.

Despite our articulation of the difficulties that are likely to arise in implementing them, most are realistic possibilities, with appropriate planning and justification. For example, subjecting expert testimony to peer review and ethical scrutiny, even if done selectively, would stimulate critical thinking about the desirability of certain behaviors on the part of experts in the courtroom and would change some experts' behaviors. Unfortunately, page limitations preclude a more detailed exploration of these and other solutions and implementing mechanisms, but the guideposts have been clearly marked.

At the same time, we need to educate potential experts about the importance of ethical behavior in the courtroom and about how the ethical principles relate to behavioral choices. This effort should be complemented by a consideration of other professional standards, but it would be greatly enhanced by further articulation of the official position of the APA (and other scientific organizations depending on the discipline of the expert) in regard to how the ethical principles should be interpreted when the scientist is serving as the expert witness.

ACKNOWLEDGMENTS

This article is based on Bruce D. Sales's Presidential Address to the American Psychology–Law Society/A Division of the American Psychological Association (APA). It was presented at the 1986 annual meeting of the APA. Recent citations are included even if the point being asserted in the text was made in the Presidential Address prior to the publication of these other articles. We thank James Fyfe, Maureen O'Connor, Kenneth Pope, and Daniel Shuman for their insightful comments on prior drafts.

REFERENCES

American Psychiatric Association's Council on Psychiatry and Law. (1992). Peer review of psychiatric expert testimony. *Bulletin of the American Academy of Psychiatry and Law, 20,* 343–352.

American Psychological Association. (1992). Ethical principles of psychologosits and code of conduct. *American Psychologist, 47,* 1597–1611.

Anderson, P. R., & Winfree, L. T. (1987). *Expert witnesses: Criminologists in the courtroom.* Albany: State University of New York Press.

Bedard, J., & Chi, M. T. H. (1992). Expertise. *Current Directions in Psychological Science, 1,* 135–139.

Black, B. (1988). Evolving legal standards for the admissibility of scientific evidence. *Science, 239,* 1508–1512.

Brief of the American Association for the Advancement of Science and the National Academy of Sciences as amici curiae in support of Merrell Dow Pharmaceuticals, Inc. Submitted to the U.S. Supreme Court in *Daubert v. Merrell Dow Pharmaceuticals, Inc.* (January 19, 1993).

Brief of the Carnegie Commission on Science, Technology, and Government as amicus curiae in support of neither party. Submitted to the U.S. Supreme Court in *Daubert v. Merrell Dow Pharmaceuticals, Inc.* (December 2, 1992).

Brief of the Group of American Law Professors as amicus curiae in support of neither party. Submitted to the U.S. Supreme Court in *Daubert v. Merrell Dow Pharmaceuticals, Inc.* (December 2, 1992).

Brodsky, L. (1991). *Testifying in court.* Washington, DC: American Psychological Association.

Brown v. Board of Education, 347 U.S. 483 (1954).

Bruce v. Byrne-Stevens & Associates Engineers, Inc., 776 P.2d 666 (Wash. 1989).

Champagne, A., Shuman, D., & Whitaker, E. (1991). An empirical examination of the use of expert witnesses in American courts. *Jurimetrics Journal, 31,* 375–392.

Christian, V. (1990). Admissability of scientific expert testimony: Is bad science making law? *Northern Kentucky Law Review, 18,* 21–40.

Committee on Ethical Guidelines for Forensic Psychologists. (1991). Specialty guidelines for forensic psychologists. *Law and Human Behavior, 15,* 655–665.

Daubert v. Merrell Dow Pharmaceuticals, Inc., 951 F.2d 1128 (9th Cir. 1991).
Daubert v. Merrell Dow Pharmaceuticals, Inc., 113 S.Ct. 2786 (1993).
Davis, K. C. (1942). An approach to problems of evidence in the administrative process. *Harvard Law Review, 55*, 364–402.
Ennis, B., & Litwack, T. (1974). Psychiatry and the presumption of expertise: Flipping coins in the courtroom. *California Law Review, 62*, 693–751.
Epstein, B. M., & Klein, M. S. (1987). The use and abuse of expert testimony in product liability actions. *Seton Hall Law Review, 17*, 656.
Faigman, D. L. (1986). The battered woman syndrome and self-defense: A legal and empirical dissent. *Virginia Law Review, 72*, 619–647.
Faigman, D. L. (1987). Discerning justice when battered women kill: Review essay. *Hastings Law Journal, 39*, 207–227.
Faigman, D. L. (1989). To have and have not: Assessing the value of social science to the law as science and policy. *Emory Law Journal, 38*, 1006–1095.
Faust, D., & Ziskin, J. (1988). The expert witness in psychology and psychiatry. *Science, 241*, 31–35.
Federal Rules of Civil Procedure.
Federal Rules of Evidence.
Freedman, A. M., & Cohen, L. P. (1993, February 11). How cigarette makers keep health question "open" year after year. *Wall Street Journal*, pp. A1–A6.
Gianelli, P. (1980). The admissability of novel scientific evidence: *Frye v. United States*, a half a century later. *Columbia Law Review, 80*, 1197.
Graham, M. H. (1986). Expert witness testimony and the Federal Rules of Evidence: Insuring adequate assurance of trustworthiness. *University of Illinois Law Review*, 43–90.
Holden, C. (1989). Science in court. *Science, 243*, 1658–1659.
Huber, P. W. (1991a). *Galileo's revenge: Junk science in the courtroom.* New York: Basic Books.
Huber, P. W. (1991b). Medical experts and the ghost of Galileo. *Law and Contemporary Problems, 54*, 119.
Loftus, E. F. (1986). Ten years in the life of an expert witness. *Law and Human Behavior, 10*, 241–263.
Loftus, E. F., & Monahan, J. (1980). Trial by data: Psychological research as legal evidence. *American Psychologist, 35*, 270.
Moenssens, A. (1984). Admissability of scientific evidence—An alternative to the Frye rule. *William and Mary Law Review, 25*, 545.
Munsterberg, H. (1908). *On the witness stand: Essays on psychology and crime.* New York: Doubleday.
Osborne, J. W. (1990). Judicial/technical assessment of novel scientific evidence. *University of Illinois Law Review*, 497–546.
Price Waterhouse v. Hopkins, 825 F.2d 458 (D.C. Cir. 1987), *cert. granted*, 108 S.Ct. 1106 (1988), 109 S.Ct. 1775 (1989).
Reilly v. United States, 863, F.2d 149 (1st Cir. 1988).
Saks, M. J. (1989). Prevalence and impact of ethical problems in forensic science. *Journal of Forensic Sciences, 34*, 772–793.
Saks, M. J. (1990). Expert witnesses, nonexpert witnesses, and nonwitness experts. *Law and Human Behavior, 14*, 291–313.
Saks, M. J. (1991). What DNA "fingerprinting" can teach the law about the rest of forensic science. *Cardozo Law Review, 13*, 361–372.
Saks, M. J. (1993). Improving APA science translation amicus briefs. *Law and Human Behavior.*
Saks, M. J., & Van Duizend, R. (1983). *Scientific evidence in litigation.* Williamsburg, VA: National Center for State Courts.

Sales, B. D., Shuman, D. W., & O'Connor, M. (in press). "Ah yes, I remember it well": Admissibility of child sexual abuse memories. *Applied Cognitive Psychology*.

Sechrest, L. (1985). Social science and social policy: Will our numbers ever be good enough? In R. L. Shotland & M. M. Marks (Eds.), *Social science and social policy* (pp. 63–95). Beverly Hills: Sage.

Shipp v. General Motors Corp., 750 F.2d 418, 422 (5th Cir. 1985).

Shuman, D. W., Whitaker, E., & Champagne, A. (in press). An empirical examination of the use of expert witnesses in the courts—Part II: A three city study. *Jurimetrics Journal*.

Spencer, J. R. (1991). The neutral expert: An implausible bogey. *Criminal Law Review*, 106–110.

State v. Long, 721 P.2d 483 (Utah 1986).

State v. Marks, 231 Kan. 645, 647 P.2d 1292 (1982).

State v. Saldana, 324 N.W. 2d 227 (Minn. 1982).

Students of California School for the Blind v. Honig, 736 F.2d 538 (9th Cir. 1984).

United States v. Telfaire, 469 F.2d 552 (D.C. Cir. 1972).

Vidmar, N. J., & Schuller, R. A. (1989). Juries and expert evidence: Social framework testimony. *Law and Contemporary Problems, 52,* 133–176.

Competence and Quality in the Performance of Forensic Psychologists

Leonard J. Haas
University of Utah School of Medicine

Mere possession of generic professional credentials cannot be used as justification of necessary and sufficient skill to perform in a forensic role. Case examples are used to illustrate problems of both competence and quality that sometimes accompany mental health clinicians to the witness stand.

Key words: expert witness, competence, psychology

Psychologists and psychological knowledge have been enthusiastically embraced by the legal system, and professional psychologists have likewise enthusiastically involved themselves in forensic practice. Indeed, a substantial number of professional and research psychologists will appear as expert witnesses at some point in their careers. Partly in response to this state of affairs, there is increasing interest in the pragmatics of forensic work, particularly in expert witnessing (e.g., Brodsky, 1991; Shapiro, 1990). As part of this literature, there is at least a modicum of attention paid to the methods of preparing properly, recognizing the boundaries of competence, and so forth. However, judging by the sort of complaints that reach ethics committees and licensing boards, more professional attention needs to be addressed to the issues of competence and quality in psychological courtroom work. The need for this inquiry can be shown by referring to a case:[1]

> Dr. F, a psychologist with essentially no forensic experience, was contacted by a former client and asked to write a letter in support of her

---

Requests for reprints should be sent to Leonard J. Haas, Department of Family and Preventive Medicine, University of Utah, 50 North Medical Drive, Salt Lake City, UT 84132.

[1]Although the case material is drawn from actual examples, features of the case examples have been altered to make them fictional composites.

attempt to obtain custody of the child after a divorce. The psychologist complied, writing a report to the mother's attorney, describing the father in a consistently negative light, alleging inferior school performance on the part of the child as a result of the father's influence, and suggesting that the son's intellectual capacity would have been better fostered under his mother's care. The letter was written without the psychologist having interviewed the son. The father obtained the services of another psychologist who evaluated all parties. This psychologist recommended that the father receive custody, in large part because the son had lived with the father and his current wife for the previous 12 years. In court testimony, Dr. F strenuously insisted that the mother showed no evidence of psychopathology, that she would be a superior parent, and that the father was destructive to the son. He was unable to provide evidence for any of these conclusions. When ethics charges were brought against Dr. F, he responded by attacking the ethics committee for its protectionist guild stance, alleging that to censure him would be to deprive him of free speech; further, he insisted that the adversary situation in the courtroom allowed him to advocate for the mother because the father had the benefit of his own counsel and psychologist.

The case illustrates a number of concerns that are examined later in this article. Consider first Dr. F's apparent attitudes toward his role, the courtroom context, and his professional peers. There is a certain amount of hubris in accepting the request of a former client in the first place, given that one has no prior experience in forensic work and given the problems of advocating for one side when it is necessary to have an equally complex understanding of the other side to competently render an assessment. Consider also the cavalier attitude toward the courtroom; "anything goes" when the other side can defend itself. Further, consider the attitude toward peers who try to critique Dr. F's behavior; they have nothing to teach him but rather are trying to restrict the exercise of what he obviously considers his enormous skills. Also consider the technical aspects of Dr. F's performance. He evaluates blindly on third party reports, which is less than competent even in a noncourtroom situation. He makes legal judgments (the mother should be awarded custody) rather than giving expert psychological testimony. In fact, his testimony is flawed in that it consists of opinions that are ordinarily based on assessment evidence; but he does not have the evidence. He also fails to indicate any awareness of alternative interpretations of the facts (e.g., the boy does not do well in school—although clear evidence would be helpful here also, and this could stem from a number of other causes beside poor fathering). There is also a deceptive element in his lack of concern with the apparently successful adjustment the boy has made while living with the father for a number of years. Overall, this psychologist failed to appreciate that he was not really being recruited as an expert witness (who testifies about scientific findings and reviews the facts of the case in light of scientific knowledge not available to the court) or as a fact witness (who testifies as to what he has observed in his direct experience relevant to the case). Rather, the psychologist has been recruited as an advocate for the mother, illegitimately using his professional credentials to support what amounted to unvalidated opinions that could potentially harm the father, the boy, and perhaps others affected by this case. Underlying these concerns, and particularly salient in light of the lack of humility shown by this psychologist, is the fact that these are well-known problems that experienced forensic and family psychologists anticipate and prevent. Even an inexperienced psychologist who consulted with a veteran forensic colleague could have acted more competently. Thus, this case shows deficits in both performance and in the professional's motive to practice competently. All of these issues bear on the question of what it means to practice competently in the courtroom.

Obviously, the mere possession of generic professional psychology credentials cannot be claimed to give evidence of the necessary and sufficient skill to perform competently as a forensic psychologist. In addition to problems already noted, the performance pressures of being on the witness stand and the seductions of highly compensated evaluations and testimony can lead to enormous temptations to be a "hired gun" for the side that obtains one's services. It is ironic that in a forum supposedly designed to ferret out "the truth", psychologists at times find it hard to adhere to this standard. Consider the following case:

> Psychologist Q offered his services as an expert witness in a fitness-to-stand-trial case. He indicated that he was a "registered psychologist, APA" and that he was a professor at a college in another state. His vitae listed department chairmanship in one section, although in another he is listed as department chair during a different time period. In fact, he was neither licensed nor an ex-department chair, and the American Psychological Association (APA) does not "register" psychologists. When confronted with the inconsistencies on cross-examination, he admitted to the inaccurate representation of his credentials. He claimed that he wanted to testify out of concern for the client and that the errors were made by a secretary.

Examining the problems with this case, we find that it exemplifies, at its root, multiple levels of dishonesty. First, the psychologist misrepresents his credentials, and then attempts to misrepresent the cause of the misrepresentation. And, again, this is done in a setting designed to ensure that statements are factual. Granted, this may be an extreme example; nonetheless, a number of observers (Fersch, 1980; Shapiro, 1990) have noted that the demand characteristics of the forensic arena seem to exert considerable pressure on even well-trained psychologists to make more absolute statements than they can justify, to find classic examples (discussed later), and to abandon the standards of competence and quality they might espouse in more tranquil environments.

But why be concerned about competence and quality? In part, to be a professional is to "hold oneself out" as a competent practitioner and to be concerned with improving the quality of one's practice (Haas & Malouf, 1989). The achievement of ever higher standards of competence and quality should be intrinsically rewarding; there is an inherent satisfaction in performing well the job one has promised to do. There is also the intrinsic satisfaction of solving a problem (in this case, the problem of helping the justice system improve its decisions using relevant psychological knowledge) and in developing methods of practice that are effective, elegant, and helpful to others.

There are also extrinsic reasons to pursue high standards. Developing greater competence and considering the nature of high-quality practice may benefit the psychologist directly, in that they help to prevent burnout (Corey, Corey, & Callahan, 1988), ethics complaints, malpractice charges, and licensing board investigations (or at least prevent resulting sanctions if such actions do take place). Adding to the pool of competent forensic psychologists may enhance the reputation of the field, whereas practicing competently in the legal arena may also enhance the reputation of the individual practitioner. Finally, there is particular need for competent, if not quality, practice in the forensic arena. The impact of poor professional practice (incompetent or simply poor quality) on human welfare, the credibility of scientific psychology, and the ability of the legal system to administer something approaching justice can be either greatly helped or greatly hindered by the practices of forensic psychologists. As Weithorn (1987) noted regarding problems with psychologists' expert testimony in child custody proceedings:

> presentation of opinions based on partial or irrelevant data; overreaching by exceeding the limitations of psychological knowledge in expert testimony and offering opinions of matters of law; loss of objectivity through inappropriate engagement in the adversary process; and failure to recognize the boundaries and parameters of confidentiality in the custody context [are among the major problems that hinder justice being served]. (p. viii)

Despite the justifications for competent work, it has been argued that identifying good practice in professional psychology (or, more specifically, in forensic psychology) is an exercise in aesthetics rather than a more objective enterprise; in other words, excellent work is whatever excellent practitioners say it is (to paraphrase Lee & Jones, 1933), and subjective judgments of competence and excellence cannot be linked to underlying concepts. This argument has been developed (and dismissed) in the philosophical literature on professional morality (Pellegrino, 1979) because the conceptual thicket can be penetrated enough to identify and specify what good work consists of (Donabedian, 1969). This article attempts to identify the dimensions of competence and the dimensions of quality in the forensic field.

COMPETENCE

Definition of Competence

Interestingly, at its root, competence is related to competition. *Competence* stems from the roots *com,* meaning together, and *peter,* meaning to seek: hence, to strive together or seek (Webster, 1956, p. 370). Consideration of the typical threshold for competent practice seems to rest on this aspect of the definition; that is, more psychologists than we would like to admit seem to consider themselves competent if they can match the abilities of the competition. This might be considered the lowest common denominator standard for competence. Moving from a consideration of the roots of the term to its actual definition, however, shows that competence means "capacity equal to requirement; adequate fitness or ability" (p. 370). In law, competence is defined as "legal . . . qualification, . . . power, or fitness" to do something (p. 370). Thus, our analysis must focus on what it is that psychologists are called on to do in courtrooms.

Commentators on Competence

Forensic psychologists, like other professionals, "profess" at the minimum to be competent at the central tasks of their chosen field. Pellegrino (1979) defined *professing* as "declaring aloud" that one possesses special knowledge and skills and that these skills will be used in the patient's interest (he referred to physicians, but the concepts are equally applicable to psychologists). Competence is a fundamental aspect of what it means to be a professional (Haas & Malouf, 1989) and encompasses knowledge, skill, and judgment (Weins, 1983). Professional competence includes both declarative expertise (knowing what) and procedural expertise (knowing how; Faust, 1986). Competence consists of appropriate professional education and training, continuing education, willingness to subject decisions to peer review, openness to criticism by colleagues, willingness to confess ignorance or error when appropriate, and concentrated and sustained efforts to deepen one's clinical craftsmanship (Pellegrino, 1979). Keith-Spiegel and Koocher (1985) emphasized, as an aspect of competence, the recognition of limitations in one's abilities, as well as knowing one's strengths and skills.

Some might argue that attaining competence occurs through obtaining the relevant credentials. However, as noted earlier, credentials are a necessary condition to practice but are not sufficient to establish professional competence. Credentials per se do not guarantee competence, although the lack of credentials would presumably be a strong indicator of incompetence to perform certain professional activities.

Competence as Defined in Psychology

If we use as our guide the revised ethics code of the APA (1992), "Ethical Principles of Psychologists and Code of Conduct," we find that the code is somewhat circular about psychological expertise; it is ethically incumbent on psychologists to be competent (Preamble, p. 1599), but this term is not defined, implicitly or explicitly, in the document. The principle devoted to competence, Principle A, only denotes psychologists's responsibility to maintain "high standards of competence" (p. 1599). There is the implication that competence proceeds from "training and experience"; more specifically, the code suggests that competence is defined as providing services and techniques for which psychologists are qualified by education, training, or experience. In addition, psychologists maintain knowledge of relevant scientific and professional information related to the services they render. This suggests that competence includes a broader understanding of related fields of knowledge. Competence also includes the idea of continuous professional development. The code (Standard 1.05, Maintaining Expertise, p. 1600) states that psychologists "undertake ongoing efforts to maintain competence in the skills they use." There is also the implication that competence, in part, consists of efforts to protect the welfare of clients. As Principle A states, "In those areas in which recognized standards do not yet exist, psychologists take whatever precautions are necessary to protect the welfare of their clients" (p. 1599). As part of this effort, "each psychologist supplements, but does not violate, the ethics code's values and rules on the basis of guidance drawn from personal values, culture and experience" (p. 1599). An additional element of competence that can be inferred from this document is the ability to recognize when one's effectiveness is compromised (Standard 1.13, p. 1601).

Psychologists are also advised to use assessment and intervention techniques in a competent manner (APA, 1992, Standard 2.02, p. 1603). A corollary of this competence is knowing to whom information should be released and to whom training should be provided (Standards 2.02b and 2.06, p. 1603). Psychologists must also know how to maintain records with appropriate safeguards to protect confidentiality in a manner that is consistent with the intended uses of the records (Standard 5.04, p. 1606).

An entire section of the code of conduct (APA, 1992, Standard 7, p. 1610) deals with forensic activities. It notes psychologists's obligation to base their forensic activities on suitable and sufficient data (Standard 7.02, p. 1610). It also implies that competent forensic work includes clear explanations of the limitations constraining generalizations that may be legitimately drawn from their work. Finally, psychologists are obligated to understand the rules governing forensic roles (Standard 7.06, p. 1610).

Competence in Relation to the Purpose of Courtroom Testimony

In light of the notion of "professional" previously noted, it is interesting to consider what the professional forensic psychologist "professes." In my opinion, psychologists profess to use scientific and professional knowledge and skills to improve an individual's quality of life and to bring to bear scientific evidence and techniques on specific problems. Applied to the courtroom setting, psychologists profess to have the tools and skills necessary to make better-than-chance assessments of an individual's fitness to stand trial, possession of mental competence, degree of psychopathology, fitness to care for a child, likelihood of acting in a violent manner, and so forth. For the most part, this is accomplished by reviewing existing scientific literature, performing scientific research, and conducting sound psychological assessments. These efforts culminate in the provision of expert testimony to the court.

The competent expert witness must know when his or her opinion is truly that of an expert and when it is no more informed than the opinion of an educated layperson. It is useful to note that the rules of evidence prohibit lay witnesses from testifying regarding their opinions. Rather, witnesses are required to testify about the facts. Experts, on the other hand, whose opinions may be based on special knowledge not available to the court or to the lay person, are entitled to give their opinions. However, those opinions must be given only within the area of their expertise.

In addition, with regard to obtained facts, the competent forensic psychologist clearly describes limitations and qualifications of findings, not just when they are based on thirdhand report. Shapiro (1990) noted that the capable expert should make reference to the specific data sources that would be important to have available for a final opinion and that were not available (p. 744). With specific regard to conducting evaluations and making predictions about future behavior, the competent forensic psychologist will have the requisite knowledge base and skill as well as the judgment to know which tools are appropriate for the job. In this context, Garb (1991) noted that

> even when mental health professionals cannot make moderately accurate predictions they can still assist judges and juries. For example, they can describe the appropriate empirical research and simply conclude that the prediction task is difficult or they may be able to help select appropriate statistical decision rules. (p. 453)

In other words, competent experts should also know the strengths and limitations of their data and decision making. It is remarkable that so often this threshold is not reached, especially as the competent forensic psychologist should know that opposing counsel (and their experts) will exert their efforts (sometimes unfairly it seems) to highlight the inadequacies and deficiencies in the psychologist's evaluation findings. Rather, there seems to be a widely noted temptation in forensic work to go beyond the limits of one's competence (Fersch, 1980; Shapiro, 1990) and to "render opinions in areas in which either the psychologist has no particular training or the state of knowledge is so meager that opinions should not be rendered" (Shapiro, 1990, p. 746). Shapiro also noted the "classic example" problem: The expert witness describes the (far from conclusive) findings as revealing a classic example of Syndrome X. A case example illustrates this only too well:

> Dr. Q, a highly experienced forensic psychologist, was asked by the mother of two boys (the custodial parent) to evaluate them to determine if they were suffering psychological or physical damage from visitation with her estranged husband. The psychologist saw the mother and saw the boys each for approximately 2 hr, and later he testified in court regarding visitation issues. He recommended no visitation. In his testimony, the psychologist repeatedly stated that the father was physically, psychologically, and verbally abusive; his source for this was verbal allegations by the sons, reports by the mother, and suggestions in the report of a previous psychologist who had evaluated the family. Asked about his confidence in his opinions, based upon only 2 hr with each child and no contact with the father himself, the psychologist stated "this is one of the clearest cases I've ever seen." He also indicated that he had no reservations about the validity and reliability of his opinions, diagnosis, and prognosis.

This is another extreme, yet telling, example of the apparently irresistible urge to go beyond one's data and to use strong language to cover up lack of evidence. This psychologist's work represents the offering of opinions without adequate data. There was no indication that the psychologist was alert to pressure that could have led to the misuse of his influence. He apparently felt that it was his duty to protect these boys and in that regard went forward despite the inadequacy of his factual base. In addition, by diagnosing the father as abusive solely on the basis of the boy's allegations, the psychologist was using inadequate assessment techniques. Again, "psychologists must remain scrupulously close to the data, present only material that is solidly documented, and present only conclusions that can be firmly supported by the data" (Shapiro, 1990, p. 46). Knowing the limits of one's testimony is fundamentally important because an expert witness should be able to help a judge or jury make more accurate judgments (Garb, 1991). If an expert witness cannot make more valid judgments than a judge or jury, then it is unlikely that the expert will be able to help a judge or jury improve the accuracy of their judgments.

There appears to be general agreement that expert witnesses should be allowed to (a) describe a person's history and mental status, (b) make diagnoses, (c) evaluate whether a person is malingering, (d) make predictions of behavior or at least describe difficulties in predicting behavior, and (e) evaluate psychological processes related to legal constructs such as competency to stand trial. In another irony, because many of the concepts used in mental health practice are somewhat vague or "open concepts" (Garb, 1989), expert witnesses apparently feel that they can define them idiosyncratically. In fact, the opposite is true; the clinician must stay abreast of the constantly evolving literature and findings being reported in the field to be as specific as possible in defining concepts and terminology.

Competence also requires the ability to recognize who is the client. This awareness may sharpen some of these ethical problems. If the psychologist considers that his or her client is the court or the justice system in the abstract, it would seem clear that the best way to serve the interests of the client is to be as honest and careful as possible (Fersch, 1980). Interestingly, the ethical obligation to terminate a professional relationship when the client is no longer receiving any benefit from it may be relevant, although difficult to implement, in this regard. It is incumbent on psychologists to become aware of the limits of their roles. They must also attempt to communicate these limitations to the relevant participants in the legal proceeding.

There may be an additional ethical dilemma for the psychologist in the courtroom who believes that there is an ethical obligation to attempt to prevent misuse of his or her work (Fersch, 1980). It appears unlikely that this is a resolvable dilemma, largely because it is not clear how this obligation could be carried out in the courtroom environment. In the courtroom, the ethics of the jurisprudence system demand an adversarial proceeding, in which opposing attorneys will attempt to present only aspects of the testimony that support their respective sides and where control over the testimony heavily resides with attorneys and the questions they pose.

Threats to Competence

The seductive power of the courtroom and the subtle gratification of being on stage as the expert can sometimes blind the psychologist to the need for particular skills and particular frames of mind necessary to both serve the court system and do justice to the complexity and integrity of the psychological profession. This section identifies several difficulties that interfere with competent practice.

Failure to understand the justice system. As noted, it is important to recognize when one is entitled to give one's opinion in court rather than simply testifying about the facts. It is also important to know when one is rendering a legal opinion versus a professional opinion that is within one's area of expertise. Although these problems are more common among psychologists who are less experienced in courtroom work, they are certainly not unknown among psychologists with many years of experience in the justice system.

A problem that also appears, regardless of experience, is that of not preparing adequately; numerous cases have been demolished by the expert psychologist not having access to his or her records, not having reviewed the findings carefully, or overlooking or omitting key material. This type of problem reflects a lack of understanding that the justice system requires evidence to support conclusions and that careful preparation is required.

Ironically, much of the effectiveness of courtroom work by psychologists hinges on their persuasive or performance skills rather than their skills at doing the psychological job. Such publications as *The Testifying Expert: Winning Strategies On and Off the Stand for the Expert Witness* ("Lawyers and Experts," 1993) illustrate this point to an extreme; this newsletter includes many advertisements and announcements of workshops that help to coach the potential expert witness in ways to dress and speak so that the message will be maximally persuasive (the content of the message is not within the scope of these preparatory efforts). Potentially, one could argue that the witness who fails to clearly carry his or her point across to the jury is not as competent as the expert showman. Clearly this is not a dichotomous judgment of competence; there is both a content dimension and a process dimension to competent expert testimony, but the testimony, regardless of the flair with which it is delivered, must be scientifically valid and germane to the issues at hand.

Unfortunately, the emphasis on style over substance can lead to cynicism about the justice system; assuming that the most dazzling presentation will sway the naive jury or dumbfound the poorly prepared opposition can lead psychologists to forget the ethic of competence. On the other hand, cynicism and incompetence can result from the psychologist feeling overwhelmed by the legal arena, assuming that the deck is stacked, and not bothering to prepare adequately. This can be compounded by the psychologist getting away with such behavior; more than one ethics complaint has elicited the response "but this is the way I did it in my previous three cases and no one complained."

Professional arrogance. Although this is more commonly a threat to the competence of senior forensic psychologists than more junior ones, it is not unknown even among psychologists who are complete novices in the courtroom. The arrogant psychologist often relies completely on his or her superb memory, thus ignoring standards of recordkeeping or documentation and exhibiting an almost complete certainty about conversations and observations that occurred long ago.

The problem of diagnosis in absentia can be considered a result of arrogance as well, although, in the many ethics complaints arising from this problem, it is simply characterized as incompetence. The psychologist who is willing to make a diagnostic statement based solely on the report of a third party is making a diagnosis based on hearsay, and with the publication of the revised "Ethical Principles of Psychologists and Code of Conduct" (APA, 1992) is likely to be committing an ethical breach. The ethical principles place the burden for diagnosis in absentia squarely on the psychologist's shoulders; it is permissible only if one can justify such a deviation from standard assessment practice.

The reliance of some senior forensic psychologists on their clinical savvy also reflects professional arrogance, and this often leads to inadequate assessment. Judgments based on intuition following a brief interview, although they may be useful as working hypotheses in ongoing treatment, can be damaging when used as the basis for expert testimony.

Advocating rather than testifying. The belief that as a psychologist one knows more than anyone in the justice system about the proper outcome for a case can be major threat to competence. Wasserstrom (1975) referred to "role-differentiated behavior" that allows the professional to suspend certain moral considerations that would hold for individuals in general. The typical example of this sort of "role morality" involves the obligation of a parent to favor the interests of his or her child over the interests of children in general. Applied to the professional role, an example would be the lawyer who is obligated to work for a client regardless of the worth of the end sought by the client. Applying this logic to the arena of forensic psychologists, it is easy to see how the demand characteristics of the legal arena might sway psychologists from their position of scientific objectivity to an advocacy position. A related problem may have more to do with a displaced faith in the adversary system; the psychologist freely advocates for his or her side and assumes that the other side can protect itself. This logic leads to greatly underestimating the potential that one's testimony might do harm to one or more participants in the process. A trenchant example of this is a recent ethics complaint in which the psychologist defended himself by noting that the court failed to follow his recommendations (which were based on inadequate assessment); therefore, no harm was caused.

Failure to attend to changes in the knowledge base. It is perhaps tautological to point out that deficient knowledge is a major threat to competence (Peterson & Bry, 1980), and yet it is important to consider the fluid nature of competence in this regard. Competence is always a relative term, especially in a field that is based on empirical findings and that is evolving at a rather rapid rate. Two decades ago, Dubin (1972) estimated that the half-life of a doctoral degree in psychology (as a measure of competence) was 10 to 12 years. No doubt the accuracy of that estimate has changed over time; in 1993, we can well imagine that the rapidity of knowledge expansion may have shrunk the "degree half-life" considerably. This is a strong argument for continuing education and continuing self-examination. A considerable number of ethics and malpractice complaints could be avoided if the psychologist were to become acquainted with (and use) current, well-validated assessment instruments, for example.

Cynicism and/or impairment. The incompetent or less-than-competent senior psychologist may be "burned out" (Corey et al., 1988) or impaired as a result of psychopathology or substance abuse (Haas & Hall, 1990). Burned out professionals are characterized by negative attitudes toward themselves, others, work, and life (Corey et al., 1988) and may experience a sense of fragmentation stemming from having attempted to do too many professional activities at the same time. Sadly, both burned-out and impaired psychologists sometimes have extreme difficulty becoming aware of their limitations, and forceful confrontation by concerned colleagues is often necessary.

Greed. Unfortunately, forensic work is seen as a lucrative line of work, and this comprises a threat to competence. In a rational world, highly rewarded activities might generate greater efforts to become competent, but a number of ethics complaints demonstrate that a small proportion of psychologists view the opportunity to provide expert testimony as an opportunity to overassess, perform lengthy reviews of material, and generally inflate their expenses. In addition, psychologists who hope to enrich themselves by showing how they can win cases may misstate their credentials or their findings.

QUALITY

Although competent practice in courtroom settings can be identified more or less easily, clearly articulating the nature of high-quality forensic work entails much more effort. Turning once again to Webster (1956, p. 1474) for a starting place, we find "quality: 'degree of excellence that a thing possesses, hence . . . 3. superiority, excellence.' " This is not terribly helpful, and yet professionals can and do distinguish subjectively (and often with great conviction) between colleagues who do competent but pedestrian work and those whose functioning is of higher quality. Conceivably, the search for the defining characteristics of quality can be so frustrating as to provoke lunacy (Pirsig,

1974); yet it is important to make clear that there are ideals beyond technical competence to which the professional can aspire. Indeed, Pirsig's novelistic treatment of the issue suggests that the achievement of quality (or striving toward it, at any rate) is what gives meaning to human activity.

Trends in published reports of expertise across a number of domains (Ericsson & Smith, 1991) suggest that 10 years or more of full-time preparation are required to obtain a superior level of performance in such arenas as chessplaying, theoretical physics, and medicine. Patel and Groen (1991) went further and suggested the following terms are useful in defining increasing levels of ability: layperson, beginner, novice, intermediate, subexpert, and expert. It is implicit in this ordering that there is a well-known domain that can be defined and that a certain amount of experience gained over time is necessary for the development of high-quality skills.

What aspect of time's passing leads to an improvement in quality? Perhaps the experience gained over years provides the opportunity to learn to link and frame information and distinguish between relevant and irrelevant information in a problem (Patel & Groen, 1991). "Analyses from several different domains of expertise have revealed that experts engage in a number of complex mental activities involving reasoning that relies on mental models and internal representations" (Ericsson & Smith, 1991, p. 31). In other words, a sophisticated internal model representing the task at hand characterizes the superior performer. This may contribute a dimension of elegance to the psychologist's work, as he or she learns to avoid underassessing, overassessing, and being distracted by highly emotional, highly intriguing, or other irrelevant aspects of the case at hand.

Apart from the sharpening of intellect and the accumulation of wisdom in the selection of tools and strategies in forensic work, there may well be a developmental personality component to the practice of quality forensic work. The virtues that form the foundation of high-quality professional character have been discussed by Jordan and Meara (1990); "virtue ethics focus on the historically formed character . . . such character development provides the basis for professional judgment" (p. 107). From this perspective, what it means to be a professional practicing with quality is to attempt to approximate the ideal professional character and to approach one's work with the intention to function with integrity.

May (1984), among others, attempted to identify professional virtues in a way that may help to flesh out the notion of quality professional practice: fidelity, prudence, discretion, perseverance, courage, integrity, public spiritedness, benevolence, humility, and hope. Consider, for example, how the psychologist who lacks fidelity might function. Dr. X, called as an expert witness, changed his position between the time of agreeing with the attorney to testify and actually appearing in court. Dr. Y, a therapist who worked with a couple on resolving their marital stresses, appeared in court on behalf of only one member of the couple to argue for custody. Consideration of some perhaps more narrow virtues such as objectivity, loyalty to the facts, recognition of the limits of psychological knowledge, and intent to benefit human welfare might also improve the ability to pursue quality in forensic work.

Moreover, we can conclude that competence is necessary but insufficient for a high-quality professional transaction. A technically competent decision or action may not necessarily be in the best interest of the client or of society. Because the Preamble of the ethics code (APA, 1992) sets an aspirational ceiling for professional actions, it is possible to conceptualize psychological work that is competent but low quality. The aspirations are clear: Psychologists are committed to increasing knowledge of human behavior and to the utilization of such knowledge for the promotion of human welfare. They employ their skills for purposes consistent with these values, and do not knowingly permit their misuse by others. Thus, we can elucidate high-quality psychological work: It is work that increases knowledge of human behavior, increases people's understanding of others, or promotes human welfare. Conversely, consider psychologists's efforts that do not demonstrably promote human welfare, although they do draw on scientific underpinnings, for example. Such efforts might be called adequate or perhaps mediocre, but the distance they fall from the ideals of the Preamble prevent such efforts from ever being called high quality.

CONCLUSION

The place of psychologists in the courts of law is more or less well-established and will continue to be important in years to come. In this context, the functioning of the forensic psychologist has important impact on the lives of those involved in the various cases, as well as on the public's and the justice system's view of the potential contributions of psychologists. Although it is not particularly difficult to list the tasks that the competent forensic psychologist should be able to accomplish, and the potential conflicts that he or she should be able to anticipate and prevent, the articulation of the skills (and states of mind) needed to put this information into practice is somewhat more difficult. In this article, I attempted to clarify the ethical obligations of the forensic psychologist and spell out the elements that contribute to competent and high-quality work.

In large part, the discussion has only elaborated on principles contained in the "Ethical Principles of Psychologists and Code of Conduct" (APA, 1992). But these standards must be elaborated by an awareness of the relevant substantive literature in one's area(s) of forensic practice; the obtaining of ongoing education in one's field of practice; and the possession of sufficient education, training, or experience to make one competent. Clearly, the skills to perform well in the courtroom are not automatically gained when one is granted a license to practice psychology or a doctoral degree.

REFERENCES

American Psychological Association. (1992). Ethical principles of psychologists and code of conduct. *American Psychologist, 44,* 1597–1611.

Brodsky, S. L. (1991). *Testifying in Court: Guidelines and maxims for the expert witness.* Washington, DC: American Psychological Association.

Corey, G., Corey, M. S., & Callanan, P. (1988). *Issues and ethics in the helping professions* (3rd ed.). Monterey, CA: Brooks/Cole.

Donabedian, A. (1969). *A guide to medical care administration: Vol. II. Medical care appraisal, quality, and utilization.* New York: American Public Health Association.

Dubin, S. S. (1972). Obsolescence or life-long education: A choice for the professional. *American Psychologist, 27,* 486–496.

Ericsson, K. A., & Smith, J. (1991). Prospects and limits of the empirical study of expertise: An introduction. In K. A. Ericsson & J. Smith (Eds.), *Toward a general theory of expertise: Prospects and limits* (pp. 1–38). New York: Cambridge University Press.

Faust, D. (1986). Research on human judgment and its application to clinical practice. *Professional Psychology: Research and Practice, 17,* 420–430.

Fersch, E. A. (1980). Ethical issues for psychologists in court settings. In J. Monahan (Ed.), *Who is the client?* (pp. 43–62). Washington, DC: American Psychological Association.

Garb, H. N. (1989). Clinical judgment, clinical training, and professional experience. *Psychological Bulletin, 105,* 387–396.

Garb, H. N. (1991). The *trained* psychologist as expert witness. *Professional Psychology: Research and Practice, 37,* 451–467.

Haas, L. J., & Hall, J. H. (1990). Impaired or unethical? Issues for colleagues and ethics committees. *The Register Report, 3,* 2–5.

Haas, L. J., & Malouf, J. L. (1989). *Keeping up the good work: A practitioner's guide to mental health ethics.* Sarasota, FL: Professional Resource Exchange.

Jordan, A. E., & Meara, N. M. (1990). Ethics and the professional practice of psychologists: The role of virtues and principles. *Professional Psychology: Research and Practice, 21,* 107–114.

Keith-Spiegel, P., & Koocher, G. P. (1985). *Ethics in psychology: Professional standards and cases.* New York: Random House.

Lawyers and experts should get into the act. (1993, August). *The Testifying Expert: Winning Strategies On and Off the Stand for the Expert Witness,* pp. 3–4.

Lee, R. J., & Jones, L. W. (1933). *The fundamentals of good medical care.* Chicago: University of Chicago Press.

May, W. F. (1984). The virtues in a professional setting. *Soundings, 67,* 245–266.

Patel, V. L., & Groen, G. J. (1991). The general and specific nature of medical expertise: A critical look. In K. A. Ericsson & J. Smith (Eds.), *Toward a general theory of expertise: Prospects and limits* (pp. 93–125). New York: Cambridge University Press.

Pellegrino, E. D. (1979). Toward a reconstruction of medical morality: The primacy of the act of profession and the fact of illness. *The Journal of Medicine and Philosophy, 4,* 32–56.

Peterson, D. R., & Bry, B. H. (1980). Dimensions of perceived competence in professional psychology. *Professional Psychology, 11,* 965–971.

Pirsig, R. (1974). *Zen and the art of motorcycle maintenance.* New York: Harper.

Shapiro, D. L. (1990). Problems encountered in the preparation and presentation of expert testimony. In E. Margenau (Ed.), *The encyclopedic handbook of private practice* (pp. 739–758). New York: Gardner.

Wasserstrom, R. A. (1975). Lawyers as professionals: Some moral issues. *Human Rights, 5*, 1–24.

Webster, N. (1956). *Webster's new twentieth century dictionary* (2nd ed.). New York: World Publishing.

Weins, A. (1983). Toward a conceptualization of competency assurance. *Professional Practice of Psychology, 4*, 1–15.

Weithorn, L. A. (Ed.). (1987). *Psychology and child custody determinations: Knowledge, roles, and expertise.* Lincoln: University of Nebraska Press.

Seven Issues in Conducting Forensic Assessments: Ethical Responsibilities in Light of New Standards and New Tests

James N. Butcher
University of Minnesota

Kenneth S. Pope
Los Angeles, California

The publication of a new ethics code for the American Psychological Association (1992), new guidelines (Committee on Ethical Guidelines for Forensic Psychologists, 1991), and two new versions of the Minnesota Multiphasic Personality Inventory (the MMPI-2, Butcher, Dahlstrom, Graham, Tellegen, & Kaemmer, 1989; and the MMPI-A, Butcher et al., 1992) provide an opportunity to review ethical aspects of forensic assessment. Seven major issues— appropriate graduate training, competence in the use of standardized tests, using tests that fit the task, using tests that fit the individual, administering tests correctly, using computers appropriately in forensic assessment, and assessing and reporting factors that may affect the meaning of test findings—are discussed. The revision of the MMPI is used to illustrate some of these issues.

Key words: expert witness, forensic assessment, standardized tests

In 1992, the American Psychological Association (APA) adopted a radically new ethics code—the "Ethical Principles of Psychologists and Code of Conduct." Over twice as long as the previous code, the new code sets forth 10 standards (2.01–2.10) relevant to general evaluation, diagnosis, and intervention, as well as 1 standard (7.02) addressing forensic assessments more specifically. During the previous year, the American Psychology-Law Society/APA Division 41 issued the "Specialty Guidelines for Forensic Psychologists"

Requests for reprints should be sent to James N. Butcher, 9631 Wyoming Circle, Bloomington, MN 55438-1628.

(Committee on Ethical Guidelines for Forensic Psychologists [CEGFP], 1991), which were endorsed by the American Academy of Forensic Psychologists. And a few years earlier, in 1989, the Minnesota Multiphasic Personality Inventory (MMPI)—the most widely used standardized psychological test for general personality assessment (e.g., Anastasi, 1988; Davison & Neale, 1990; Goldstein, Baker, & Jamison, 1980; Lubin, Larsen, & Matarazzo, 1984; McConnell, 1974; Waskow & Parloff, 1975), as well as for forensic personality assessment (Lees-Haley, 1992; Pope, Butcher, & Seelen, 1993)—was revised for the first time since it was introduced in the late 1930s and early 1940s.

The appearance of new standards and guidelines relevant to forensic assessment and of new versions of an assessment instrument widely used in forensic settings provides an opportunity for those who conduct forensic assessments and serve as expert witnesses to reconsider their practices in this area. The purpose of this article is to note seven major issues confronting forensic psychologists and others who use psychological tests in light of these revisions and other general standards for sound assessment. Because of its popularity and because of its recent revision, the MMPI-2 and MMPI-A are used to illustrate how ethical issues are reflected in the design, validation, and uses of standardized psychological tests. Finally, on the assumption that not all readers are familiar with the origins, psychometric characteristics, and methodology of the original MMPI or its two revised versions (MMPI-2 and MMPI-A), these aspects of the test are summarized in the context of the examples presented.

APPROPRIATE GRADUATE TRAINING

The first general principle set forth by the new ethics code emphasizes that psychologists must maintain awareness of the boundaries of their own competence and that they must limit their professional activities to those in which their competence is established by education, training, and experience (APA, 1992). Similarly, Section III.A. of the "Specialty Guidelines for Forensic Psychologists" sets forth an explicit responsibility for psychologists conducting forensic work to limit their practice to those areas in which they possess specific knowledge, skill, experience, and education (CEGFP, 1991). This ethical duty to practice only with competence obviously applies to conducting psychological assessment. Indeed, those looking for creative rationalizations to evade this responsibility when conducting assessments will find all loopholes closed; Section 2.01(a) of the ethics code specifically states that "psychologists perform evaluations, diagnostic services, or interventions only within the context of a defined professional relationship" (APA, 1992, p. 1603). As a professional activity carried out only within the context of a defined professional relationship, assessment clearly and explicitly falls within the domain of ethical standards set forth by the ethics code.

There are diverse aspects to ensuring that an individual is competent to conduct an assessment. For example, he or she must have adequate education or training in the general area (e.g., clinical assessment to determine whether individuals suffer from mental or emotional disorders or personnel assessment to determine whether individuals should be hired for specific jobs), in the population of those being assessed (e.g., candidates for employment as police officers or those standing trial and claiming an insanity defense), in the theory and use of standardized tests (e.g., regarding validity, reliability, or confounding factors), in the specific standardized tests and other methods of assessment (e.g., MMPI-2, Wechsler Adult Intelligence Scale–Revised, and Halstead–Reitan Neuropsychological Test Battery), and so on. In this section, we discuss one of the most fundamental aspects of competence in forensic assessment—obtaining the requisite graduate education and training. A degree in personality psychology, for example, does not signify adequate and appropriate training to testify as an expert witness in trials focusing on the efficacy of certain tests as used by police departments to screen employment applicants. Similarly, a degree in experimental psychology does not reflect adequate and appropriate training to conduct assessments of plaintiffs in personal injury cases.

Reviewing APA policy documents can help psychologists determine whether they meet the educational criteria to practice within a particular specialty area. In 1976, APA adopted a set of requirements for those wishing to change specialties (Conger, 1976). For example, those already holding doctorates in other areas of psychology who sought to practice in such specialty areas as clinical, counseling, or school psychology must obtain what would be in essence a second doctorate in the new specialty area. In a subsequent policy statement, Abeles (1982) set forth specific requirements for the doctoral-training programs providing such respecialization:

The American Psychological Association holds that respecialization education and training for psychologists possessing the doctoral degree should be conducted by those academic units in regionally accredited universities and professional schools currently offering doctoral training in the relevant specialty, and in conjunction with regularly organized internship agencies where appropriate. Respecialization for purposes of offering services in clinical, counseling, or school psychology should be linked to relevant APA approved programs. (p. 656)

When a psychologist attends only to ensuring doctoral-level training from a particular type of program (e.g., clinical), he or she may overlook extremely important matters about the nature, scope, and depth of the graduate program. If, for example, a psychologist possessing a doctorate from an APA-approved clinical training program and an APA-approved clinical internship is asked by an attorney to conduct a clinical assessment to determine whether a defendant was insane at the time he or she committed a certain crime, the psychologist must recognize that this assessment is in fact a forensic assessment. The individual must ask whether his or her specific graduate training program and internship provided an adequate foundation for conducting this type of task. (If the individual fails to ask himself or herself this question or fails to answer it candidly, the attorney conducting the cross-examination in any subsequent trial may dwell on it at length.) The APA must ask itself if it considers that training provided by some, most, or all of its APA-approved doctoral-level graduate programs and internships in, for example, clinical psychology, provides adequate and relevant educational background for forensic practice.

COMPETENCE IN THE USE OF STANDARDIZED TESTS

Beyond holding an appropriate doctoral degree, psychologists seeking to conduct forensic assessments that utilize standardized instruments must ensure that they have requisite education, training, and supervised experience in the use of such tests. This is another aspect of the requisite competence mentioned in the previous section and emphasized by both the "Ethical Principles of Psychologists and Code of Conduct" (APA, 1992) and the "Specialty Guidelines for Forensic Psychologists" (CEGFP, 1991). It is a responsibility that also derives from the ethical mandates to remain knowledgeable about relevant scientific and professional information and to rely on this knowledge when making professional judgments and carrying out professional tasks (APA, 1992, Sections 1.05 and 1.06). The *Standards for Educational and Psychological Testing* (1985; see also Anastasi, 1988; Pope, Butcher, & Seelen, 1993) provides a more extended discussion of the psychometric and related concepts that form an essential component of the knowledge important to those who conduct forensic assessments.

Those who present expert testimony based on such tests as the MMPI, MMPI-2, or MMPI-A are likely in for a deservedly hard time on cross-examination if they do not adequately understand and cannot clearly explain terms such as *validity, reliability, standardization, central tendency, variance, correlation, inferential statistics, descriptive statistics, specificity, sensitivity, social approval bias, ideographic, nomothetic,* and *standard score*. Familiarity with the general principles, concepts, and techniques of standardized assessment, however, is only the foundation on which specific expertise with specific instruments must rest. Experts who use versions of the MMPI as a basis for their testimony, for example, must be able to articulate to the jury (or judge if there is no jury) and to answer vigorous cross-examination questions about terms such as *rational scale development, the purified sample, the linear versus uniform* T-*scales, validity scales* (e.g., *Cannot Say, F,* True Response Consistency [*TRIN*], and Variable Response Inconsistency [*VRIN*]), *the* K-*correction, clinical scales* (e.g., Depression and Paranoia), and *content scales* (e.g., Social Discomfort and Work Interference). To offer expert testimony based on the MMPI, MMPI–2, or MMPI–A without such knowledge can result in ethical sanctions. For example, the APA's Committee on Scientific and Professional Ethics and Conduct (now termed the Ethics Committee) reported a typical case in which one psychologist charged another psychologist with incompetence, especially in the area of psychological testing. The committee "found that the person had no training or education in principles of psychological testing but was routinely engaged in evaluations of children in child custody battles" (Hall & Hare-Mustin, 1983, p. 718).

USING TESTS THAT FIT THE TASK

Those who conduct forensic assessments on a regular basis may be vulnerable to a special occupational hazard: Having assembled a standard battery of tests with which they are comfortable, they may use that battery without evaluating whether the tests are appropriate for the specific assessment task at hand for each new case. A standard battery assembled by a psychologist for addressing issues relevant to criminal trials, for example, may be inadequate for evaluating a party to an administrative hearing. It is the expert's professional and ethical responsibility to ensure that the test (or tests) be adequately validated for its purpose. If the expert has any doubts about this issue, it is important to conduct a literature review or consult a colleague to determine whether research published in peer-reviewed scientific and professional journals provides adequate evidence that a test or battery of tests can accomplish the task (e.g., to determine whether an individual suffers from neuropsychological impairment, possesses characteristics that would make him or her unfit to serve as custodial parent, or is currently psychotic in a way that would make him or her unfit to stand trial). For example, one psychologist was charged with misusing a battery of tests—including the MMPI—in an incompetent attempt to evaluate whether an individual was suffering from a personality disorder. The APA Ethics Committee obtained the test report, the raw data, and other relevant information about the assessment. In addition to its customary review, the committee submitted the materials to two diplomates with extensive experience in testing for independent reviews of the case. The committee concluded that most of the tests were inappropriate for the uses to which they were being put.

> The only test used by the complainee that has established validity in identifying personality disorders is the MMPI, and none of the conclusions allegedly based

on the MMPI are accurate. We suspect that the complainee's conclusions are based upon knowledge of a previous psychotic episode and information from the psychiatric consultant, whose conclusions seem to have been accepted uncritically. The complainee's report is a thoroughly unprofessional performance, in our opinion. Most graduate students would do much better. (Sanders & Keith-Spiegel, 1980, p. 1098)

Those who administer, score, and interpret psychological tests must be constantly alert to the ways that seemingly subtle factors may affect a test's capability to serve as the basis for inferences in a particular assessment situation. For example, the various forms of the MMPI have been useful in suggesting appropriate treatment modalities (e.g., individual therapy, group therapy, or hospitalization) for prospective patients (e.g., Butcher, 1990; Butcher & Williams, 1992; Graham, 1987; Greene, 1980). However, we need to incorporate information about the specific purpose for which the test is used in the evaluation for a full and appropriate assessment. The University of California, Los Angeles' Post Therapy Support Program, founded in the early 1980s to provide services to people who were sexually intimate with a previous therapist, used the MMPI in an attempt to identify patients who might benefit from group therapy. They found, however, that the traditional MMPI indicants revealing that a person would not be able to function well in or benefit from group treatment did not seem to work with this special population. Many of those for whom the general MMPI research literature had suggested that group therapy was contraindicated "managed to work quite well within the group context and to benefit substantially from this modality" (Pope & Bouhoutsos, 1986, p. 76; see also Pope, 1994; Pope, Sonne, & Holroyd, 1993).

Selecting or reviewing each test for a forensic evaluation is not simply a matter of ensuring that it has been previously used for the task at hand. The research published in peer-reviewed scientific and professional literature must provide sufficient evidence that the test accomplishes the task. The fact that a test has been repeatedly used, for example, to predict future violence is not a particularly meaningful factor in choosing a test for that purpose unless research findings have shown that the test is effective at distinguishing those who are at substantial risk to commit violence from those who are not at substantial risk. Moreover, the test must accomplish its purpose with sufficient sensitivity and specificity for the task at hand. The principle that one must choose tests for which there is adequate research evidence of efficacy was stated clearly by Messick (1980), who emphasized that in psychological assessment, "validity has always been an ethical imperative" (p. 1020). This principle is also set forth clearly in the *Standards for Educational and Psychological Testing* (1985): "Validity is the most important consideration in test evaluation" (p. 9). Similarly, the new ethics code emphasizes: "Psychologists rely on scientifically and professionally derived knowledge when making scientific or professional judgments . . ." (APA, 1992, Section 1.06, p. 1600; see also CEGFP, 1991, Section VI.A). Weiner (1989) provided an illustration of the failure to rely on adequate scientifically or professionally derived knowledge:

> A psychologist commenting on the assessment of alleged sexual abuse was heard to identify a "certain sign": If a girl sees Card IV on the Rorschach as a tree upside down, then she has been a victim of sexual abuse. Whatever tortuous rationale might be advanced on behalf of such an influence, there is not a shred of empirical evidence to support it. Indeed, there is precious little evidence to support any isomorphic relationship between specific Rorschach responses and specific behavioral events. Psychologists who nevertheless use Rorschach responses in this way are behaving unethically, by virtue of being incompetent. (pp. 829–830)

It is important to remember that evidence for validity will change over time, thus placing a special burden on the forensic witness to stay abreast of recent developments. For instance, during the decades following its initial appearance, the MMPI was the subject of thousands of published research studies, defining the areas in which the evidence supported its validity. The obvious challenge in revising the instrument was to preserve—to the greatest extent possible—the continuity of demonstrable validity between the previous and the newer versions, while modifying those aspects over which the passage of time had cast a shadow. As described next, the passage of time had not only revealed defects and limitations in the original instrument but had also brought about significant changes in the population that the MMPI was designed to assess and in the standard methods of administration (for a more detailed discussion of these issues, see Pope, Butcher, & Seelen, 1993).

The revision process included two major approaches to preserve and extend the validity of the instrument. First, as an examination of the actual scales shows, the traditional validity and clinical scales were kept relatively intact (i.e., these scales—for the most part—contain the same items in revision as they did in the original). These basic validity and clinical scales reflect the same constructs they have been measuring since the MMPI's inception in the 1940s. Forensic practitioners must be knowledgeable about the psychometric analyses defining the nature of the continuity in validity (e.g., Tellegen & Ben-Porath, 1993).

Second, a new array of validation studies specifically focusing on the MMPI-2 and MMPI-A began to emerge before the instruments were formally released for general use. Experts using any form of the MMPI need to be adequately aware of this growing body of literature to the degree that it is relevant to a specific assessment task at hand (e.g., Ben-Porath, Butcher, & Graham, 1991; Butcher, Graham, Williams, & Ben-Porath, 1990; Butcher et al., 1992; Egeland, Erickson, Butcher, & Ben-Porath, 1991; Hjemboe, Almagor, & Butcher, 1992; Hjemboe & Butcher, 1991; Keller & Butcher, 1991). However time-consuming, bothersome, and burdensome this responsibility may seem (e.g., searching the literature or reviewing the studies), it tends to be much less aversive than learning about the existence, findings, and implications of each of these studies as one sits on the witness stand, with the court reporter recording every word and the well-prepared attorney conducting a skilled cross-examination.

Even when a test is not revised, the research literature tends to expand rapidly. Professionals must constantly update their knowledge of new findings. In a discussion of this issue, Weiner (1989), then editor of *Journal of Personality Assessment,* concluded: "The passage of just a few years . . . is sufficient to land practitioners who have not kept current on the doorstep of unethicality" (p. 830). Similarly, the new code underscores this ethical responsibility: "Psychologists who engage in assessment . . . maintain a reasonable level of awareness of current scientific and professional information in their fields of activity, and undertake ongoing efforts to maintain competence in the skills they use" (APA, 1992, Section 1.05, p. 1600). This responsibility to keep abreast of the current literature is even more pressing when a test is modified and renormed, as illustrated by the revision of the MMPI.

USING TESTS THAT FIT THE INDIVIDUAL

Section 7.02 of the new ethical code (APA, 1992) emphasizes that conclusions about an individual must be based on an adequate examination of the individual: "Except as noted in (c), below, psychologists provide written or oral forensic reports or testimony of the psychological characteristics of an individual only after they have conducted an examination of the individual adequate to support their statements or conclusions" (p. 1610). Similarly, the "Specialty Guidelines for Forensic Psychologists" (CEGFP, 1991, Section VI-H) state that

> Forensic psychologists avoid giving written or oral evidence about the psychological characteristics of particular individuals when they have not had an opportunity to conduct an examination of the individual adequate to the scope of the statements, opinions, or conclusions to be issued. (cited in Pope, Butcher, & Seelen, 1993, p. 206)

In the appraisal of individual clients, a single test such as the MMPI may not be considered adequate to serve as the complete assessment. Moreover, the use of test scores alone to make forensic decisions about individuals, in the absence of obtaining other, substantial information on the client to support the clinical decisions, can be inappropriate. However, test experts can legitimately testify about the test itself (without actually seeing the client), as long as testimony is explicitly qualified as addressing the psychometric and related qualities of the test. For example, it is appropriate for an expert on the Wechsler Adult Intelligence Scale–Revised, the Halstead–Reitan Neuropsychological Test Battery, or the MMPI–A to testify about the meaning of particular test scores or the adequacy of a particular interpretation of the test that another psychologist provided.

Assuming that the expert's testimony will address the individual's psychological status and characteristics based on standardized psychological testing of that individual, there is a fundamental responsibility to ensure that the tests are appropriate for the individual. Even if the tests have been carefully selected on the basis of demonstrable validity (as supported by research published in peer-reviewed scientific and professional journals) in addressing the tasks at hand (e.g., assessing psychological characteristics relevant to serving as custodial parent, competence to stand trial, or chronic psychological injury suffered as a result of an automobile accident), there are significant factors that can affect whether the tests are appropriate for a specific individual. Examples of three such factors are presented next.

The Passage of Time

A test that the literature supports as effective for a specific assessment task may not be valid for a particular individual because of the passage of time. Changes in either the relevant population (of which the individual is a member) or in the standard procedures for administering or scoring the test may diminish the relevance of the validation research for the assessment of the individual. It was, in fact, this issue that formed part of the major impetus for revising the MMPI.

The original MMPI norms, developed mostly on response data collected from visitors to the University of Minnesota Hospital in the 1930s, had served as the standard of normality since the instrument's publication. Many investigators (see e.g., Butcher, 1972, 1994; Colligan, Osborne, & Swenson, 1984; Pancoast & Archer, 1989) noted problems with the original sample and resultant norms. The major problem was that the original norms, when used to evaluate contemporary test takers, tended to overpathologize. In other words, contemporary test takers may appear to suffer from more distress and dysfunction than they do in actuality (see Pope, Butcher, & Seelen, 1993, for a review of this research).

The MMPI Restandardization Project administered the MMPI to diverse sets of contemporary people. Their group mean MMPI scores are shown on the original norms developed by Hathaway and McKinley (1940). Contemporary individuals show scale elevations between ½ and 1 full standard deviation above the original MMPI normals. One reason why there is a misleading tendency for the original norms to overpathologize contemporary test takers is that when the original norms were developed, individuals were encouraged to omit items that they felt did not apply to them. Thus, many of the original normative individuals omitted a large number of items (around 30). In contemporary practice, however, test takers are encouraged to respond to all items, if possible. As a result, contemporary test takers respond to more items that can raise their scores on each of the scales and thus (inaccurately) appear to show more pathology.

This issue raised in this subsection, like the one presented in the following subsection, is rooted in the principle—stated in both the "Ethical Principles of Psychologists and Code of Conduct" (APA, 1992) and the "Specialty Guidelines for Forensic Psychologists" (CEGFP, 1991) and cited at the beginning of this section of the article—that psychologists bear a grave responsibility to ensure that the test fits (i.e., is appropriate for) the individual. Moreover, the necessity of attending carefully to norms, procedures, validating studies, and so forth, that may have become outdated is also rooted in the psychologist's responsibility to "maintain a reasonable level of awareness of *current* scientific and professional information" (APA, 1992, Section 1.05, p. 1600; italics added). Finally, Section 2.07 of the ethical principles specifically requires that "psychologists do not base . . . decisions or recommendations on tests and measures that are obsolete and not useful for the current purpose" (APA, 1992, p. 1603).

Geographic and Educational Representativeness

A second factor that can cast doubt on the validity of an otherwise acceptable test when used with a specific individual is the degree to which the individual fits the test norms in terms of variables such as geographic locale and formal education. Allowing these factors to result in distorted or misleading testimony about the findings of a forensic examination would violate explicit statements, cited previously, that assessment findings must be based on an adequate evaluation of the individual (APA, 1992; CEGFP, 1991).

The original MMPI normative sample, for example, tended to be rural in character, having been drawn from the Minnesota area. The mean educational level was around that of the eighth grade. The original MMPI normative group is, at best, an unusual reference group for contemporary test takers.

The Restandardization Committee sought to achieve at least three goals in developing a new normative sample. First, the committee sought to develop contemporary norms based on a larger sample that would be more geographically and educationally reflective of the contemporary United States. Second, the committee sought to maintain, insofar as possible, the original clinical and validity scales, making changes only for such reasons as eliminating objectionable items (e.g., items that were objectionable on religious grounds), updating items whose wording or content was so dated as to be meaningless to many contemporary test takers, and omitting items that were not scored on any of the clinical and validity scales. Few essential changes were made to these basic scales in an effort to preserve the empirical basis of the MMPI and maintain the relevance of much of the considerable body of research that was conducted during the last 50 years. Third, the committee sought to broaden the item pool to provide content for new measures that might be more relevant to contemporary test takers.

Beginning in 1982, the MMPI Restandardization Committee started gathering normative data for two new forms of the instrument: A form for contemporary adults (MMPI-2) and a form for contemporary adolescents (MMPI-A). The revised MMPI booklets were changed in three ways: (a) some items were rewritten to improve and modernize the language of the items; (b) objectionable item content, some of which had been the subject of lawsuits when used in personnel screening (see, e.g., *Soroka v. Dayton Hudson Corporation*, 1990), were deleted; and (c) new items were added to provide a more comprehensive assessment.

To broaden the geographic base of the normative sample, large and heterogeneous samples of normal individuals from across the United States were recruited. For the MMPI-2, a sample of 1,138 men and 1,462 women were randomly solicited from California, Minnesota, North Carolina, Ohio, Pennsylvania, Virginia, and Washington. For the MMPI-A, a total of 805 boys and 815 girls, between the ages of 14 and 18 and from both public and private schools were obtained in California, New York, North Carolina, Ohio, Pennsylvania, Virginia, and Washington. The MMPI-2 and MMPI-A normative samples are similar to the national population on education level and ethnic group membership (Butcher, Dahlstrom, Graham, Tellegen, & Kaemmer, 1989; Tellegen & Ben-Porath, 1992).

The psychologist conducting a forensic assessment bears an inescapable responsibility to ensure that the instruments and methods of assessment fit the individual geographically and educationally. He or she owes this responsibility to the court, to society in general (on whose behalf the justice system functions), and, not least, to the individual being assessed. Fulfilling this responsibility may require overcoming an understandable professional inertia: The forensic practitioner may have assembled a standard battery of tests with which he or she is comfortable. It may be a great temptation to administer this same battery in virtually every forensic assessment without taking time to ask whether each test makes sense in terms of the individual's geographic and educational background. Furthermore, certain tests or forms of tests have become so widely known and accepted that it appears—at least superficially—that they are appropriate for almost everyone; it may be dangerously easy for a forensic practitioner to select an array of such tests almost reflexively without examining each in detail to determine whether it adequately fits the individual to be assessed. Ethical practice requires that, in each forensic case, the psychologist first conduct an assessment of the test instruments themselves to ensure they fit the individual prior to using tests to conduct a forensic assessment of the individual.

Avoiding Ethnic and Racial Bias

A third factor that can affect the validity of an otherwise useful test is the intrusion of ethnic or racial bias. Evaluating the degree to which this factor may affect the validity of a test is a significant ethical responsibility.

> Psychologists attempt to identify situations in which particular interventions or assessment techniques or norms may not be applicable or may require adjustment in administration or interpretation because of factors much as individuals' gender, age, race, ethnicity, national origin, religion, sexual orientation, disability, language, or socioeconomic status. (APA, 1992, p. 1603; see also the chapters "Assessment, Testing, and Diagnosis" and "Cultural, Contextual, and Individual Differences" in Pope & Vasquez, 1991, pp. 87–100 and pp. 130–138.)

Imagine an expert witness breezing through a cross-examination about his or her forensic evaluation. Things are going well until suddenly the attorney asks: "Isn't it true that your clinic where you conducted this assessment has a 'Whites-Only' sign out in front and does not admit non-White clients?" It is probably difficult for the reader to imagine such a scene, in part because it seems so unlikely and outrageous that a professional would practice in such a setting. But consider how the judge, jury, and witness might react if the question were: "Isn't it true that you used a personality test whose norms excluded all people of color and diverse ethnic background and for which normality was defined, on a de facto basis, as 'Caucasian' "? How could the expert witness explain to the judge and jury the difference between practicing in a Whites-only clinic and using a test for which the norms were defined on a Whites-only sample?

The original MMPI, whose norms—as noted in the previous section—were created in the 1930s, drew as its normative sample an exclusively White group of people. Those of Asian, Black or African American, Hispanic, Native American, and other racial or ethnic groups and backgrounds played no role in defining what constituted normal responses to the hundreds of items on the MMPI. What are the ethical implications of using a test that defines its norms—and thus its assumptions of what is normal—using a Whites-only reference group? Faschingbauer (1979) wrote one of the most eloquent statements of the dilemmas of attempting to draw inferences about contemporary individuals using a psychometric instrument normed on such a limited sample:

The original Minnesota group . . . seems to be an inappropriate reference group for the 1980s. The median individual in that group had an eighth-grade education, was married, lived in a small town or on a farm, and was employed as a lower level clerk or skilled tradesman. None was under 16 or over 65 years of age, and all were white. As a clinician I find it difficult to justify comparing anyone to such a dated group. When the person is 14 years old, Chicano, and lives in Houston's poor fifth ward, use of the original norms seems sinful. (p. 375)

In a fascinating study, Erdberg and his colleagues (Erdberg, 1970, 1988; Gynther, Fowler, & Erdberg, 1971) discovered that, for a rural sample, all White test takers could be distinguished from all-Black test takers on the basis of one particular item from the original MMPI. Submitting the MMPI profiles for this rural sample to one of the widely used computer scoring and interpretation services, they also found that the computer-generated interpretations falsely indicated that 90% of the Black test takers, who showed no other evidence of suffering from significant pathology or of any clinical abnormalities, showed profiles associated with psychiatric patients.

The revision process leading to the creation of the MMPI–2 and MMPI–A involved careful attention to these issues. The MMPI–2 and MMPI–A normative samples are more representative of the United States and included a broad range of ethnic minorities. Researchers have investigated the usefulness of the revised versions of the test with those of different racial and ethnic backgrounds. Shondrick, Ben-Porath, and Stafford (1992), for example, found that Black and White men who had been court ordered for psychological evaluation produced nearly identical MMPI–2 profiles. In another cross-cultural study, Lucio and Reyes (1992) found that Mexican college students taking a Spanish version of the MMPI–2 showed essentially no difference on the MMPI–2 clinical scales than college students from the United States who took the MMPI–2 as reported by Butcher, Graham, Dahlstrom, and Bowman (1990).

Although the foundations and rationales for the psychologist's responsibility to ensure that tests not only avoid racial or ethic bias but also adequately fit the individual in all other significantly relevant ways have been cited previously, it is possible to view this responsibility from yet another perspective. Psychologists who offer testimony about forensic assessments take an oath prior to testifying: They swear or affirm that they will tell the whole truth. When psychologists present testimony that is distorted, misleading, or downright wrong because it is based on tests that embody racial or ethnic bias or that otherwise do not adequately fit the individual being assessed, they violate this oath to tell the whole truth. The testimony embodies half-truths and/or half-lies as if they were the whole truth.

ADMINISTERING TESTS CORRECTLY

It is important for standardized tests to be used in a standardized manner. The power and effectiveness, as well as the validity and reliability of standardized instruments, are assured only by using standardized procedures for administration, scoring, and interpretation. Shortcuts and improvisation are tempting to most of us in light of our crowded schedules and desire for creative expression. However, to alter the instructions or scoring system makes, by definition, a standardized test nonstandardized. In most cases, departing from the standardized method of administration, scoring, and interpretation cuts the vital link between the test and the validating research from which the test draws its power. The new ethics code underscores this responsibility:

> Psychologists who develop, administer, score, interpret, or use psychological assessment techniques, interviews, tests, or instruments do so in a manner and for purposes that are appropriate in light of the research on or evidence of the usefulness and proper application of the techniques. (APA, 1992, Section 2.02[a], p. 1603)

Although the "Specialty Guidelines for Forensic Psychologists" (CEGFP, 1991) does not explicitly mention the nonstandardized (mis)use of standardized tests, the responsibility to use such tests in a way that preserves their validity is implicit in Section VI(A)'s emphasis on the duty to maintain knowledge of scientific and professional developments and to apply this knowledge in a manner that accords with accepted scientific and clinical standards (see also *Standards for Educational and Psychological Testing*, 1985).

Part of the proper application for almost all standardized tests involves adequate monitoring of administration (Committee on Professional Standards of the APA, 1984; see also Pope, Tabachnick, & Keith-Spiegel, 1987). The problem was highlighted when a complaint was filed with the Committee on Professional Standards regarding a psychologist who had given his client an MMPI to take home. The committee found that whenever a psychologist

> does not have direct, first-hand information as to the condition under which the test is taken, he or she is forced (in the above instance, unnecessarily) to assume that the test responses were not distorted by the general situation in which the test was taken (e.g., whether the client consulted others about test responses). Indeed the psychologist could have no assurance that this test was in fact completed by the client. In the instance where the test might be introduced as data in a court proceeding it would be summarily dismissed as hearsay evidence. (Committee on Professional Standards of the APA, 1984, p. 664)

USING COMPUTERS APPROPRIATELY IN FORENSIC ASSESSMENT

Do computerized methods of scoring and interpreting standardized psychological tests provide an adequate scientific or professional basis for forensic decision making? Certainly the use of such methods has become widespread. In one national survey of clinical psychologists, less than 40% of the participants reported never using a computerized test interpretation service (Pope et al., 1987). Ziskin (1981) suggested that such services may actually have advantages for forensic assessments.

> I would recommend for forensic purposes the utilization of one of the automated . . . services. One obvious advantage is the minimizing or eliminating of the possibility of scoring errors or errors in transposition of scores. Also, these systems are capable of generating more information about an individual than the individual clinician is usually capable of simply by virtue of their ability to deal with greater amounts of information. Another advantage is the reduction of the problems of examiner effects, such as biases entering into the collection, recording, and interpretation of the data. (p. 9)

There are at least three crucial considerations in using computerized methods of scoring and interpretation. First, can the professional be confident that the mechanics of such services are error-free? That is, the professional must have some basis for testifying—should this issue be raised in court—that he or she is confident there are no bugs in the scoring program, virtually no likelihood that answer sheets became switched when fed into the computer (so that a printout purportedly for one examinee is actually based on the answer sheet of another individual), and so on.

Second, is there adequate evidence that the computer transforms raw scores and profiles into interpretative statements? This issue should never be taken on faith. It is possible that the interpretive statements have no research or other validity whatsoever but simply reflect the programmer's guesses about what certain scores or profiles suggest about the individual who took the test. The new ethics code emphasizes the psychologist's responsibility to ensure that "assessments, recommendations, reports, and psychological diagnostic or evaluative statements are based on information and techniques . . . sufficient to provide appropriate substantiation for their findings" (APA, 1992, Section 2.01a, p. 1603; see also Section 7.02, p. 1610). When a psychologist relies on information generated by a computerized interpretation service, this information must be scrutinized by the psychologist with the same care he or she uses in considering other sources of information. The "Specialty Guidelines for Forensic Psychologists" (CEGFP, 1991, Section F3) sets forth the special responsibilities of the psychologist to ensure that such third-party information (in this case, the information supplied by a computerized-scoring and interpretation service) has been obtained in compliance with the standards of the profession and to disclose the origins of the data (in this case, the basis of the computerized decision making or interpretive rules).

Third, the degree to which the interpretive statements in the computer-generated report actually apply to the individual who is being assessed needs to be determined. Although the use of a computer may lend an air of authority or even infallibility to the interpretive statements, inferences drawn on an actuarial basis from the standardized instrument such as the MMPI are hypotheses that must be evaluated in the light of other information. This issue is addressed in the following section.

The question as to whether computer-derived psychological reports stand alone as veridical personality information about clients is important to consider. Computer-derived descriptions are essentially textbook or prototype descriptions of a particular test pattern developed by examining patterns of test results and behavioral correlates. For example, an MMPI-2 computer-based narrative report on a client is not a report about that particular patient but is a summary of the most appropriate test descriptors for the particular set of test scores the individual produced. Any time those scores are read into the computer, the exact descriptions will be printed out. The generalization that people who produce those scores are alike (and thus receive those personality descriptions) in terms of symptoms and attitudes and are different from people who produce other patterns of scores is derived from the validity research supporting the test.

ASSESSING AND REPORTING FACTORS THAT MAY AFFECT THE MEANING OF TEST FINDINGS

Even when all of the factors noted thus far have been carefully attended to, there are numerous factors that can influence the test data and their meaning (e.g., distractions while a client is taking a test or a client taking a test while heavily medicated). Such factors must be included in a forensic report or forensic testimony because they affect the accuracy of interpretations, as noted in the new code:

> When interpreting test results, including automated interpretations, psychologists take into account the various test factors and characteristics of the person being assessed that might affect psychologists' judgments or reduce the accuracy of their interpretations. They indicate any significant reservations they have about the accuracy or limitations of their interpretations. (APA, 1992, Section 2.05, p. 1603)

Because such factors can obscure or distort assessment findings and inferences in a variety of subtle (as well as not-so-subtle) ways, those reporting the results of forensic evaluations have a special obligation to disclose information that will prevent misunderstanding. Section VII(a) of the "Specialty Guidelines for Forensic Psychologists" states clearly that

> Forensic psychologists make reasonable efforts to ensure that the products of their services, as well their own public statements and professional testimony, are communicated in ways that will promote understanding and avoid deception, given the particular characteristics, roles, and abilities of various recipients of the communications. (cited in Pope, Butcher, & Seelen, 1993, p. 202)

In forensic settings, one of the prominent factors that can affect the meaning of test findings is an individual's possible motivation to respond deceptively. Forensic assessments often involve questions of credibility that may be much less salient in other settings. The defendant in a capital case may be strongly motivated to convince others that he or she meets the legal criteria of insanity. The convict who is being considered for parole may rely on sophisticated skills in attempting to present a good picture. The plaintiff pressing a bogus personal injury suit may be quite creative in describing deep and chronic dysfunction and distress. Such motivation—completely understandable in light of the circumstances—must be taken into account during a forensic assessment.

In some cases, the assessment instrument may help the forensic evaluator identify ways an individual might attempt to present a distorted picture of himself or herself. For example, the revision process for the MMPI paid special attention to the needs for empirically based measures that help the expert witness in this regard. Several new measures were developed for the MMPI-2 to improve the detection of deviant response sets. An additional infrequency scale *(FB)* was developed to assess random, confused responding, or faking of items that appear toward the back of the MMPI-2 booklet. The *Back F* scale operates in a manner similar to the original *F* scale which appears earlier in the MMPI-2 booklet. In addition, two new measures were designed to assess inconsistent responding, a situation that frequently occurs in forensic assessment. These scales, the *VRIN* and *TRIN,* operate on the assumption that individuals, to be consistent, should respond to similar item content in a similar manner. The new validity scales, as well as those originally contained in the MMPI, have been extensively studied in several recent articles (Berry et al., 1991; Graham, Watts, & Timbrook, 1991; Wetter, Baer, Berry, Smith, & Larsen, 1992), and several recent evaluations of the utility and effectiveness of MMPI-based measures of test validity in detecting malingering and underreporting of symptoms have been published (see Baer, Wetter, & Berry, 1992; Pope, Butcher, & Seelen, 1993; Schretlen, 1988; Wetter et al., 1992). Forensic witnesses must be aware of and familiar with this literature, as well as the capabilities of other tests in this regard.

It is also important to be thorough, objective, and balanced when communicating test results that will be used in court (Pope, 1994; Pope, Butcher, & Seelen, 1993; Weiner, 1987). Appropriate reservations about the findings and possible limiting factors need to be included in the report, as well as information that supports the conclusions being made.

CONCLUSION

The publication of both a new ethics code (APA, 1992) and new guidelines for forensic psychologists (CEGFP, 1991), as well as the recent appearance of two revisions MMPI-2 and MMPI-A; Butcher et al., 1989; Butcher et al., 1992, respectively) of perhaps the most widely used personality test, provided the opportunity for discussing seven fundamental responsibilities of psychologists conducting forensic assessments. It is worth emphasizing again that these are but a few of the many ethical standards relevant to forensic assessment (see in the "Ethical Principles of Psychologists and Code of Conduct," APA, 1992, those statements relevant to, for example, maintaining documentation in forensic work, Section 1.23, p. 1602; avoiding recommendations based on test data that are outdated, Section 2.07a, p. 1603; and avoiding or at least clarifying multiple and potentially conflicting roles, Section 7.03, p. 1610). These new documents also provide opportunities to rethink other aspects of our professional responsibilities relevant to forensic practice. Though discussion of these issues is beyond the scope of this article, this concluding section notes three of the most important questions confronting forensic practitioners.

First, to what extent is our training in these responsibilities adequate? Ideally, the kinds of responsibilities discussed in this article should be a basic part of the education of anyone who begins to conduct forensic assessments. They should be internalized as important values so that they become second nature to the psychologist and will not be easily forgotten, fudged, or rationalized away in the often stressful, demanding, contentious atmosphere of the American adversarial system of justice. Yet there are a number of distressing reports of expert witnesses who seem either to be unaware of these responsibilities or to have no allegiance to them (e.g., Pope & Vetter, 1992). Individual psychologists and the profession as a whole must candidly confront the issue of education and training in the ethics of forensic work.

Second, the occurrence of unethical forensic practice leads also to another question: Are our mechanisms of accountability adequate? What happens when we become aware that another psychologist has violated one of these fundamental standards of forensic practice? Do we tend to turn away and take no action, perhaps because we are uncertain about what the standards are and what constitutes substandard or unethical practice, perhaps because we shy away from encountering the wrath of a colleague, perhaps because we fear being sued by the colleague, perhaps because we assume—rightly or wrongly—that nothing will come of our attempts at intervention, or for other reasons? The revision of our ethical standards should prompt thorough consideration of why we have such standards, what purposes we intend them to serve, whether we believe that practicing in accordance with them is important (and if so, how important), how we expect them to be implemented, and what sanctions, if any, we believe should be imposed when forensic practitioners violate an important standard. Thus, the occasion of creating a new code provides a stimulus and opportunity to rethink our efforts to implement standards and to hold accountable those who violate them.

Third, to what extent are the documents that codify our standards adequate to the current practice of forensic psychology? One section of this article emphasized the evolution of normative data, administrative and interpretive procedures, and research bases for psychological tests. A person well trained to administer, score, and interpret a standardized test 10 years ago may well be incompetent to use that test today if he or she has not secured additional training, kept up with the current research literature, or learned that the test has been revised. But it is not only the domain of testing that evolves. The forensic setting, the legislation and case law that affect expert testimony, the factors that can subtly but powerfully influence the forensic psychologist's judgment, and participation in the legal system have also changed. To what extent do the ethical principles and other statements of professional standards adequately address the dilemmas currently faced by psychologists who conduct forensic assessments?

The psychologist who conducts forensic assessments holds a sometimes overwhelming power over the lives of others. The results of a forensic assessment may influence—perhaps even determine—whether a person receives custody of his or her child, is forced to pay damages to another litigant, returns home from the courtroom, or spends years in prison. In some cases, the assessment results may literally determine whether a person accused of a capital crime lives or dies. Whatever other implications this power has, it mandates that we never take it for granted or treat it carelessly. The explicit ethical and professional standards reviewed in this article are the profession's attempt to ensure that this power is used competently, carefully, appropriately, and responsibly. Our responsibility as forensic practitioners includes not only upholding these standards in our own work of conducting assessments but also constantly rethinking the nature of these standards, their presence in our education and training, the degree to which the profession ensures accountability or, alternatively, passively tolerates and tacitly accepts or encourages violations, and the care with which we spell out responsibilities that fit the current and constantly evolving demands of forensic assessment.

ACKNOWLEDGMENT

We express our deep appreciation to Bruce Sales, PhD, JD, whose editorial suggestions were extremely helpful.

REFERENCES

Abeles, N. (1982). Proceedings of the American Psychological Association, Incorporated, for the year 1981. Minutes of the annual meeting of the Council of Representatives. *American Psychologist, 37,* 632–666.

American Psychological Association. (1992). Ethical principles of psychologists and code of conduct. *American Psychologist, 47,* 1597–1611.

Anastasi, A. (1988). *Psychological testing* (6th ed.). New York: Macmillan.

Baer, R. A., Wetter, M. W., & Berry, D. T. (1992). Detection of underreporting of psychopathology on the MMPI: A meta analysis. *Clinical Psychology Review, 12,* 209–225.

Ben-Porath, Y. S., Butcher, J. N., & Graham, J. R. (1991). Contribution of the MMPI-2 scales to the differential diagnosis of schizophrenia and major depression. *Psychological Assessment: A Journal of Consulting and Clinical Psychology, 3,* 634–640.

Berry, D. T., Wetter, M. W., Baer, R. A., Widiger, T. A., Sumpter, J. C., Reynolds, S. K., & Hallam, R. A. (1991). Detection of random responding on the MMPI-2: Utility of F, Back F, and VRIN scales. *Psychological Assessment: A Journal of Consulting and Clinical Psychology, 3,* 418–423.

Butcher, J. N. (Ed.). (1972). *Objective personality assessment: Changing perspectives.* New York: Academic.

Butcher, J. N. (1990). *Use of the MMPI-2 in treatment planning.* New York: Oxford University Press.

Butcher, J. N. (1994). Psychological assessment of airline pilot applicants with the MMPI-2. *Journal of Personality Assessment, 62,* 31–44.

Butcher, J. N., Dahlstrom, W. G., Graham, J. R., Tellegen, A., & Kaemmer, B. (1989). *Minnesota Multiphasic Personality Inventory-2 (MMPI-2): Manual for administration and scoring.* Minneapolis: University of Minnesota Press.

Butcher, J. N., Graham, J. R., Dahlstrom, W. G., & Bowman, E. (1990). The MMPI-2 with college students. *Journal of Personality Assessment, 54,* 1–15.

Butcher, J. N., Graham, J. R., Williams, C. L., & Ben-Porath, Y. S. (1990). *Development and use of the MMPI-2 Content scales.* Minneapolis: University of Minnesota Press.

Butcher, J. N., & Williams, C. L. (1992). *MMPI-2 and MMPI-A: Essentials of clinical interpretation.* Minneapolis: University of Minnesota Press.

Butcher, J. N., Williams, C. L., Graham, J. R., Archer, R., Tellegen, A., Ben-Porath, Y. S., & Kaemmer, B. (1992). *MMPI-A manual for administration, scoring, and interpretation.* Minneapolis: University of Minnesota Press.

Colligan, R. C., Osborne, D., & Swenson, W. M. (1984). *The MMPI: Development of the contemporary norms.* New York: Praeger.

Committee on Ethical Guidelines for Forensic Psychologists. (1991). Specialty guidelines for forensic psychologists. *Law and Human Behavior, 15,* 655–665.

Committee on Professional Standards of the American Psychological Association. (1984). Casebook for providers of psychological services. *American Psychologist, 39,* 663–668.

Conger, J. J. (1976). Proceedings of the American Psychological Association, Incorporated, for the year 1976. Minutes of the annual meeting of the Council of Representatives, August 29 and September 2, 1975, Chicago Illinois, and January 23-25, 1976, Washington, DC. *American Psychologist, 31,* 406-434.

Davison, G. C., & Neale, J. M. (1990). *Abnormal psychology: An experimental clinical approach* (5th ed.). New York: Wiley.

Egeland, B., Erickson, M., Butcher, J. N., & Ben-Porath, Y. S. (1991). MMPI-2 profiles of women at risk for child abuse. *Journal of Personality Assessment, 57,* 254-263.

Erdberg, P. (1970). MMPI differences associated with sex, race, and residence in a southern sample (Doctoral dissertation, University of Alabama, 1969). *Dissertation Abstracts International, 30,* 5236B.

Erdberg, P. (1988, August). *How clinicians can achieve competence in testing procedures.* Paper presented at the annual meeting of the American Psychological Association, Atlanta.

Faschingbauer, T. R. (1979). The future of the MMPI. In C. S. Newmark (Ed.), *MMPI: Clinical and research trends* (pp. 373-398). New York: Praeger.

Goldstein, M. J., Baker, B. L., & Jamison, K. R. (1980). *Abnormal psychology.* Boston: Little, Brown.

Graham, J. R. (1987). *The MMPI: A practical guide* (2nd ed.). New York: Oxford University Press.

Graham, J. R., Watts, D., & Timbrook, R. (1991). Detecting fake-good and fake-bad MMPI-2 profiles. *Journal of Personality Assessment, 57,* 264-277.

Greene, R. L. (1980). *The MMPI: An interpretive manual.* New York: Grune & Stratton.

Gynther, M. D., Fowler, R. D., & Erdberg, P. (1971). False positives galore: The application of standard MMPI criteria to a rural, isolated, Negro sample. *Journal of Clinical Psychology, 27,* 234-237.

Hall, J. E., & Hare-Mustin, R. T. (1983). Sanctions and the diversity of complaints against psychologists. *American Psychologist, 38,* 714-729.

Hathaway, S. R., & McKinley, J. C. (1940). A multiphasic personality schedule (Minnesota): I. Construction of the schedule. *Journal of Psychology, 10,* 249-254.

Hjemboe, S., Almagor, M., & Butcher, J. N. (1992). Empirical assessment of marital distress: The Marital Distress Scale (MDS) for the MMPI-2. In C. D. Spielberger & J. N. Butcher, (Eds.), *Advances in personality assessment* (Vol. 9, pp. 141-152). Hillsdale, NJ: Lawrence Erlbaum Associates, Inc.

Hjemboe, S., & Butcher, J. N. (1991). Couples in marital distress: A study of demographic and personality factors as measured by the MMPI-2. *Journal of Personality Assessment, 57,* 216-237.

Keller, L. S., & Butcher, J. N. (1991). *Use of the MMPI-2 with chronic pain patients.* Minneapolis: University of Minnesota Press.

Lees-Haley, P. R. (1992). Psychodiagnostic test usage by forensic psychologists. *American Journal of Forensic Psychology, 10,* 25-30.

Lubin, B., Larsen, R. M., & Matarazzo, J. (1984). Patterns of psychological test usage in the United States: 1935-1982. *American Psychologist, 39,* 451-454.

Lucio, E., & Reyes, I. (1992, July). *Adaptation of the MMPI-2 for college students in Mexico.* Paper presented at the meeting of the International Congress of Psychology, Brussels, Belgium.

McConnell, J. V. (1974). *Understanding human behavior.* New York: Holt, Rinehart & Winston.

Messick, S. (1980). Test validity and the ethics of assessment. *American Psychologist, 35,* 1012-1027.

Pancoast, D. L., & Archer, R. P. (1989). Original adult MMPI norms in adult samples: A review with implications for future developments. *Journal of Personality Assessment, 53,* 376-395.

Pope, K. S. (1994). *Sexual involvement with therapists: Patient assessment, subsequent therapy, forensics.* Washington, DC: American Psychological Association.

Pope, K. S., & Bouhoutsos, J. C. (1986). *Sexual intimacy between therapists and patients.* New York: Praeger.

Pope, K. S., Butcher, J. N., & Seelen, J. (1993). *MMPI/MMPI-2/MMPI-A in court: Assessment, testimony, and cross-examination for expert witnesses and attorneys.* Washington, DC: American Psychological Association.

Pope, K. S., Sonne, J. L., & Holroyd, J. (1993). *Sexual feelings in psychotherapy.* Washington, DC: American Psychological Association.

Pope, K. S., Tabachnick, B. G., & Keith-Spiegel, P. (1987). Ethics of practice: The beliefs and behaviors of psychologists as therapists. *American Psychologist, 42,* 993–1006.

Pope, K. S., & Vasquez, M. J. T. (1991). *Ethics in psychotherapy and counseling: A practical guide for psychologists.* San Francisco: Jossey-Bass.

Pope, K. S., & Vetter, V. A. (1992). Ethical dilemmas encountered by members of the American Psychological Association: A national survey. *American Psychologist, 47,* 397–411.

Sanders, J. R., & Keith-Spiegel, P. (1980). Formal and informal adjudication of ethics complaints against psychologists. *American Psychologist, 35,* 1096–1105.

Schretlen, D. (1988). The use of psychological tests to identify malingered symptoms of mental disorder. *Clinical Psychology Review, 8,* 451–476.

Shondrick, D. D., Ben-Porath, Y. S., & Stafford, K. (1992, May). *Characteristics of individuals undergoing court-ordered evaluations.* Paper presented at the 27th Annual Symposium on Recent Developments in the Use of the MMPI (MMPI-2), Minneapolis.

Soroka v. Dayton Hudson Corporation, 753 Cal. Rptr. App.3d 654I, Cal.Rptr 2d77 (Cal. App. 1 Dist, 1990).

Standards for educational and psychological testing. (1985). Washington, DC: American Psychological Association.

Tellegen, A., & Ben-Porath, Y. S. (1992). The new uniform T-scores for the MMPI-2: Rationale, derivation, and appraisal. *Psychological Assessment, 4,* 145–155.

Tellegen, A., & Ben-Porath, Y. S. (1993). Code-type comparability across MMPI and MMPI-2 norms: Some necessary clarifications. *Journal of Personality Assessment, 61,* 489–500.

Waskow, I. E., & Parloff, M. B. (Eds.). (1975). *Psychotherapy change measures: Report of the Clinical Research Branch Outcome Measures Project* (DHEW Publication No. ADM 74–120). Rockville, MD: National Institute of Mental Health.

Weiner, I. B. (1987). Writing forensic reports. In I. Weiner & A. Hess (Eds.), *Handbook of forensic psychology* (pp. 511–528). New York: Wiley.

Weiner, I. B. (1989). On competence and ethicality in psychodiagnostic assessment. *Journal of Personality Assessment, 53,* 827–831.

Wetter, W., Baer, R. A., Berry, D. T., Smith, G. T., & Larsen, L. (1992). Sensitivity of MMPI-2 validity scales to random responding and malingering. *Psychological Assessment, 4,* 369–374.

Ziskin, J. (1981). Use of the MMPI in forensic settings. In J. N. Butcher, W. G. Dahlstrom, M. D. Gynther, & W. Schofield (Eds.), *Clinical notes on the MMPI* (Whole No. 1–19). Nutley, NJ: Hoffman-La Roche Laboratories/National Computer Services.

The Use of Empathy in Forensic Examinations

Daniel W. Shuman
School of Law
Southern Methodist University

Key words: empathy, expert witness, forensic examination

The interaction of a myriad of legal and ethical rules create the responsibility for psychiatrists and psychologists conducting court-ordered examinations to warn the examinee that the results of the examination will be reported to the court. For instance, the U.S. Supreme Court has ruled that the Fifth Amendment privilege against self-incrimination precludes using, during the capital-sentencing portion of that case, information obtained during a court-ordered competence to stand trial examination unless the defendant was given a Miranda-type warning that what is disclosed may be used in court before the examination begins (*Estelle v. Smith,* 1980). In many states, the physician–patient or psychotherapist–patient privilege permits psychiatrists and psychologists to testify to the results of a court-ordered examination only if they informed the examinee that the results of the examination would not be privileged (e.g., Maryland Courts, 1993; Texas Rules of Evidence, 1993). And, numerous ethical rules recognize psychiatrists' and psychologists' obligation to inform the examinee that a report will be prepared and made available to certain named persons and of the possible legal consequences of that report (American Psychiatric Association, 1984; Committee on Ethical Guidelines for Forensic Psychologists [CEGFP], 1991; Rappeport, 1981).

This article begins where that warning ends. A warning about the purpose and potential use of a court-ordered psychiatric or psychological examination is necessary, but is it sufficient? Once the examiner has explained the purpose and potential use of the examination in clear and unambiguous language, should the examiner be permitted to use any technique short of physical

---

Requests for reprints should be sent to Daniel W. Shuman, School of Law, Southern Methodist University, Dallas, TX 75275.

violence to gain information? For example, should the court-ordered examiner be permitted to use therapeutic relationship building as a tool to gather information during an assessment?

A psychiatrist or psychologist who provides both assessment and therapeutic services to a person risks that the objectivity of the assessment services may be adversely affected by the therapeutic services and that the efficacy of the therapeutic services may be adversely affected by the assessment services. The specter of a patient witnessing a devastating cross-examination of a therapist gives rise to a myriad of therapeutic concerns. Correlatively, the therapeutic role may cause the forensic examiner to weigh heavily the patient's response to the examiner's testimony, resulting in a loss of objectivity. It is best to separate assessment and therapeutic functions in both civil and criminal cases (CEGFP, 1991). This conclusion holds true whether the psychiatrist or psychologist is court-appointed or privately retained.

These results will not occur uniformly in civil and criminal cases, however. Certain civil cases, for instance, may mix court-ordered examiner's roles in ways that are less likely to occur in criminal cases. A psychiatrist or psychologist conducting a court-ordered examination in a child custody case may, utilizing "the best interests of the child" standard, appropriately recommend a therapeutic outcome for the parties—parents and child. For example, a psychologist conducting a court-ordered examination in a child custody dispute in which the father seeks custody only to hurt the mother may recommend that custody not be awarded to a father and that postdivorce counseling be a condition of unrestricted visitation. This result may be in the best interests of the child, who avoids becoming a pawn in a parental game; the mother, who avoids becoming entangled in a battle over issues left over from the marriage; and the father, who is not saddled with a responsibility he did not really want and who is now provided with an alternative solution to address issues left over from the marriage.

Although most civil cases do not utilize a "best interests" test, they still present markedly different concerns from criminal proceedings. For example, criminal proceedings involve issues of pretrial confinement, risk of imprisonment or execution, imbalance of resources, and later appointment of counsel for the defendant—issues not present in civil proceedings. And, with the exception of child custody and guardianship issues, examinations by court-appointed psychiatrists and psychologists are rare in civil cases (American Bar Association, 1983). In criminal cases, conversely, examinations by court-appointed psychiatrists and psychologists occur regularly regarding competence to stand trial, mental disability and criminal responsibility, and sentencing (Shuman, 1986). Increasingly, refusing to speak with the court-appointed examiner precludes a criminal defendant's presentation of expert testimony in support of an insanity defense (*Muhammad v. State,* 1987).

For these reasons, the importance of drawing a bright line between forensic assessment and therapeutic services is most apparent in criminal cases, and the rest of the article focuses on the use of empathy in court-ordered examinations in criminal cases with one exception. Although civil commitment proceedings defy reductionist civil or criminal labels (*Addington v. Texas,* 1983), the use of governmental power to confine and coerce treatment argues persuasively in favor of their inclusion under the criminal label for the purposes of this article. Finally, I do not intend to imply through the exclusion of civil cases that the use of empathy is appropriate in court-ordered examinations in civil cases; I do, however, think that the issue is more complex and requires more extensive treatment than this forum permits.

A PROBLEM OF LAW?

The stakes in criminal proceedings are high—life and liberty hang in the balance. And, the role of the court-ordered examiner is often thought to be central on questions of competence to stand trial, criminal responsibility, and sentencing. The court-ordered examiner is, therefore, expected to provide the court with an informed opinion. Indeed, the examiner's reputation is a function of the thoroughness of the examination. Thus, there are powerful incentives for the examiner to utilize all available information-gathering skills when conducting the examination.

Is the use of therapeutic relationship building and information-gathering skills in a forensic examination really a legal problem? Why is it not resolved by the obligatory warning about the purpose and use of the examination? The warning alerts defendants that this is not therapy and that the intended use of the examination requires vigilance. This analysis seems to underlie the intuitive response of forensic examiners who do not perceive the use of therapeutic skills in forensic examinations as problematic.

There is a rational basis for the criminal defendant to speak with the examiner because refusal may preclude raising an insanity defense. However, there is no rational basis for the defendant to discuss wrongful conduct with the examiner when that information is not already known to law enforcement authorities and when it might result in the rejection of the insanity defense or the imposition of a harsher sentence. Because the purpose of the examination is not therapeutic, disclosure of such information will not serve a useful purpose for the defendant. Indeed, it is surprising when such disclosures are made given that the examiner warned the defendant that inculpatory remarks will be reported to the court. Then why might they occur? If the examiner utilizes an empathetic relationship-building technique, as recommended by Hall (1987), responds emotionally to the defendant's hurt and anger and communicates that response to the defendant, then the defendant may be persuaded that an alliance exists with the examiner, misinterpret the relationship as therapeutic, and reveal the commission of previously undiscovered crimes (Rosenbaum, 1991).

When faced with a therapist's admonition that certain information may have to be disclosed to third persons whom patients threaten with violence (*Tarasoff v. Regents of the University of California,* 1976) or to governmental entities in cases of child abuse, most patients do not, because of the admonition, refrain from discussing these issues with therapists (Shuman & Weiner, 1987). Some suggest that this candor may have the opposite effect (American Psychiatric Association, 1984). Patients may be enticed by the candor of the warning to believe that increased trust in the therapist is justified. This increased trust may result in the patient's revelation of more, rather than less, potentially damaging information than might be expected following a warning about disclosure to third persons.

At the very least, a warning is easily neutralized. One study of the effect of a Fifth Amendment warning on people awaiting civil commitment hearings found that it had little impact on willingness to speak to staff (Miller, Maier, & Kaye, 1985). Moreover, studies of the effect of the Miranda warning in normal populations do not reveal that it has reduced the number of confessions (Leiken, 1970; Special Project, 1967). Thus, there is little reason to expect that a warning about the consequences of the forensic examination would help mentally ill criminal defendants maintain an appropriate perspective on the examination.

Even for the nonmentally disordered, "being jailed following an arrest for an alleged criminal offense is for many an upsetting, threatening, and depressing experience" (Dunn & Steadman, 1982, p. 3). Criminal defendants suffering from mental or emotional problems bear these problems as an additional burden when trying to keep the role of the examiner in perspective. This is significant because criminal defendants suspected of suffering from mental or emotional problems are likely to be confined in a jail prior to a ruling on their competence (Wexler, 1971). The stress of criminal prosecution and confinement can be expected to exacerbate preexisting mental or emotional problems. Mental health services for pretrial detainees are woefully inadequate. And, criminal defendants are unlikely to find a sympathetic ear among fellow inmates. Because fellow inmates who are willing listeners may well be informants (*United States v. Henry,* 1980), the forensic examiner is likely to be the only mental health professional available to speak with the criminal defendant. Thus, it is not surprising that "many defendants develop anticipation of a therapist–patient connection with an evaluator whose ultimate work-product they may later come to regard as patently antithetical to their interests" (Wells, 1985, p. 94).

The behavior of the examiner also may be a significant part of the problem. The examiner's "uniform" may induce an inappropriately relaxed mindset in the defendant. The uniforms worn by law enforcement personnel are intended to make people hypervigilent (Bickman, 1974; Volpe & Lennon, 1988). It is intended that the uniforms cause us to act in a more law-abiding manner. The uniforms worn by mental health professionals are not intended to induce the same hypervigilence. To the contrary, they are intended to result in relaxation and minimization of resistance (Hubble & Gelso, 1978).

In addition, the examiner is, by selection, training, and experience, likely to be skilled at helping people to be comfortable when discussing uncomfortable things. The authority of a therapist in a traditional, voluntary therapeutic relationship to order hospitalization or reveal confidential communications is purposefully limited (Shuman & Weiner, 1982). The use of empathy in a therapeutic relationship when the therapist has limited authority over the patient reduces, but does not completely avoid, the risk of abuse or conflict (Brodsky, 1989). However, the use of these same skills in a forensic examination in which treatment by the examiner is not contemplated presents a markedly different scenario.

A potential solution beyond warnings is for the law to require that lawyers be present during the examination or that the examination be videotaped. Because empathy involves not only verbal activities but also nonverbal activities such as facial expression, vocal intonation, and body language (Goldstein & Michaels, 1985), being able to watch what the examiner does may provide an added safeguard. Yet, it is unlikely that the subtle evidence of this problem will be captured by the videotape or be perceived by the lawyers.

The judicial system is unlikely to be capable of resolving this problem adequately. Lawyers are capable of structuring formal warnings and ascertaining whether they were given. This is the sort of task for which they are trained and at which they excel. They are adept at literal interpretation. Lawyers are less likely to be capable of grasping the subtext of communications between examiner and defendant. This is not the sort of task for which they are trained, at which they excel, or in which they rejoice. For example, the U.S. Supreme Court has been unwilling to scrutinize police use of persuasive interviewing styles following a Miranda warning (*Brewer v. Williams,* 1977).

The prospect of an expanded warning to address this problem is also less than satisfying. A warning that the purpose of the examination is not therapeutic and that the results will be reported to the court is already required. An embellished warning to be on guard against techniques that erroneously imply a therapeutic relationship is simultaneously too much and not enough. Requiring an embellished warning that focuses on techniques that may erode the warning is too much in that it may cause most defendants to refuse to participate in the interview in its entirety; reliable psychiatric and psychological interpretation of information gained in appropriate ways may provide unique, helpful insights to the courts (Shuman, 1986).

An embellished warning is not enough in that empathetic techniques are intended to break down resistance and to encourage disclosure without self-censorship. When a skilled examiner uses these techniques, there is reason to question the ability of a mentally ill criminal defendant to avoid their intended effect. "Skilled interviewers . . . will create a relationship in which the examinee can readily forget he/she has been warned" (Stone, 1984, pp. 213–214). Thus, although the use of empathy in forensic evaluations is precipitated by the legal setting, it is not readily resolvable by a legalistic response. The use of empathy in forensic examinations must, instead, be addressed in the realm of professional ethics.

THE ETHICAL INQUIRY

There are at least two sets of ethical guidelines for forensic examiners that might be expected to provide direction on the use of empathy in forensic examinations—the American Psychological Association Division 41's Ethical Guidelines for Forensic Psychologists" (CEGFP, 1991) and the American Psychiatric Association Task Force on the Role of Psychiatry in Sentencing. Whereas the former document does not address the use of empathy in forensic examinations, the latter does. It concludes in absolute terms only that when the person being examined appears to be mistakenly approaching the examination as therapy, does the examiner have an obligation to reinform the subject of the purpose of the examination or terminate the examination?

> The use of empathetic techniques and tools of clarification and interpretation may lower a subject's usual defenses. It is difficult to provide guidelines to regulate such behavior, however, because in many cases these techniques represent the essence of the psychiatric examination. In addition, empathetic statements may be necessary to prevent the subject from suffering harm as the result of discussing psychologically distressing topics. A particularly troubling situation arises when the defendant responds to an empathetic interviewer by revealing damaging information as a penitential act or as an expression of guilt. One must ultimately rely on the judgment of the individual psychiatrist in this type of situation. What can be said is that the psychiatrist should consider terminating the examination whenever it appears that the subject is confused about the purpose of the encounter. A subject who appears to be slipping into a "therapeutic" mindset should be reminded of the nontherapeutic intent of the assessment before the examination proceeds further. (American Psychiatric Association, 1984, p. 203)

This conclusion is pragmatic and finds that empathy is permissible, even desirable, in forensic examinations "to prevent the subject from suffering harm as the result of discussing psychologically distressing topics" (p. 203). But it finds the use of empathy impermissible when the subject slips into a "therapeutic mindset" (p. 203).

This approach places the examiner and the subject in an untenable position. The forensic examiner and the subject are expected to distinguish between the use of empathy as a therapeutic tool, which is not permitted, and the use of empathy "to prevent the subject from suffering harm as the result of discussing psychologically distressing topics" (p. 203), which is permitted. The distinction drawn by the American Psychiatric Association's task force between a nontraumatic discussion of a psychologically distressing topic and therapy is illusory. Therapy is helping people feel comfortable when discussing psychologically distressing subjects (Wolberg, 1967). Reliance on a mentally disordered criminal defendant to distinguish between a therapeutic and a nontherapeutic but nonharmful discussion of a psychologically distressing topic is unrealistic. And, research reveals that therapists do not accurately assess the level of empathy perceived by patients (Kurtz & Grummon, 1972). Thus, even if the distinction drawn by the task force were not illusory, it is unlikely that the distinction could be applied accurately.

Halleck (1986), one of the authors of the task force report (American Psychiatric Association, 1984), and others (e.g., Szasz, 1963) approached the issue in terms of double agent—the white coat syndrome. He stated, "Most people view a doctor or psychotherapist as somebody whose only obligation is to help people. While offenders may be cynical and suspicious of authority figures, they too have been trained to trust doctors" (p. 170). Although this contextualization provides an important perspective on the role of the forensic examiner, it ignores an important variable. Most criminal defendants come from a segment of society that lacks adequate health care (Segalman & Basu, 1981). They are unlikely to have had regular preventive health care from a family physician. Instead, they are likely to have used clinics and emergency rooms for health care, with intermittent contact from different physicians. There is reason to doubt that the bulk of criminal defendants come from a tradition of long-term, trusting doctor–patient relationships that would condition them to disclose fully to their doctor for therapeutic reasons. Mental health care for the poor, in particular, has been largely unavailable and ineffective when available (Garfield, 1986; Lerner, 1972). Although thoughtful psychiatrists and psychologists may experience ambiguity in approaching a forensic role (Stone, 1984), it is not at all clear that criminal defendants experience ambiguity in approaching the forensic examiner.

An analysis of the use of empathy in forensic examinations is more appropriately framed in terms of fairness. Rather than approach the problem as a function of the trust in doctors that criminals bring to the forensic relationship, it is more useful to ask how psychiatrists and psychologists get people to trust them and whether the techniques used to gain this trust are fair. It is fair to ask why fairness counts, particularly because fairness is a familiar word in the legal lexicon but is less familiar as a psychiatric or psychological concern.

The role of the forensic examiner is to provide information about a person's mental or emotional condition. This information is gathered during a forensic relationship that is unbalanced (Perlin, 1991); it is not a voluntary relationship that a patient chooses to enter or terminate. The participants do not share a common goal of patient benefit. The rules of confidentiality do not apply. It is an adversarial relationship arising out of a judicial proceeding, with the examiner having the capacity to influence the result of a judicial proceeding against the defendant. Thus, the fairness of the use of empathy in a forensic relationship to gain the trust of the examinee is an appropriate ethical inquiry.

Such an inquiry requires a more detailed exploration of empathy than has been presented so far. Empathy is often conceptualized as having cognitive and affective components (Gladstein, 1983). The cognitive component involves an intellectual response to another person—thinking as that person does. The affective component involves an emotional response to another person—feeling as that person does. Rogers (1975), an advocate of the importance of empathy in therapy, provided a definition of empathy that merges these two concepts and offers insights into its clinical application:

> It means entering the private perceptual world of the other and becoming thoroughly at home in it. It involves being sensitive, moment to moment, to the changing felt meanings which flow in this other person, to the fear or rage or tenderness or confusion or whatever, that he/she is experiencing. It means temporarily living in his/her life, moving in it delicately without making judgments, sensing feelings of which he/she is scarcely unaware, but not trying to uncover feelings of which the person is totally unaware, since this would be too threatening. It includes communicating your sensing of his/her world as you look with fresh and unfrightened eyes at elements of which the individual is fearful. (p. 2)

Empathy may be important to help a therapist form a therapeutic bond with a patient (Book, 1988; Westen, 1985). Framed in these terms, empathy seems only a tool for good. This construct contributes to the common misconception that "empathy *always* produces altruistic, helping, or caring responses" (Henderson, 1987, p. 1583). It does not (Hoffman, 1981). In the abstract, empathy is neither positive nor negative. A therapist may use empathy to help a patient; a car dealer may use empathy to sell a car.

The deception implicit in the myth that empathy invariably leads to helpful or caring behavior is fostered by empathetic resonation, a part of the empathy cycle that also includes expressed and received empathy (Barrett-Leonard, 1981). The therapist responds to the patient's expression of anger, for example, and then reflects that response to the patient. For example, "That must have really made you angry," or "I can feel how angry you are about that." The reflection implies an understanding and concern that may justify an inappropriate level of trust. When viewed in this context, empathy becomes part of a "covert process" (Ham, 1987, p. 22).

However, one may argue that given the therapeutic value of empathy, the ethical principle of beneficence, which requires the therapist to act in the best interests of the patient (Pellegrino & Thomasma, 1988), justifies disregarding the patient's autonomy (Beauchamp & Childress, 1989) in voluntary psychotherapy and makes the use of empathy fair. Although there is disagreement about the importance of empathy for effective therapy, at least for client-centered therapies, effective treatment may include the use of empathy (Gladstein, 1987; Rogers, 1957). The strongest argument that deception may be fair occurs when the relationship is voluntary, the participants share the common goal of benefiting the patient, and the deception is of significant therapeutic value (Patterson, 1985). These same considerations are not present in a court-ordered examination of a criminal defendant. The defendant's best interests are not relevant. The relationship is not voluntary. And, the goal of the relationship is not therapeutic. Thus, the beneficence rationale that may justify the fairness of using empathy in therapy is not present in a court-ordered criminal examination.

WHAT CAN FORENSIC EXAMINERS DO?

What might a forensic examiner do if she or he agrees that it is unethical to use therapeutic relationship-building skills that inaccurately imply a therapeutic relationship; of what might such an examination consist? To keep this problem in perspective, it is important to remember that there are sources of information available to the forensic examiner that do not pose these ethical problems. For example, none of this criticism is relevant to the use of psychological tests. There are a large number of psychological tests that have been evaluated for use in the forensic context (Grisso, 1986). These tests may pose problems of validity and reliability, but they do not pose problems of empathy.

In addition, psychiatrists and psychologists can and should use information about the defendant that has been lawfully collected by other sources. Witness statements and physical evidence do not involve problems of empathy. Whether personal interviews by the examiner with other witnesses are required is a question of validity and reliability, not empathy.

Nonetheless, it is unethical to render a psychiatric or psychological opinion in the absence of a personal examination when the opportunity to do so exists (American Psychiatric Association, 1984; CEGFP, 1991). I do not suggest that a psychiatrist or psychologist do otherwise (Shuman, 1986). A personal examination is a necessary, although not a sufficient basis for a reliable forensic opinion. It is, however, incumbent on the ethical forensic examiner to address the use of empathy in the examination.

A reliable and ethical court-ordered psychiatric or psychological examination of a defendant requires a distinction between the receptive and reflective use of empathy. *Receptive empathy* is the perception and understanding of the experiences of another person. *Reflective empathy* is the communication of a "quality of felt awareness" of the experiences of another person (Barrett-Leonard, 1981, p. 91; Traux & Mitchell, 1971). It is neither possible nor desirable for a psychiatrist or psychologist to conduct an examination and be unaware of the cognitive and affective experiences of the defendant during the examination. Indeed, what the defendant thought or felt at some relevant point in time is important. This awareness, or receptive empathy, is an inherently human aspect of communication to which psychiatrists and psychologists are particularly attuned during their training. This awareness may inform the judge (or jury) of the relevance of behavior he or she might otherwise have ignored.

The receptive use of empathy in a forensic examination does not avoid all ethical problems. Psychological research indicates that measured disclosure of personal information may create feelings of trust and closeness with the listener (Cvetkovich, Baumgardner, & Trimble, 1984). Classical psychoanalysis is based on a patient working through transference issues with a therapist who engages only in receptive empathy and interpretation (Luborsky & Spence, 1971).

Unlike the conflicts surrounding the receptive use of empathy, the reflective use of empathy presents a bright ethical line that the ethical examiner should not cross. It is unfair for the forensic examiner to reflect the defendant's cognitive or affective experiences in a manner that erroneously implies a therapeutic alliance or a comfort level that would lead the defendant to slip into a therapeutic mindset. Psychiatrists and psychologists are trained to enhance therapeutic relationships by employing certain "joining" techniques with their patients (Minuchin & Fishman, 1981). These joining techniques go beyond the inherently human awareness of receptive empathy and are entirely inappropriate in a court-ordered examination of a criminal defendant.

Avoiding reflective empathy does not mean that the forensic examiner cannot speak to the defendant. It is possible to ask how the defendant felt or what the defendant thought without reflecting those thoughts or feelings to the defendant in a manner that induces a therapeutic mindset. For example, when a defendant appears sad or angry, it is unnecessary for the examiner to reflect empathetically "you seem sad," or "I'll bet that made you angry." If the examiner finds it necessary to clarify an ambiguous response, it is possible to frame an inquiry in a nonempathetic form: "I am not sure that I understood your response; were you angry?" An ethical forensic examiner may appropriately use receptive empathy to perceive and understand the defendant's affect and/or cognition. However, an ethical forensic examiner should not use reflective empathy to communicate that interpretation or understanding to the defendant in a manner that implies a therapeutic alliance.

OTHER RISKS IN THE USE OF REFLECTIVE EMPATHY

The use of reflective empathy in a forensic examination poses additional risks—patients may come to doubt the loyalty of their therapists, and courts and legislatures may fashion rules that limit forensic examinations or psychiatric and psychological evidence. More serious than these risks is that, in the process of seducing forensic examinees, psychiatrists and psychologist are themselves seduced. The integrity of their identity is lost.

The failure to distinguish between forensic assessment and therapeutic encounters abrades the tenets by which psychiatrists and psychologists define their profession. Their assertion that their dominant responsibility is to their patients is an important moral claim, even in the legal sphere. It has helped to maintain their focus on their professional identity and concomitant obligations to their patients (Stone, 1976), and it has defined a unifying ethical tenet of psychiatry and psychology. It describes who psychiatrists and psychologists are and what is expected of them. The use of reflective empathy in a forensic assessment to imply a therapeutic relationship diffuses that focus and embraces the legal pragmatism. It threatens psychiatry and psychology by the actions of psychologists and psychiatrists.

Finally, the use of reflective empathy risks undermining the Fifth Amendment privilege against self-incrimination. The argument by a psychiatrist or psychologist that reflective empathy must be used in forensic examinations to inform the court fully is a covert assault on that privilege. The privilege against self-incrimination rests on the premise that the government may not require individuals to be agents of their self-destruction (Uviller, 1987). The government must do its own criminal investigation and may not rely on the defendant to prove its case. To argue that reflective empathy is necessary to achieve full disclosure from the accused assumes that it is necessary and appropriate to rely on evidence from the accused to prove the government's case. This argument is even more insidious coming from a profession that has identified itself with concerns about individual rights and liberties.

Recasting the actors further clarifies the issue. Imagine that criminal suspects are arrested by street police, but interrogated by a second level of officers. The second level of officers are police psychiatrists and psychologists who use their therapeutic skills to investigate crime. The point of the example is that if psychiatrists or psychologists are indistinguishable from the police in criminal investigations, the professional identity of psychiatrists and psychologists is profoundly altered.

Perhaps the refusal to use reflective empathy in a forensic examination will make it less complete. Maybe those psychiatrists and psychologists who refuse to use reflective empathy will be offered fewer opportunities to participate in the judicial process. But if ethical forensic practice is merely doing that which lawyers entreat and the law allows, then psychiatry and psychology have relinquished control and failed to articulate meaningful criteria for ethical forensic practice.

ACKNOWLEDGMENTS

Preparation of this article was supported by the M.D. Anderson Foundation.

I thank Paul Appelbaum, Emily Atlas, William May, Fred Moss, Michael Perlin, Bruce Sales, Walter Steele, and David Wexler who provided helpful comments on an earlier draft. Many of the insights in this article grew out of a long running conversation with John Zervopoulos. I am grateful for our agreeable disagreements.

REFERENCES

Addington v. Texas, 441 U.S. 418 (1983).
American Bar Association, Section on Litigation. (1983). *Emerging problems under the rules of evidence.*
American Psychiatric Association, Psychiatry in the Sentencing Process. (1984). A report of the task force in the role of psychiatry in the sentencing process in issues in forensic psychiatry. In *Issues in forensic psychiatry* (pp. 181–215). Washington, DC: American Psychiatric Press.
Barrett-Leonard, G.T. (1981). The empathy cycle: Refinement of a nuclear concept. *Journal of Counseling Psychology, 28,* 91–100.
Beauchamp, T., & Childress, J. (1989). *Principles of biomedical ethics* (3rd ed.). New York: Oxford University Press.
Bickman, L. (1974). The social power of a uniform. *Journal of Applied Social Psychology 4,* 47–61.
Book, H.E. (1988). Empathy: Misconceptions and misuses in psychotherapy. *American Journal of Psychiatry, 145,* 420–424.
Brewer v. Williams, 430 U.S. 387 (1977).
Brodsky, A.M. (1989). Sex between patient and therapist: Psychology's data and response. In G. Gabbard (Ed.), *Sexual exploitation in professional relationships.* Washington, DC: American Psychiatric Association.
Committee on Ethical Guidelines for Forensic Psychologists. (1991). Specialty guidelines for forensic psychologists. *Law and Human Behavior, 15,* 655–665.
Cvetkovich, G., Baumgardner, S., & Trimble, J. (1984). *Social psychology.* New York: Holt, Rinehart & Winston.
Dunn, C., & Steadman, H. (1982). *Mental health services in local jails: A report of a special national workshop* (DHHS Publication No. ADM 82-1181). Rockville, MD: U.S. Department of Health and Human Services.
Estelle v. Smith, 451 U.S. 454 (1980).
Garfield, S. (1986). Research on client variables in psychotherapy. In S. Garfield & A. Bergin (Eds.), *Handbook of psychotherapy and behavior change* (pp. 213–256). New York: Wiley.
Gladstein, G.A. (1983). Understanding empathy: Integrating counseling, developmental, and social psychology influences. *Journal of Counseling Psychology, 30,* 467–482.
Gladstein, G.A. (1987). The role of empathy in counseling: Theoretical considerations. In G.A. Gladstein (Ed.), *Empathy and counseling* (pp. 1–20). New York: Springer-Verlag.

Goldstein, A., & Michaels, G. (1985). *Empathy: development, training and consequences.* Hillsdale, NJ: Lawrence Erlbaum Associates, Inc.

Grisso, T. (1986). *Evaluating competencies: Forensic assessments and instruments.* New York: Plenum.

Hall, H. (1987). *Violence prediction: Guidelines for the forensic practitioner* (pp. 8, 64–65). Springfield, IL: Thomas.

Halleck, S. (1984). The ethical dilemmas of forensic psychiatry: A utilitarian approach. *Bulletin of the American Academy of Psychiatry & Law, 12,* 279–288.

Halleck, S. (1986). *The mentally disordered offender* (DHHS Publication No. ADM 86-1971). Rockville, MD: U.S. Department of Health and Human Services.

Ham, M.D. (1987). Counselor empathy. In G.A. Gladstein (Ed.), *Empathy and counseling* (p. 21–29). New York: Springer-Verlag.

Henderson, L. (1987). Legality and empathy. *Michigan Law Review, 85,* 1574–1653.

Hoffman, M.L. (1981). The development of empathy. In J. Ruston & R. Sorentino (Eds.), *Altruism and helping behavior: Social, personality and developmental perspective* (pp. 41–63). Hillsdale, NJ: Lawrence Erlbaum Associates, Inc.

Hubble, M., & Gelso, C. (1978). Effect of counselor attire in an initial interview. *Journal of Consulting Psychology, 25,* 581–584.

Kurtz, R., & Grummon, D. (1972). Different approaches to the measurement of therapist empathy and their relationship to therapy outcomes. *Journal Consulting and Clinical Psychology, 39,* 106–115.

Leiken, L.S. (1970). Police interrogation in Colorado: The impact of Miranda. *Denver Law Journal, 47,* 1–53.

Lerner, B. (1972). *Therapy in the ghetto: Political impotence and personal disintegration.* Baltimore, MD: Johns Hopkins University Press.

Luborsky, L., & Spence, D. (1971). Quantitative research on psychoanalytic therapy. In A. Bergin & S. Garfield (Eds.), *Handbook of psychotherapy and behavior change* (pp. 419–420). New York: Wiley

Maryland Code Ann. Courts & Judicial Proceedings, § 9–109 (d)(2) (Supp. 1993).

Miller, R.D., Maier, G.J., & Kaye, M.K. (1985). Miranda comes to the hospital: The right to remain silent in civil commitment. *American Journal of Psychiatry, 142,* 1074–1077.

Minuchin, S., & Fishman, H.C. (1981). *Family therapy techniques.* Cambridge, MA: Harvard University Press.

Muhammad v. State, 494 So 2d 969 (Fla. 1986), cert denied, 479 U.S. 1101 (1987).

Patterson, E.G. (1985). The therapeutic justification for withholding medical information: What you don't know can't hurt you, or can it? *Nebraska Law Review, 64,* 721–771.

Pellegrino, E., & Thomasma, D. (1988). *For the patient's good: The return of beneficence in health care.* New York: Oxford University Press.

Perlin, M. (1991). Power imbalances in therapeutic and forensic relationships. *Behavioral Science & Law, 9,* 111–128.

Rappeport, J. (1981). Ethics in forensic psychiatry. In S. Bloch & P. Chodoff (Eds.), *Psychiatric ethics* (p. 255). New York: Oxford University Press.

Rogers, C.R. (1957). The necessary and sufficient conditions of therapeutic personality change. *Journal of Consulting Psychology, 21,* 95–103.

Rogers, C.R. (1975). Empathic: An unappreciated way of being. *Counseling Psychologist, 5* (2), 2–10.

Rosenbaum, R. (1991). *Travels with Dr. Death and other unusual investigations* (pp. 230–231). New York: Viking.

Segalman, R., & Basu, A. (1981). *Poverty in America.* Westport, CT: Greenwood.

Shuman, D.W. (1986). *Psychiatric and psychological evidence.* Colorado Springs: Shepard's/McGraw-Hill.

Shuman, D.W., & Weiner, M.F. (1982). The privilege study: An empirical examination of the psychotherapist–patient privilege. *North Carolina Law Review, 60,* 893–942.

Shuman, D.W., & Weiner, M.F. (1987). *The psychotherapist–patient privilege: A critical examination.* Springfield, IL: Thomas.

Special Project. (1967). Interrogations in New Haven: The impact of Miranda. *Yale Law Journal, 76,* 1519–1648.

Stone, A. (1976). The Tarasoff decisions: Suing psychotherapists to safeguard society. *Harvard Law Review, 90,* 358–378.

Stone, A. (1984). The ethical boundaries of forensic psychiatry: A view from the ivory tower. *Bulletin of the American Academy of Psychiatry & Law, 12,* 209–219.

Szasz, T. (1963). *Law, liberty and psychiatry.* New York: Macmillan.

Tarasoff v. Regents of the University of California, 17 Cal.3d 425, 131 Cal. Rptr. 14, 551 P.2d 334 (1976).

Texas Rules of Evidence, Rule 510 (d) (4) (1993).

Traux, C., & Mitchell, K. (1971). Research on certain therapist interpersonal skills in relation to process and outcome. In A. Bergin & S. Garfield (Eds.), *Handbook of psychotherapy and behavior change* (pp. 299–344). New York: Wiley.

United States v. Henry, 447 U.S. 264 (1980).

Uviller, R.H. (1987). Evidence from the mind of the criminal suspect: A reconsideration of the current rules of access and restraint. *Columbia Law Review, 87,* 1137–1212.

Volpe, J., & Lennon, S. (1988). Perceived police authority as a function of uniform hat and sex. *Perceptual and Motor Skill, 67,* 815–824.

Wells, S.H. (1985). The 1984 ABA criminal justice mental health standards and the expert witness: New therapy for a troubled relationship. *Western State University Law Review, 13,* 79–104.

Westen, D. (1985). *Self & society: Narcissism, collectivism, and the development of morals.* New York: Cambridge University Press.

Wexler, D. (1971). Special project: The administration of psychiatric justice: Theory and practice in Arizona. *Arizona Law Review, 13,* 1–254.

Wolberg, L. (1967). *Techniques of psychotherapy* (Vol. 1). New York: Grune & Straton.

Social Responsibility Ethics: Doing Right, Doing Good, Doing Well

Charles R. Clark
Ann Arbor, Michigan

The ethics of social responsibility is discussed in reference to six case vignettes drawn from forensic psychology. A definitional model of social responsibility is proposed, and two unequal components of the concept—respect for the individual and concern for social welfare—are identified. The sources of ethical conflict in regard to social responsibility are enumerated. Scholarly criticism of the value orientation of forensic psychology is reviewed, and forensic psychology is contrasted with social policy advocacy efforts made by organized psychology. The social responsibility obligations of psychologists in the microethical sphere, where their actions affect individuals, are diffentiated from the obligations psychology has when operating in the macroethical sphere of social policy. The ethical problems inherent in policy advocacy brought about by individual psychologists working with individuals are underscored: the inevitable element of deception, the violation of role integrity, and the circumvention of social structures and institutions that safeguard the rights of individuals.

Key words: expert witness, social responsibility, ethics

Like other fields, psychology has had difficulty articulating coherent ethics concerning social responsibility. Far from wishing to stand apart from social values, psychology has repeatedly affirmed its fundamental commitment to human welfare. But this value orientation appears naturally to militate against a social science's aspirations to objectivity. Questions inevitably arise: How can psychologists maintain objectivity yet work to benefit society? If it is not simply true that what is good for psychology is good for society, how can psychologists maintain a social conscience together with scientific rigor? Does psychology's talk about social responsibility mean anything? Is there actual content to an ethics of social responsibility?

Requests for reprints should be sent to Charles R. Clark, 117 North First Street, Suite 103, Ann Arbor, MI 48104-1343.

CASE VIGNETTES: DILEMMAS

A psychologist in a community mental health agency performs certification examinations for civil commitment. Criteria for commitment provide that a mentally ill person must be dangerous to self or others in order to be hospitalized involuntarily. The police bring in for examination an obviously psychotic man, well known to the agency as a chronic schizophrenic who is noncompliant with recommended outpatient treatment. The police arrested him because of property damage, a broken window, in a downtown store. The psychologist privately acknowledges that the man is not demonstrably dangerous to others or himself: He is not and, to the agency's knowledge, has never been assaultive; he is not suicidal and takes basic care of himself. Concerned that this homeless and mentally ill man will otherwise wait some weeks or months in jail before the criminal offense is disposed of, and certain that the man would benefit from treatment, the psychologist certifies him as committable.

A psychologist who has been treating the 8-year-old child of separated parents at the request of the child's mother learns that the mother and father are contesting custody of the child in the pending divorce proceedings. The focus of treatment has been the child's fears and anxieties before and after visits with her father, and the mother's concerns that the child may have been sexually abused by him. The psychologist is soon asked by the mother's attorney to offer an opinion on the custody question, particularly whether the child needs to be in the continued custody of her mother as she has been during the separation and what sorts of visitation arrangements with the father would be most appropriate. Feeling very certain from treating the child that she needs to remain with her mother, and feeling in any case that custodial placement with the mother is preferable, especially for girls of this age, the psychologist acquiesces to the lawyer's request. Without conducting further evaluation of the child, the mother, or the father, whom the therapist has never met, the psychologist offers the opinion that custody should be awarded to the mother, and that, in light of the child's anxieties and the uncertainty of what may have occurred during past visits, visitation with the father should be halted until he has been evaluated psychologically.

A psychologist devoted to treating women who have suffered spousal abuse, sexual abuse, and other victimization is asked by an attorney to evaluate a woman she is representing who is alleging sexual harassment in the workplace. Convinced of the importance to the victim of not discrediting complaints of this sort, the psychologist does not explore the woman's report in a critical manner. On interview, the woman indicates anger but reports no real experiences of acute emotional distress; standard psychological testing points to no clear clinical symptomatology. The psychologist is aware that the woman will have no chance of winning at trial unless emotional damage can be demonstrated, and the psychologist is concerned about the importance of recognizing the damage produced by sexual harassment in our society—damage often not recognized as such even by its victims. When reanalysing the interview and test data, the psychologist finds significant evidence of the woman's uninsightful denial of emotional conflict and distress related to the harassment and indications that, in fact, due to personality and historical factors, she was particularly vulnerable to the psychological effects of sexual harassment. Consequently, the psychologist finds it possible to testify that the woman has suffered significant emotional damage as a result of sexual harassment.

A psychologist is called on to evaluate juvenile offenders charged with serious felonies relative to the question of whether they should be tried as adults and face adult criminal penalties. The psychologist is convinced that prison is harmful to adults, but is especially destructive to youngsters, and feels that for all its limitations juvenile placement and treatment at least offer hope of rehabilitation. Although the psychologist is ostensibly conducting evaluations addressing established legal criteria for the transfer of juvenile cases to adult jurisdiction, the psychologist in every case offers the opinion that the youngster should remain in the juvenile system.

A psychologist employed in a court agency is in great turmoil about the role psychologists are expected to take in regard to a new statute that provides for expert testimony in mitigation of the death penalty in capital cases. Participation by agency psychologists in mitigation evaluations is encouraged, but they may decline to participate on grounds of conscientious objection. The psychologist resolves the dilemma by deciding to conduct such evaluations only if a case review reveals the likelihood of mitigating factors and to decline participation if it appears that it may be necessary to testify that no mitigating factors are present. As it turns out, the psychologist does not find it necessary to decline participation in any of the cases referred to the agency.

A psychologist who has studied the reactions of populations to environmental disasters has agreed to conduct an evaluation of residents of a neighborhood where a toxic waste dump is located. The psychologist is certain from the results of research that a variety of psychological effects occur in such situations, and the psychologist is committed as well to the view that the international corporate giants that have generated toxic waste must be held accountable before any major reform in environmental policy can occur. The psychologist designs an assessment strategy for the case aimed at ensuring that the psychological effects known to be associated with such situations will be demonstrated. Expert testimony is offered indicating that every one of the area residents has suffered adverse psychological impact from the toxic waste dump.

In these vignettes, psychologists sensitive to social issues—the plight of the homeless and untreated mentally ill, child sexual abuse and parenting, sexual harassment in the workplace, the need for treatment services for juvenile offenders, the morality of the death penalty, and the effects of irresponsible environmental actions—confront limited options in individual cases. It appears to psychologists that they may either strike a blow for social justice, human rights, and humane treatment or permit individuals to be further victimized by negative social forces. Each of these psychologists wishes to proceed responsibly and do what is right; each is guided by social values, not simply scientific knowledge or method. In none of the cases is there any indiction of primarily self-interested motives. Yet, in each of these cases, whether the psychologist is aware of it, lurks an ethical dilemma: To what extent is professional conduct to be guided by social values, unassailably correct though they may be?

Not incidentally, all six of the case vignettes outlined earlier concern forensic psychology. It is not that other areas of psychology—research, teaching, and treatment—do not offer their own social responsibility ethical dilemmas. Indeed, it is in regard to these more traditional areas of psychology that the psychological ethics of social responsibility were first identified. In many instances, however, the social responsibility problems are hidden and more difficult to dissect out of more traditional psychological activities. In some ways, the ethical dilemmas may appear less acute in these areas where there may be little obvious question of *cui bono*. There may be no evident disagreement, for example, between how therapist and client view treatment goals. To be sure, conflicts and concerns may exist in terms of value assumptions that are unarticulated and unrecognized even by the treating psychologist (e.g., beliefs in personal responsibility or ethnic and gender biases)—values that inevitably affect the psychologist's behavior and societal well-being generally. In forensic psychology, by contrast, the adversarial nature of the legal system throws value conflicts into sharp relief. Questions of who benefits from the service and whether actual harm may not be done, at least from the standpoint of one of the persons affected by the psychologist's behavior, are not at all obvious. It may be questionable whether there can be any agreement on what a good result might be given diverse points of view. And so forensic psychology, rich in ethical ambiguity, offers a convenient focus for a broader discussion of social responsibility ethics, but one with relevance to psychology in general.

DEFINING SOCIAL RESPONSIBILITY

Social responsibility ethics is introduced in the stated objectives of the American Psychological Association (APA, 1989): "The objects of the American Psychological Association shall be to advance psychology as a science and profession and as a means of promoting human welfare . . ." (p. 1).

Definitional Model

In its broadest form, the ethics of social responsibility concerns this goal of promoting human welfare; yet such a conventional and often-stated value risks being ignored as trite. Without further delineation and content, the ethics of social responsibility would fail to direct psychologists' behavior in particular ways. Thus, a definitional model must be posited to serve as a heuristic for exploring this area further.

The least controversial definition of social responsibility may be what it is not. Social responsibility, as it involves an interest in furthering human welfare, stands in clear distinction to self-interest on the part of psychologists. This carries the implication that psychological activity motivated simply by economic factors—the maximization of personal wealth—or other forms of self-interest is not socially responsible and is unethical.

Whereas social responsibility is a duty owed to society at large, it is clearly not a duty to meet community standards or the expectations of society as such. In some cases, the only socially responsible answer to community values may be to oppose them.

Beyond this scope, social responsibility may be seen as distinguishable from ethical duty owed to clients, students, or research participants as such; to employers, employees, and colleagues as such; to institutions or governments; and to the field and profession of psychology. Ethical obligations pertain to all of these individuals and groups, such as the assurance of competence and protection of confidentiality. But unless social responsibility is simply the syncretistic sum of all other ethical obligations, it must be distinguishable from them. Social responsibility must then involve ethical obligations owed to individuals outside their particular relationships with psychologists, relationships that impose various ethical duties of their own. It must constitute an ethical obligation to persons as individual representatives of society at large, with diverse identities and membership in various social groups.

Using this definitional heuristic—an ethical obligation that extends beyond self-interest and also beyond the particular relationships in which psychologists encounter individuals—the content of social responsibility ethics, at this point in the analysis relatively inchoate, may be brought into focus.

1981 "Ethical Principles of Psychologists." The broad, general objective of the APA to further human welfare is mirrored in the recently superseded "Ethical Principles of Psychologists" (APA, 1981, 1990; referred to hereafter as ethical principles). A number of specific references to social responsibility have been identified (Keith-Spiegel & Koocher, 1985). To begin with, the preamble to the ethical principles provides:

> Psychologists respect the dignity and worth of the individual and strive for the preservation and protection of fundamental human rights. They are committed to increasing knowledge of human behavior and of people's understanding of themselves and others and to the utilization of such knowledge for the promotion of human welfare. (APA, 1981, p. 39)

Further definition of social responsibility emerges in particular principles. Principle 1.a enjoins psychologists as researchers to "provide thorough discussion of the limitations of their data, especially where their work touches on social policy or might be construed to the detriment of persons in specific age, sex, ethnic, socioeconomic, or other social groups" (p. 390).

Principle 1.f, addressed to practitioners rather than researchers, warns psychologists that "they bear a heavy social responsibility because their recommendations and professional actions may alter the lives of others," and requires them to be "alert to personal, social, organizations, financial, or political situations and pressures that might lead to misuse of their influence" (p. 390).

Principle 3.a requires psychologists as teachers to "recognize and respect the diverse attitudes" that students may have regarding topics that may give offense. Principle 3.b states that in employment settings "psychologists do not engage in or condone practices that are inhumane or that result in illegal or unjustifiable actions," including "actions based on considerations of race, handicap, age, gender, sexual preference, religion, or national origin in hiring, promotion, or training." Principle 3.c addresses psychologists in general and directs them "to avoid any action that will violate or diminish the legal and civil rights of clients or of others who may be affected by their actions" (p. 391).

Principle 6.a enjoins psychologists to be "continually cognizant of their own needs and of their potentially influential position vis-à-vis persons such as clients, students, and subordinates. They avoid exploiting the trust and dependency of such persons" and "make every effort to avoid dual relationships that could impair their professional judgment or increase the risk of exploitation" (p. 393).

General Principle 9 advises that the "decision to undertake research rests upon a considered judgment by the individual psychologist about how best to contribute to psychological science and human welfare," and that the psychologist "carries out the investigation with respect and concern for the dignity and welfare of the people who participate . . ." (p. 394).

Even in General Principle 10, the central ethical principle of the advancement of human welfare is reinforced: "An investigator of animal behavior strives to advance understanding of basic behavioral principles and/or to contribute to the improvement of human health and welfare. In seeking these ends, the investigator ensures the welfare of animals and treats them humanely" (p. 395).

Although not included by Keith-Spiegel and Koocher (1985) as a specific aspect of social responsibility ethics, Principle 6.d encourages psychologists to "contribute a portion of their services to work for which they receive little or no financial return" (p. 393).

It is not clear how enforceable most social responsibility references in the old ethical principles were. Many, such as the preamble and the general principles, seemed to be a mix of aspirational and mandatory language. Even when they appeared to be stated in directive terms, the provisions were not consistently treated as enforceable, for example, the pro bono language in 6.d: "They contribute a portion of their services to work for which they receive little or no financial return" (p. 393). The new code attempts to address this ambiguity.

1992 "Ethical Principles of Psychologists and Code of Conduct." The recently enacted successor document to the ethical principles (APA, 1981) is in the format of a preamble and general principles, intended to represent aspirational goals to guide conduct, and ethical standards, enforceable rules of conduct that are intended to represent minimal requirements (APA, 1992). By design, the ethical standards that constitute the code of conduct incorporate the central ethic of social responsibility. However, given the new document's stated goal of separating aspirational and enforceable language, particular standards no longer make reference to social responsibility as such in its broad meaning; that language is confined to the preamble and general principles.

On the other hand, there are a multitude of standards that specifically address issues of individual rights and differences and the influence of social values on psychologists in more explicit and directive terms than before. These new standards arguably do not create new ethical responsibilities, but rather they explicate and emphasize responsibilities psychologists have always had. They cast in clearly mandatory language the sections of the old ethical principles that were embedded in a confusing mix of aspirational and enforceable terminology. Some of the new standards closely mirror the language of the old ethical principles but make it clear that these are minimal, not aspirational, requirements.

A nonexhaustive list of the new code standards that bear on individual rights and differences and on social values includes: 1.08 Human Differences; 1.09 Respecting Others; 1.10 Nondiscrimination; 1.11 Sexual Harassment; 1.12 Other Harassment; 1.15 Misuse of Psychologists' Influence; 1.17 Multiple Relationships, Section (a); 2.04 Use of Assessment in General and with Special Populations, Section (c); 6.03 Accuracy and Objectivity in Teaching; 6.07 Responsibility, Sections (a) and (d); and 7.01 Professionalism (in forensic activities).

Far from abandoning general social responsibility language, however, the preamble to the new "Ethical Principles of Psychologists and Code of Conduct" states that the goal of psychologists is "to broaden knowledge of behavior, and where appropriate, to apply it pragmatically to improve the condition of both the individual and society," and that psychologists "respect and protect human and civil rights, and do not knowingly participate in or condone unfair discriminatory practices" (p. 3). Further, one of the six general principles, Principle F, treats social responsibility explicitly:

> Psychologists are aware of their professional and scientific responsibilities to the community and the society in which they work and live. They apply and make public their knowledge of psychology in order to contribute to human welfare. Psychologists are concerned about and work to mitigate the causes of human suffering. When undertaking research, they strive to advance human welfare and the science of psychology. Psychologists try to avoid misuse of their work. Psychologists comply with the law and encourage the development of law and social policy that serve the interests of their patients and clients and the public. They are encouraged to contribute a portion of their professional time for little or no personal advantage. (APA, 1992, p. 4)

Principle F is not the sole reference in the general principles to social responsibility. Principle B, Integrity, urges psychologists to "strive to be aware of their own belief systems, values, needs, and limitations and the effect of these on their work" (p. 3).

Principle D, Respect for People's Right and Dignity, states that psychologists "accord appropriate respect to the fundamental rights, dignity, and worth of all people. They respect the rights of individuals to privacy, confidentiality, self-determination, and autonomy" and are "aware of cultural, individual, and role differences, including those due to age, gender, race, ethnicity, national origin, religion, sexual orientation, disability, language, and socioeconomic status" (p. 3). Further, Principle D holds, "Psychologists try to eliminate the effect on their work of biases based on those factors, and they do not knowingly participate in or condone unfair discriminatory practices" (p. 4).

Although the explicit social responsibility language in the new ethical principles is not stated in enforceable language (and how could the requirement that psychologists strive to advance human welfare be enforced?), it was nonetheless intended that social responsibility ethics would be enforceable as it found expression in particular standards. Operationalizing social responsibility in the new code was accomplished most readily in regard to a respect for individual rights and differences and in regard to the influence of social values on psychologists. Except to the extent that the preamble injunction to improve the condition of society can be translated into such specific standards, it must remain aspirational.

1986 "Canadian Code of Ethics for Psychologists." In marked departure from the APA at that time, the Canadian Psychological Association set out to provide not only an articulation of ethical principles, values, and standards but also a proposed method for ethical decision making (Canadian Psychological Association Committee on Ethics, 1986). In addition, the four basic ethical principles around which ethical standards were organized were ordered "according to the weight each should be given when they are in conflict" (pp. ii–iii). Of highest priority is Principle I, Respect for the Dignity of Persons. Principle II, Responsible Caring, is followed by Principle III, Integrity in Relationships, and finally, Principle IV, Responsibility to Society.

Whereas the Canadian code seems to differentiate social responsibility from respect for individuals and make it a subordinate consideration, a review of Principle I reveals it to have much in common with the social responsibility definition introduced previously: responsibility to act beyond simple self-interest and to consider the characteristics of individuals beyond the scope of particular role relationships.

Respect for the Dignity of Persons involves the fundamental beliefs that "each person should be treated as a person or an end in him/herself, not as an object or a means to an end" and that

> all persons have a right to have their innate worth as human beings appreciated and that this worth is not enhanced or reduced by such differences as culture, ethnicity, colour, race, religion, gender, sexual preference, physical or mental abilities, age, socio-economic status, and/or any other preference or personal characteristic, condition or status. (p. 1)

This principle involves respect for rights of privacy, self-determination, and autonomy; an appreciation of the need to take special precautions to safeguard the rights of those who are vulnerable; and a commitment to equal justice and nondiscrimination.

Yet clearly, the Canadian code's first Principle of Respect for the Dignity of Persons is not simply co-extensive with the definition of social responsibility adopted here. Principle IV, Responsibility to Society, although seen as subordinate to all of the others, is the only principle to make explicit reference to human welfare broadly considered. The principle states that "Two of the legitimate expectations of psychology as a discipline are that it will increase knowledge and that it will conduct its affairs in such ways that it will promote the well-being of all human beings" (p. 16). Psychological knowledge is to be used for beneficial social purposes, namely, in a reference to the three superordinate principles, those purposes that reflect respect for the dignity of persons, responsible caring, and integrity in relationships. Psychologists have an ethical responsibility to try to correct misuse of psychological knowledge in this regard. Psychologists respect social structures and avoid unwarranted or unnecessary disruptions of them. Actions to produce social change are carried out through an educative process that seeks consensus within society through democratic means, although criticism and advocacy of rapid change may be necessary at times. The principle also holds that "psychology as a whole needs to be self-reflective about its place in society and about the ways in which it might be contributing to or detracting from beneficial societal changes" (p. 16).

Synthesis

It is important not to ignore the differences in possible conceptions of social responsibility ethics. As best illustrated by the Canadian code, there may be two components or factors comprising social responsibility. One factor, viewed in the Canadian code as primary, is a concern about humans as individuals; the other factor is a concern for social change and betterment. The Canadian prioritization is one with which most psychologists would doubtlessly agree; when the two values are in conflict, concern about individuals must take precedence over a desire for social improvement.

In fact, concern about social change and betterment appears to be grounded in respect for the rights, dignity, and worth of the individual. It is the reduction of human suffering and furtherance of human rights—rights to fair and equitable treatment, to confidentiality, to privacy, and to self-determination and autonomy—that are at the basis of psychology's concern about society in general. Although social responsibility can be conceptualized as more than unidimensional, it does appear to be essentially unified around, and even reducible to, the central ethical value of respect for the individual. Not coincidentally, in the efforts to create enforceable standards of social responsibility in the new APA (1992) "Ethical Principles of Psychologists and Code of Conduct," the standards all appear to pertain to respect for individual rights and differences and to the effect of the psychologist's values on individuals.

At the outset of the previous discussion of a definitional model of social responsibility, it was proposed that social responsibility is distinguishable from the variety of ethical obligations owed to individuals as participants in professional relationships, individuals such as therapy clients, students, or research subjects. Social responsibility extends beyond those particular relationships and beyond the particular ethical obligations they entail, which will differ according to the relationship. It is not a contradiction of this position to assert that concern for the individual as such, rather than for the individual as participant in particular professional relationships, is at the heart of social responsibility ethics.

Social responsibility involves, more fundamentally than other ethical obligations, certain key values in respect to human welfare, values that ultimately pertain to individuals. Social responsibility is in essence the collection of social values that gives any psychological activity its ethical character; in this sense, all other ethical obligations are subordinate to it. As used here, social responsibility ethics is the delineation of psychology's broadest overarching ethical imperative, and it involves the subordination of private and personal goals to a greater consideration of human welfare. It incorporates central social values and applies them to general professional conduct. It is respect for and concern about the individual that informs and organizes social responsibility obligations. Social responsibility is ultimately responsibility owed to individual human beings.

ETHICAL CONFLICTS AND SOCIAL RESPONSIBILITY

The six vignettes presented at the beginning of this article can be examined in terms of their approximation of an ideal of social responsibility. It may readily be seen that, as an ethical principle, the concept of social responsibility has been developed enough to permit the identification of clear ethical conflicts but not nearly well enough to suggest clear resolutions.

In all six of the vignettes, there is a working assumption by the psychologist that the social concerns that inform the psychologist's behavior—concern for the homeless and mentally ill, the sexually abused children of divorce, victims of sexual harassment, juvenile offenders, convicts facing the death penalty, and the victims of irresponsible environmental policy—are and ought to be paramount considerations. In every instance, social concern and social values are permitted to sweep aside other possible considerations, including competing social values.

Case Vignettes: Conflicts

In the first case, a psychologist agrees to facilitate the civil commitment of a homeless man who, although mentally ill, is not demonstrably dangerous to himself or anyone else. Here, concern about the man's welfare and status and about the likely harm produced by incarceration versus the likely benefits of treatment are allowed to override considerations of the man's autonomy and rights and of the law intended to protect those rights. Clearly, this is a clash of social values, a clash that results in an action dictated by the psychologist's personal view of the priority of values. What appears to the psychologist to be the individual's best interests is accorded precedence over the social good embodied by the law. Still, one must ask whether the psychologist is not obliged to make some choice among the unattractive alternatives here, especially when the social structures designed to protect individual rights and assure social welfare ignore the particular features of the individuals subject to them. Is this not simply a clash of individual social conscience with a law that may work for many but may fail in the individual case?

In the instance of the psychologist who agrees to provide an opinion regarding child custody and visitation but who never evaluated the child's father, concern about the effects of possible child sexual abuse and separation from the mother are permitted to override considerations not only of objectivity and accuracy—themselves not clearly elements of social responsibility as such—but also a broader understanding of the child's best interests. The child's best interests may be seen to demand fairness in assessment, and an obligation to consider the father as a person. It is not so much that the father has rights as a father that are not protected in an assessment process that excludes him, but that the child has rights to a father. Ostensibly advocating the interests of the child, the psychologist is actually advocating a result based on a particular set of social values but ones that are in conflict with other values. Still, the psychologist may contend that the limitations of the opinion offered to the court, especially the absence of any assessment of the father, were made clear in the report, and that, in any event, as the child's therapist, the psychologist is truly the child's advocate and must speak to the child's best interests in light of the available information. Would it not be socially irresponsible to stand aside and permit continued victimization of the child? In this instance, there is no intent by the psychologist to permit private value considerations to override social welfare as it is embodied in legal procedures; the psychologist values social responsibility but fails to discern any clash of social values in the behavior.

The psychologist evaluating a woman in a sexual harassment lawsuit enters the evaluation of the plaintiff with a strong commitment to women who have been victimized in just the way they alleged and to social change regarding the way women are treated. The psychologist fails at first to find evidence of emotional damage. Aware of the consequences of such a failure for this woman, the psychologist takes a second, closer look at the data and finally finds indications of emotional damage. Is this a case of finding only what is looked for? Have the psychologist's social concerns interfered with objectivity and judgment? The psychologist would deny such suggestions and assert that this was simply a more difficult case of sexual harassment than usual in terms of identifying the particular psychological factors affecting the victim. Moreover, the data on which the report and testimony were based were clearly spelled out, so there can be no question of deception; the psychologist would even admit that at first there appeared to be no clinical evidence of harm. As someone committed to righting a great wrong in society, would it be ethical for the psychologist not to have looked exhaustively for indications of harm so that this woman could obtain justice and treatment?

In the case of the psychologist faced with evaluating juvenile offenders in regard to their eligibility for transfer to adult jurisdiction, it is not the particular problems presented by an individual that lead to a decision that established social value mechanisms must be overridden. In this instance, the social policy that affects an entire class of individuals—juveniles—is viewed as harmful and wrong. The psychologist systematically thwarts the aims of the social policy that permits the imprisonment of youngsters by reporting in each case that the juvenile fails to meet the criteria for transfer of jurisdiction. The actions of the psychologist, however, are performed in respect to individual cases and are presented to the court as such, as the result of psychological evaluation of individuals rather than as the result of a general social value considerations. Although there is a duplicitous aspect to this behavior on the part of the psychologist, one must ask how the social good of providing appropriate treatment for juveniles could be accomplished otherwise. If a psychologist who cares about this issue does not perform such evaluations, who will?

The psychologist faced with the dilemma of how to respond to a new statute requiring psychological evaluation of factors that would mitigate sentencing in capital punishment cases has struck a compromise that appears at first blush to be both honest and socially responsible. This psychologist takes no stand on the death penalty as such, but because of social value considerations cannot countenance contributing as a mental health professional to state-sanctioned executions. By the expedient of agreeing to participate only when there appears to be a likelihood of testimony in favor of mitigation, the psychologist concludes that at least no harm will be done in any case, and positive good will result for those defendants who are chosen by the psychologist for evaluation. In additional, such selective and positive participation in death penalty proceedings does not amount to support for the death penalty as such. Experience in producing initial reviews of death penalty cases assures the psychologist that it is relatively easy to find some basis for a positive report in mitigation. The ethical issues here involve the operation of social value considerations as a biasing factor, albeit not one recognized as such by the well-meaning psychologist, and the honesty of producing opinions that are greatly affected by value considerations never made explicit to the sentencing court. The psychologist, confronted with this objection, might assert that the repeated findings of mitigating factors are objective, and that the bases of the psychologist's opinions on mitigation are always made clear and can be judged on their own merits. Moreover, the psychologist continues to view as a real possibility that there may be no mitigating factors in evidence in particular cases, and he or she views each case as one that can be approached with an open mind.

The case of the psychologist who devises an assessment protocol in a toxic tort case directed to demonstrate emotional impact of environmental damage is concerned that the very real psychological effects evident from research may not otherwise be understood or considered adequately in the litigation, that justice to the plaintiffs will not be done, and that the offending corporations will not be deterred from continuing environmentally destructive practices. Because the psychological effects of such situations have been observed repeatedly, there is every reason to believe that they exist in this case as well. The assessment strategy created for this case, the psychologist would contend, serves the interests both of the individuals involved and of society in general; to become involved in an assessment of the plaintiffs that might support the defendant corporations in this matter would be unconscionable and, in its environmental impact, socially irresponsible. This case involves the subordination of the professional assessment of individuals to social value assertions; but the psychologist may argue that unlike other situations in which social concerns are permitted to dominate professional activity, the individuals involved are only likely to benefit, not be harmed. The defendants are corporate entities that have a demonstrated record of social irresponsibility. In any conflict between individuals harmed by environmental pollution and such corporations, social responsibility, the psychologist may say, demands advocacy for the plaintiffs.

Each of the vignettes involves the operation of personal agendas by psychologists that reflect social values. In none of the cases, as they are (artificially) presented here, is there evidence of primary self-interest on the part of the psychologist. In each case, there is an attempt to identify the socially responsible course of action. If there are genuine ethical conflicts here, where do they lie? Keith-Spiegel and Koocher (1985) wrote about the source of conflict in regard to social responsibility:

> ... many well-meaning public activities of psychologists are evaluated variously by others, depending on whose ox is being gored. Differences in opinion include conflicts over what approaches are acceptable to achieve a humane goal as well as whether certain goals are themselves "good" or in the best public interest. (p. 442)

General Principles and Operational Goals

In all of the cases considered, there have been assumptions or inferences made that general principles of social responsibility can or must be realized as particular operational goals. An injunction that psychologists promote social good presupposes that the social good can be identified. But although many may agree about the desirability of social responsibility, a consensus on its implementation is unlikely.

Psychologists may agree that it is important to respect people as individuals, promote their independence and autonomy, and support equitable and just treatment of everyone. However, does this necessarily involve support for abolition of restrictive legislation aimed at homosexuals, opposition to the death penalty, contraception and abortion rights, and assisted suicide? Certainly there are psychologists passionately committed to these social positions who would assert that social responsibility demands such stances. But does this mean that others who do not hold these positions or who actually oppose them are not socially responsible?

Clearly, social responsibility is relative in practice, even if the imperative to act in a socially responsible way is absolute in general. Paradoxically, two psychologists could be equally ethical in allowing social welfare considerations to explicitly inform their work yet work to promote diametrically opposed social results. Indeed, social responsibility demands a commitment to promoting tolerance for divergent social viewpoints, even viewpoints opposed to tolerance.

In the various vignettes presented in this article, the actions taken by the psychologists have all been based on certain assumptions about what constitutes socially responsible behavior, for example, keeping juvenile offenders out of prison. Many of these assumptions are debatable but are not treated as such by the psychologist in question. The ethical conflict in this regard does not stem simply from the fact that social value positions are taken; it would be unrealistic to speak of the valueless social action. Instead, the ethical conflict involves the willingness to permit social values to operate covertly and unacknowledged, as though they were unrebuttable or absolute. Doing so disregards the reality that—particularly in adversarial settings—someone else would contradict a value position if it were known; permitting social values to operate covertly and unacknowledged denies the prospective opponent access to important information and the issue a fair hearing.

Relative Values

Even among those precise social values for which there is agreement, there may well be conflict over priority. Conflicts among two or more social goods recognized as such by the psychologist are featured in all of the case vignettes presented. When it is seen as important to promote a person's rights to autonomy as well as the person's access to beneficial treatment, for example, which of the two clashing values takes precedence? Again it cannot be the simple fact that choices are made among competing alternative social imperatives that creates an ethical conflict; hard choices must often be made. Instead, the problem arises when there is neither acknowledgment of any choice being made nor of the rationale underlying the choice. To make such choices known, of course, is to invite debate at least, but then such choices among competing social values are inherently debatable. Psychologists who fail to make such ethical decision making clear are arrogating to themselves the responsibility for determining outcomes that affect others and society in general.

Strategies and Tactics

Even if there would be no dispute over which particular social effect is necessary or desirable, there may still be conflict regarding the means by which that end is achieved. Ethical conflicts do not pertain only to deception of self or of others regarding the social values underlying professional behavior. In many instances, the conflict includes the tactics adopted by the professional to implement values. An eagerness to achieve a particular social good will often lead to a distortion of a professional role.

The social ethics of a professional choice involves the extent to which, in order to further some desired social goal, the psychologist crosses role boundaries or violates role integrity. There is a duality of role obligation in undertaking to serve as a child's therapist and as a supposedly objective expert witness with an opinion about the child's best interests in a custody dispute. There is frequent incompatibility in terms of role integrity between any effects-oriented stance by a psychologist, no matter how desirable the effect may appear from a social responsibility point of view, and the psychologist's duties to science and objectivity.

In many instances, the question is whether any psychologist whose behavior is so determined by explicit social agendas can ethically perform as a psychologist. It is not a question of how a psychologist should proceed to implement social values and goals in a given situation, but whether the psychologist should be acting in that situation at all. In breaching role boundaries, such as that between an objective observer and treater on one hand and a frank advocate on the other, there is the real risk of an abrogation of the rights and interests of the individuals involved in the situation and a subversion of the social structures, such as the law, erected to safeguard and promote those rights and interests. In many situations, it is not enough to acknowledge to oneself the nature of the social values that impel certain actions, and it is not sufficient to make certain everyone else is aware of operating value assumptions. There is no good way to do what should not be done at all.

MACROETHICAL AND MICROETHICAL SOCIAL RESPONSIBILITY

Social Policy of Psychology and of Psychologists

Unfortunately, the task of knowing what is the right thing to do is not always simple; first, it is necessary to know what it is psychology as a discipline represents. The social values of psychology are apparent in the policy positions and advocacy efforts of organized psychology on national and local levels. These organized efforts in turn result from the contributions of various individual psychologists. The social-value viewpoints of psychology as a discipline are also conveyed by the choice of research topics, writing, and teaching—all of these activities typically being identified with individual psychologists rather than with organized psychology.

Despite the apparent positions of psychology as a discipline, it can never be said that psychology speaks with one voice. Questions of who ought to speak for psychology and what psychology's positions truly are naturally arise. The extent to which individual psychologists should even be drawn into social activism and advocacy is impossible to prescribe and remains an essentially personal choice. So, too, are the social policy goals psychologists choose to work toward and, to a great extent, the means they adopt to implement them. Because psychology must maintain respect for divergent viewpoints within the profession, the ethics of individual participation in efforts to affect society as a whole must remain aspirational, an essential truth reflected in the new bifurcated ethical principles. Although psychology as a whole sees itself as oriented toward enhancing human welfare, it cannot require particular actions, or even types of activism, of individual psychologists.

On the other hand, active participation in social policy development is not only clearly permissible but is necessary for any discipline that holds itself out as existing to advance human welfare. Yet, there are potential pitfalls in any such activity. Policy positions may be adopted that may appear in retrospect to be fundamentally mistaken or to entail unforeseen and undesirable consequences; the involvement of science in the eugenics movement earlier in the century is a case in point. In a post-Holocaust era, the enormity of the moral errors to which science lends itself is impossible to underestimate. But the possibility of error is not clearly, or always, an ethical concern as such; not all errors are ethical lapses. Put another way, ethical sensitivity alone is no protection from error, including errors that carry the gravest social consequences. The ethics of such activity do inevitably focus on questions of accuracy in representation; however worthy a social cause may seem to be on other grounds, neither the nature and results of research nor the actual policy positions of professional organizations should be misrepresented to support it.

Ethical concerns thus focus on means–ends conceptualizations; not every method of advocating social justice or human welfare is necessarily ethical.

Ethical Complexity of Social Activism

Whatever debate there may be regarding goals and methods, the ethics of large-scale social activism and advocacy by psychology and by individual psychologists working to achieve general social change is inherently simpler than social responsibility ethics involving individual psychologists acting on a smaller scale. If advocacy is not only permissible but necessary on what may be termed the *macroethical level,* it does not automatically follow that social advocacy should be exercised on the more limited *microethical level.* In fact, as the case vignettes illustrate, social value considerations operating in particular cases that involve individuals give rise to ethical compromise and conflict. It may appear that there is an ethical double standard, if not a double bind, regarding social responsibility; what may be desirable for organized psychology to advocate openly may bias individual applications of psychology. The essential question is how psychologists can work to advance human welfare and still maintain role integrity as objective students of human behavior.

The sophisticated psychologist understands that social value considerations pervade all psychological work, and that a pure science free of value considerations is neither possible nor desirable. Choices remain as to whether to engage in particular activities, whether or how to limit the influence of value considerations, and whether to make social value considerations manifest and overt in communications. The simple fact of conflicts over role expectations in expert testimony, for example, does not provide the psychologist "with a license to do any old thing he or she wishes, but rather presents alternative challenges . . ." (Saks, 1990, p. 311). The inevitability of value considerations does not simply mean that the psychologist can surrender ethical responsibility and give those considerations full and unrestricted range. Viewing value orientation from a different perspective, namely that values are not simply inevitable but potentially positive influences, Vachon and Agresti (1992) argued cogently for systematic training of counseling psychologists in recognizing and working with values; this sensible proposal would not support the advocacy of social programs or policy in such work.

Role Violation and Deception

Because advocacy of social value positions by psychologists on the microethical level of individual action on behalf of individuals so often involves deception—the assumption of an objective posture while engaged in essentially subjective activity—it threatens role integrity. For example, if the psychologist who is motivated by a desire to keep a mentally ill person out of jail instead of a desire to apply the commitment law strictly were to make that value position explicit rather than permit it to operate covertly, the psychologist's opinion in that case might well be discounted as social advocacy rather than clinical science. And if the psychologist whose motivation in performing evaluations of juvenile offenders is to keep all such youngsters out of adult jurisdiction and prisons were to make that objective known, it is unlikely the psychologist would continue to receive referrals for such evaluations. Thus, activities aimed at achieving particular social effects are likely to conflict with other ethical obligations to avoid misrepresentation and deception.

Role Violation and Social Effects

At an even deeper level than the question of deception in such value-influenced activity by psychologists is the problem of its effect on individuals and on the social structures dedicated to protecting the individual's rights and autonomy. Although ostensibly acting to protect the best interests of the individual in the case of the psychologist who drafts a child custody opinion without evaluating the father, for example, the psychologist is acting to protect the best interests of the individual as the psychologist sees them. This involves a misplaced and even arrogant confidence by the psychologist in his or her own discernment of the answer to the sort of question that legal procedures were created to address. It pits the best interests of an individual as the psychologist views them against a broader conception of that person's interests and against the interests of other individuals and institutions. Outside the legal arena, a psychologist undertaking in therapy to direct a client to a particular course of action in line with the psychologist's social values—for example, to agree to an abortion or to agree not to have one; to commit to a marriage or to end it—may similarly be assuming a superior viewpoint on the client's best interests and thwarting more legitimate means, including the client's own moral judgment, of resolving such questions.

Other Causes of Role Violations

It is clearest in regard to social responsibility on the microethical level that psychologists' individual actions must respect the rights and dignity of the individual. This is best conveyed by the enforceable injunctions in APA's (1992) "Ethical Principles of Psychologists and *Code of Conduct,*" injunctions perhaps inevitably understood as behaviors in which psychologists must not engage. Psychologists must not engage in racial or ethnic prejudice, for example, or in sexual exploitation or harassment. Participation in immoral activity is an ethical violation. But the implicit and explicit orientation of psychological activity on the individual level to achieve particular social effects beyond avoiding such violations is far more problematic.

The vignettes presented in this article are artificially free of both obvious corrupt self-interest and purely emotional motivations on the part of the psychologists involved. To be sure, social value considerations are not alone among biasing factors that lead to the compromise of psychologists' role integrity and are not the most pernicious sources of bias. In the forensic realm, the most troubling violations of role integrity stem from pure self-interest on the part of the expert witness, who may stoop to conscious prostitution, including outright lying, in order to make money or further a career—in effect, to do well rather than do good. Problems of advocacy based in financial and other relationships—the "hired gun" or "whores for hire" (Golding, 1990) issue—are less debatable than social responsibility ethics, and are addressed by simple prohibition, which is essentially what is done in the "Specialty Guidelines for Forensic Psychologists," (IV.B and VI.C, Committee on Ethical Guidelines for Forensic Psychologists, 1991) "Ethical Principles of Psychologists and Code of Conduct" (APA, 1992; but see Standards 7.03, 7.04, and 7.05). It is far from certain how effective such admonitions can ever be with individuals who must be motivated not by social value considerations but by the lack of them.

Much more common is the bias that stems from sincere personal reactions to an individual or an issue—variations and analogs of what psychodynamic theory posits as countertransference. These reactions will operate either positively, for example, as urges to help the client or to see matters as the client does, or negatively, as when a client's complaints are dismissed and the client is seen as insincere and manipulative. These biases, which if unchecked may also lead to violations of role integrity, do not stem so much from social value assumptions (although they could not possibly be absent) but more immediately from the psychologist's own emotional reactions and cognitive prejudices.

Compromising Role Integrity for Good Reasons

Despite the need on the macroethical level for psychology to support human welfare, a particular social value orientation can bias a psychologist's activities with individuals just as self-interest and personal reactions can. Yet, there is nothing about the virtue of any social policy position that permits the abrogation of scientific objectivity in any particular case. The psychologist wishing to strike a blow for social justice in respect to a forensic assessment, no less than in respect to other assessments, treatment, or research, is risking the loss of role integrity and a range of other negative consequences, including harm to particular individuals.

It may be that in particular cases there occurs a happy convergence of social justice and good result, at least a good result from a client's point of view. Certainly, it would be unrealistic to expect the psychologist not to wish for both. But true social responsibility on an individual level will often require the suspension of efforts to achieve particular social effects and, in many cases, the actual suspension of activities that are hopelessly biased by social value considerations. In a forensic assessment, an effects-oriented psychologist may feel that a particular opinion will accomplish some social good; but doing good may be different from doing right.

It is a sad aspect not only of forensic psychology but of other applications of psychology that the right action or response by the psychologist may accomplish no good at all, at least not in any immediate or obvious sense. The good, both social and personal, is of course relative. A psychotherapy client may conceive a good result in treatment to be the resolution of feelings of guilt and misgiving about a course of action that from another perspective, such as that of the therapist, may be self-destructive or harmful to others. But there are many instances in which good, as those involved in a matter might conceive it, simply cannot be accomplished by honest and objective psychological work. In any such instance, the socially responsible psychologist's only consolation may be that in conveying bad news in an assessment, in failing to gratify a therapy patient's strongest desires, or in publishing data disconfirming the efficacy of a socially valued intervention, the psychologist is upholding not only role integrity but the integrity of social institutions and processes on which individual rights and dignity ultimately rely for protection.

Case Vignettes: Concluding Discussion

In the first case, that of the psychologist who is performing a civil commitment evaluation, it may be that everyone involved, including the police, the prosecuting and defense attorneys, and the subject of the petition himself agrees that a hospital is preferable to jail. But a false certification of him as dangerous and, therefore, committable cannot be justified on the grounds of social justice. Whether the psychologist's failure to cooperate in diverting this homeless man from jail would serve to spur the legal system on to finding more appropriate and honest solutions to the social problems the man represents (and most likely it would accomplish no such thing), distorting clinical findings to provide what appears to be a good solution to this individual's immediate problem requires deception and misrepresentation of the psychologist's actual findings and involves a fundamental violation of role boundaries.

In the second case, that of the psychologist who is treating the child of divorcing parents, the psychologist cannot responsibly offer an opinion on custody in the circumstances described here, which include a failure to evaluate the father. If the essential rationale for the psychologist's opinion that the child should remain with the mother is the psychologist's a priori social convictions regarding the importance of the mother as a parenting figure, the psychologist should simply say so; chances are an opinion evidently based on nothing more than such a programmatic point of view would not be accorded great weight, but at least the basis for the opinion would be explicit. If the rationale for the opinion is the psychologist's concern, stemming from the very equivocal suggestions of sexual abuse, that the child may be at risk of victimization by the father, the psychologist should consider refraining from offering that opinion. The psychologist would have access to no more information about this putative sexual abuse than the court would, unless the psychologist took additional steps, including evaluating the father. But those additional steps may require of the psychologist an objectivity that is no longer possible due to the therapeutic relationship with the child. From a practical point of view, the father may, sensibly, be most reluctant to submit to examination by a psychologist who is already aligned with the mother who is contesting custody. The psychologist must also consider that no amount of warning about the limitations of the data on which the custody opinion is based, including the psychologist's failure to see the father, may be sufficient to offset the impact of an expert opinion offered by a psychologist working with the child in question. Above all, the psychologist must consider that the child's best interests may be poorly appreciated by any of the individuals with whom contact has already been established, especially the child and the mother. A valid determination of the best interests of the child may require more than what the psychologist has done to date or is capable of reconciling with existing role obligations.

In the third case, which involves a sexual harassment complaint, the psychologist's failure to find evidence of the expected psychological harm prompted a reexamination of the data. The psychologist's new construal of the data to support an opinion that the woman experienced harm seems at best to represent self-deception on the examiner's part prompted by the psychologist's eagerness to correct a social wrong. In a larger sense, an unwillingness to report negative findings (also seen in cases involving other social issues, e.g., racial discrimination and child sexual abuse) may be counterproductive of actual social change, because it may foster the impression that positive reports of psychological harm resulting from social injustice are usually influenced more by an expert witness' social agenda than by objective findings. But whether this search for positive findings was socially pragmatic or not, the psychologist involved has compromised scientific and clinical objectivity to become an advocate, an advocate not of the findings as they occurred but of a desired social effect.

In the fourth case, a psychologist is unwilling to abet the placement of any juvenile offender in the adult correctional system. In each case, the psychologist's recommendations support retention of juvenile court jurisdiction. Masquerading as objective clinical findings, such opinions involve an essential element of deception. The psychologist must bear the ethical burden of establishing that such means are justified by the end and neither create the risk of additional harm nor represent a fundamental compromise of role integrity.

Even when assuming the injustice of juvenile treatment in an adult correctional system, the psychologist's solution to the social dilemma of juvenile crime carries a number of risks—perhaps to the juvenile and to potential victims of the juvenile's criminal activity and certainly to the position of psychology itself, which may be discredited once it becomes clear that the psychologist's opinions have been fueled by a social agenda rather than objective findings. It is always possible for the psychologist to pursue such a social agenda honestly and effectively on the macroethical level either by writing or by supporting professional organizational advocacy. Naturally, to the extent that a psychologist such as this one is identified with a sociopolitical position, questions will be raised about the objectivity of any opinions on individual cases. In fact, it will be difficult for this psychologist to conclude honestly that his or her evaluations of juvenile offenders for placement in adult jurisdiction could be objective. Participation in these evaluations ought to proceed from an acknowledgment of the justice of the legal procedure if not of each individual consequence of the procedure.

In the fifth case, that of the psychologist facing a dilemma in respect to the death penalty, no firm position has been taken about the morality or social acceptability of the death penalty itself. The psychologist would admit to no actual bias against the death penalty. Regardless, the psychologist's unacknowledged agreement to become involved only in cases in which it appears possible to testify about mitigating factors introduces a structural bias: By design, the only opinions offered on the question of mitigation will be those in which the psychologist has something good to say. Again, this pattern cannot be maintained continuously, and the structural bias will eventually become clear and lead to the discounting of the examiner's opinions. The psychologist must consider that this particular response to a social responsibility dilemma is an expedient rather than a solution. Partial participation in social processes such as this cannot be sustained and is not ultimately responsive to the ethical dilemmas raised: The psychologist who is "in for a penny" is "in for a pound." Full participation implies an acknowledgment that the social process is at least not immoral or socially irresponsible. If the socially responsive psychologist has questions about the underlying values of state-sponsored executions, those questions must be resolved prior to participation in related evaluations.

In the sixth case, that of the toxic tort assessments, the psychologist has identified an assertedly objective position with what is viewed as a socially responsible position: The two are inseparable. A macroethical position explicitly informs microethical decisions. By assuming that toxic exposure (supposing there was actual exposure in this case) leads to psychological effects and by entering this case solely to find the expected effects, the psychologist has begged the question of whether the effects are actually present in this particular case. In creating an assessment strategy that is simply sensitive to the expected psychological effects but cannot distinguish those apparent effects from other psychological factors, the psychologist has not designed an honest test of any hypothesis. In pitting individuals against corporate entities in frankly advocating for the plaintiffs, the psychologist has arrogated to himself or herself the authority to set social policy, deciding that the social good in this instance is to be found in support of the individuals' claims. Pragmatically, the psychologist's opinions may easily be challenged on the basis of sociopolitical bias and methodological flaws and may not prevail to achieve the desired effect and strike a blow for responsibility in environmental policy. But whether such a position is effective, the psychologist has not offered the court objectively based findings and, in seeking a particular social effect, has done nothing to support the social institutions and processes designated to create and implement social policy.

SUMMARY

Two arenas of social responsibility can be distinguished in which two ethical strategies must apply. In the macroethical sphere of efforts by organizations and by individuals serving as representatives of their field, psychology must proceed from its core social values to advocate for social welfare in respect to particular issues. Psychology is ethically bound to represent accurately the extent of scientific knowledge about the issue at hand and the actual extent of organizational support for or professional consensus on the social policy positions it assumes.

In the microethical sphere of their impact on smaller groups and individuals, psychologists must consider the need to refrain from advocacy for particular social values or changes in order to maintain role integrity. Psychologists need to appreciate their own social value assumptions and impulses and to analyze the ways in which these factors compromise professional roles and objectivity. To the extent that the impact of these deep value considerations on their work can be controlled, it ought to be. As Vachon and Agresti (1992) contended, values may be understood as necessary and positive components of at least some psychological activity, but unacknowledged value assumptions and their unrestrained operation can be detriments to the welfare of individuals affected by a psychologist's work.

In addition to appreciating their own value assumptions, psychologists must appreciate the values implicit in the activities they undertake. If the underlying values of the individual, group, or institution with which the psychologist is working are in essential conflict with the psychologist's own values, consideration must be given to whether any such work will inevitably lead to ethical compromise. It cannot be expected that it will be ethically tenable to pretend to acquiesce to social values that are in conflict with the psychologist's own values and to work covertly to subvert them in order to achieve a good and socially responsible result. Doing so will require substantial deception, subert the scientific objectivity to which psychologists must aspire, and be ethically and socially irresponsible.

REFERENCES

American Psychological Association. (1981). Ethical principles of psychologists. *American Psychologist, 36,* 633–638.

American Psychological Association. (1989). *Bylaws.* Unpublished booklet.

American Psychological Association. (1990). Ethical principles of psychologists. *American Psychologist, 45,* 390–395.

American Psychological Association. (1992). Ethical principles of psychologists and code of conduct. *American Psychologist, 47,* 1597–1611.

Canadian Psychological Association Committee on Ethics. (1986). *A Canadian code of ethics for psychologists* (3rd draft). Unpublished manuscript.

Committee on Ethical Guidelines for Forensic Psychologists. (1991). Specialty guidelines for forensic psychologists. *Law and Human Behavior, 15,* 655–665.

Golding, S. L. (1990). Mental health professionals and the courts: The ethics of expertise. *International Journal of Law and Psychiatry, 13,* 281–307.

Keith-Spiegel, P., & Koocher, G.P. (1985). *Ethics in psychology: Professional standards and cases.* New York: Random House.

Saks, M.J. (1990). Expert witnesses, nonexpert witnesses, and nonwitness experts. *Law and Human Behavior, 14,* 291–313.

Vachon, D.O., & Agresti, A.A. (1992). A training proposal to help mental health professionals clarify and manage implicit values in the counseling process. *Professional Psychology: Research and Practice, 23,* 509–514.

Ethical Concerns of Nonclinical Forensic Witnesses and Consultants

Jeffrey E. Pfeifer
University of Regina

John C. Brigham
Florida State University

Current research suggests that nonclinical forensic psychologists[1] are appearing increasingly more often in the legal arena. We argue that many of the ethical dilemmas that face these psychologists differ from those encountered by clinical forensic psychologists. To test the accuracy of this assertion, 37 nonclinical forensic psychologists were surveyed to identify some of the ethical issues and dilemmas they have encountered while engaging in expert testimony or pretrial consulting. Respondents were asked also about how they have resolved these ethical issues and whether they were aware of the "Specialty Guidelines for Forensic Psychologists" (Committee on Ethical Guidelines for Forensic Psychologists, 1991). Results of the survey are discussed in terms of the need for additional regulatory guidelines or professional standards that speak directly to the ethical issues confronting nonclinical, forensic expert witnesses and consultants.

Key words: expert witness, forensic psychology, ethical dilemmas

Blau (1984) suggested that psychologists have played a continually increasing role in the judicial system since the *Jenkins v. United States* decision. According to Smith (1989, p. 147), "Judge Bazelon's decision in *Jenkins v. United States* [1962] accepted psychologists . . . as appropriate mental health experts . . .

Requests for reprints should be sent to Jeffrey E. Pfeifer, Department of Psychology, University of Regina, Regina, Saskatchewan, Canada S4S 0A2.

[1]Although the term *forensic psychologist* is commonly employed to refer to clinical psychologists who engage in legally related research, evaluations, or testimony, we employ the definition proposed by the CEGFP (1991, pp. 656–657) which, "specify the nature of desirable professional practice by forensic psychologists, *within any subdiscipline of psychology (i.e., clinical developmental, social, experimental)*" [italics added].

[which] led to the general acceptance of psychologists, and later other mental health professionals, as qualified expert witnesses." This "general acceptance" by the courts appears to have been actively welcomed by numerous clinicians who have since flocked to the courts in large numbers (Evans, 1987). Indeed, Faust and Ziskin (1988) estimated that psychologists and psychiatrists are now involved in the presentation of clinical evidence in over 1 million cases per year in the United States.

This increased psychological presence in the courtroom, however, has been paralleled by an equally intense debate regarding the propriety of such clinically related forensic testimony (see, e.g., Howard, 1986; Otto, 1989; Saks, 1990; Smith, 1989). Often, the major issue of contention revolves around the ethical concerns that arise when members of one profession (i.e., psychology) are introduced into another profession (i.e., the law) that may be based on different professional standards or regulatory guidelines (see, e.g., Fitch, Petrella, & Wallace, 1987; Hollien, 1990; Slovenko, 1987). In response to the concern over the ethical issues that face clinical forensic psychologists who enter the legal arena, a set of "Specialty Guidelines for Forensic Psychologists" was developed and published (Committee on Ethical Guidelines for Forensic Psychologists [CEGFP], 1991).

Yet, clinical forensic psychologists have not been the only ones to enter the legal arena in the capacity of expert witnesses or pretrial consultants (Yuille, 1989). Increasingly, as identified by our survey responses, forensic psychologists have begun to testify in a wide array of nonclinical areas (see Table 1). Unlike the issue of expert testimony by clinical forensic psychologists, the ethical issues involved in nonclinical forensic expert testimony or pretrial consultation have been given relatively little attention (an exception is the special issue of *Law and Human Behavior* edited by McCloskey, Egeth, & McKenna, 1986a). Therefore, in an attempt to gather preliminary information about the contours of existing or potential ethical dilemmas for nonclinical forensic psychologists, the following informal survey was conducted. We hope that this information will stimulate empirical research about many of the issues discussed herein.

BIOGRAPHICAL DATA OF SAMPLE

To sample nonclinical forensically inclined academics, questionnaires that asked about experiences with ethical dilemmas and issues involving forensic activity were sent to a small sample of academics who had published recent articles on forensic topics. In addition, copies of the questionnaire were made available to all participants at the 1992 biennial American Psychology–Law Society meeting. Questionnaires were to be completed anonymously and mailed back; responses were received from 37 Canadian and U.S. academically

TABLE 1
Description of Cases Reported by Survey Respondents

Case Type	Remuneration	Pro Bono
Accuracy of eyewitness identification	564	84
Product liability	475	0
Pretrial research (including change of venue)	156	7
Jury selection	130	23
Death penalty issues	64	16
Trademark infringement	30	1
Juvenile treatment	30	0
Cults and religious groups	25	12
Disability issues	25	0
Transfer of juveniles to criminal courts	20	0
Discrimination	18	0
Conformity, compliance, group dynamics	15	1
Guardianship	15	0
Child custody evaluations	8	12
Prison and jail crowding	6	0
Joinder issues	6	0
Posttrial juror interviews	4	0
Issues in accidental injury cases	4	0
Issues of cognition and speech perception	3	0
Rape trauma syndrome	1	0
Jury instructions	1	0
Evidence of previous criminal activity	1	0
Aging and mandatory retirement	1	0
Coerced confession	1	0
Evaluations of child witnesses	0	6

Column header: Number of Cases Involved In

based psychologists. Academically based psychologists were sampled because we felt that they were most likely to be the individuals called on to engage in nonclinical forensic expert testimony or pretrial research.

Respondents ranged from 29 to 72 years of age and included 33 men and 4 women. All members of the sample held PhDs; 4 members also held JDs. Reported experience as a consultant/expert ranged from 1 to 24 years, and respondents estimated that, on average, 84% of their income was derived from their faculty salary, 7.5% from legal consulting or expert testimony, and 8% from other sources (including royalties and nonlegal professional consultation). Twenty members of the sample described themselves as social psychologists, 4 as cognitive psychologists, 2 as developmental psychologists, 2 as consulting scientists, 1 as an experimental psychologist, 1 as a legal (nonclinical) psychologist, and 1 as a law psychologist. Another 6 respondents described themselves as forensic psychologists; 3 of the 6 received their PhDs in nonclinical areas (social, experimental, or developmental), whereas the remaining 3 respondents received their PhDs in clinical psychology. However, these 3 respondents identified themselves as primarily academic psychologists who engaged in little private practice and interacted with the courts primarily through nonclinical forensic testimony or pretrial research.

ETHICAL ISSUES AND CONCERNS

Respondents were asked to comment on a number of questions regarding ethical issues that they have encountered while engaging in expert testimony or pretrial consultation. Listed next are the questions posed and a summary of the answers that were received.

> Question 1: In deciding whether or not to work on a case, or while working on a case, what (if any) ethical/moral conflicts or issues have you faced?

Of the individuals who reported ethical/moral conflicts in their decision to work on a case, a number voiced concern over whether there was a sufficient level of professional knowledge available to testify and whether they would be able to address the possible limitations of their research or testimony.

Closely related to this issue was concern that attorneys, and the legal system in general, may misuse psychological testimony or research for their own ends. Specifically, a number of individuals noted ethical concerns ranging from cases in which there existed, "subtle pressure not to be so open in my answers to the opposing side," to "attorneys [who] did not want to provide all of the information asked for and needed, especially if it did not help their case." This dilemma led at least one respondent to discontinue work in the legal field, "I'm not convinced lawyers want to use the scientific evidence in the service of justice. Rather, their goal is to win, and I'm not comfortable in that setting."

Another major ethical dilemma reported by respondents surrounded the issue of accepting a case when it appears that the employing party may be guilty or morally culpable. This dilemma is illustrated by one respondent who stated that, "In one case, after rehearsing my testimony (eyewitness accuracy case), the lawyer and his assistant asked me if I thought their client was guilty. I demurred. Then they said (in unison), I think he's guilty as hell." Similarly, another respondent suggested that the "main conflict [involved] assisting the criminal defense when [the] defendant appear[ed] guilty and dangerous."

Not all respondents, however, were unsettled only by the possibility that they may be aiding in the release of a guilty defendant. At least one individual noted the opposite scenario, "I agonize a lot about the possibility that my efforts might have the effect of sending an innocent person to prison." In either case, it is readily apparent that many members of our survey sample placed some weight on the perceived level of guilt (or moral culpability) of a prospective client.

Remuneration also raised ethical concerns for respondents. Apprehension regarding the question of payment for services ranged from whether testimony would be perceived as tainted (i.e., a hired gun) to concern for the cost of expert assistance to the client. At least one respondent voiced some concern over accepting a large fee from victims/defendants who already face large legal expenses.

Finally, individual respondents also mentioned ethical dilemmas in the areas of witness preparation, the granting of media interviews before a trial has concluded, and the potential problems involved in imparting case facts to a mock juror during pretrial simulations. The ethical implications of this final issue were described by one individual as follows, "on one occasion, a mock juror we hired for pretrial simulations took the results to opposing counsel who used it to inform their decision about [a] settlement offer."

Question 2: How have you resolved these issue(s) in the past?

Respondents suggested a number of approaches for resolving current ethical dilemmas. First, in terms of dealing with the issue of whether sufficient professional knowledge is available to comment on a particular case and whether the limitations of this research should be reported, respondents appeared to clearly agree that, "in instances where it [the literature] is not strong, [it is best to] decline to offer testimony or to comment."

Respondents appeared equally certain that, for the most part, psychologists should attempt to report the possible limitations of the research that they are employing as a basis for their testimony. At least one individual dealt with this, "by making the limits of th[e] research very clear and refusing to testify in court on anything other than my assessment of the data." Similarly, this preference for ensuring that the possible limitations of research are attended to was echoed by a number of other respondents, including one who noted that when working on a case the, "defense attorney is informed that I will only give testimony if allowed to make an initial set of remarks [that ensure that the qualifications of the data presented are made known]." Another individual noted that when discussing a case with an attorney, "I tell them I am there to testify about what the research says, that it may hurt their client, and it's their decision to put me on the stand."

Similarly, all individuals who described ethical dilemmas involving the attempted misuse of psychological research or testimony by attorneys reported dealing with this situation by informing the attorney that they would not go beyond the general knowledge of the field in which they were testifying. This belief is summed up by two individuals who suggested that forensic psychologists, "limit [their] work to those areas [they] really know and where there is a logical connection to the case at hand," and not "allow[ing] the lawyer to dictate what will or will not be *your* testimony. If this is clear up front, *you* will not be put into untenable positions."

Although these responses indicate a general agreement in terms of dealing with the ethical implications by fully presenting information that is within the confines of accepted psychological knowledge, there is less agreement over what to do when one perceives that the client is guilty (or is morally culpable). Responses to this dilemma took one of two directions. For some respondents, this dilemma was resolved by replacing the concern about defendant guilt with a belief in the integrity of the judicial system and, therefore, testifying. These respondents indicated their preference for this approach by deciding that it is the function of the court to determine the guilt of a defendant. According to one respondent, this was accomplished, "by recognizing that the *process* is there to decide [on guilt], not me."

Second, and perhaps more surprising, a number of respondents suggested that the dilemma was resolved by the expert refusing to testify in a case when they believed that the defendant was guilty. According to one respondent, "I won't testify in cases where there is other, direct evidences besides the [eyewitness] IDs to implicate [the defendant]." Another respondent was even more adamant about forensic psychologists' concern for representing only the right side,

> In general, I wish to be convinced that I am testifying for the side in a lawsuit who I believe should win the case. If there is any doubt, as there has been in a number of cases, I ask to read the briefs and to examine the harshest evidence introduced by the other side. Until my doubts are satisfied, I will refuse to accept work on a case. In several situations I have withdrawn my name from consideration.

Finally, in response to the ethical concerns regarding remuneration, at least one respondent resolved the question of tainted testimony by refusing all payment: "Since I do not accept a fee, I am not troubled that I said whatever it was I said in order to profit." Several other psychologists said that they approached this issue on a case-by-case basis. They appeared to weigh a number of variables such as the client's ability to afford their services, the degree to which payment might taint the perception of the testimony, and whether payment was on a contingency basis.

Aside from these responses to dealing with specific ethical dilemmas, a review of answers to this question indicate two other interesting trends. First, of the 37 psychologists surveyed, 3 individuals indicated that they remain unsure about how to resolve many of the ethical dilemmas they face. In addition, 4 other individuals indicated that the ethical dilemmas they have encountered have led to their reluctance to continue to appear as an expert witness or engage in pretrial consultation.

Question 3: What suggestions do you have for other academics who may face the same issue(s)?

Responses to this question can be separated into three distinct categories: (a) relying on personal beliefs/values, (b) being cognizant of the findings and limitations of the field of specialization that you represent, and (c) actively seeking a better understanding of the legal system. To begin with, a number of individuals who responded to this question suggested that academics should rely on their personal beliefs or values when attempting to deal with ethical dilemmas because there were few alternatives available. According to one respondent, individuals who find themselves faced with an ethical dilemma should, "go with [their] conscience and may cognitive dissonance work well for [them]."

In addition, respondents suggested that academics who may face similar ethical dilemmas should deal with them by ensuring that their theoretical and/or research base is a strong one and that they will be given an opportunity to state the limitations of the research. According to one individual, this may be accomplished by, "explain[ing] to attorneys that by qualifying the research yourself, it helps inoculate your testimony against the other side's attack."

Other respondents suggested that academics may face fewer ethical dilemmas if they gain a working knowledge of the legal system before entering it as an expert witness or a pretrial consultant. Specifically, it was suggested that psychologists interested in participating in the legal arena should, "be acquainted with the adversary process [and] if [they] cannot accept it, recognize [they] do not belong in court." Similarly, another respondent warned other psychologists that, "you may be asked to round off sharp edges of scientific testimony and to anticipate before you get too deeply involved that there will be pressures to go beyond the data."

This concern for not going "beyond the data," even under pressure from members of the legal community, was echoed by other respondents, including one who cautioned others to, "be aware [that] the legal system has different 'rules of the game' by which they play. Do not get sucked into that game. Lawyers respect us when we hold our positions on issues, ideas, etc." This alludes to the ethical issue that may arise when psychologists are asked to enter an arena with differing professional standards or regulatory guidelines. However, at least one respondent offered a solution to this potential problem, "Remember that you are first and foremost a psychologist and therefore should adhere to the principles and ethics of your discipline."

Question 4: Have you ever withheld pertinent information during testimony because it would hurt the side that retained you?

A few individuals answered that they had withheld pertinent information. One of them argued that the basis for this action could be found in the adversarial process,

> I have not testified on direct examination about the fact that same-race IDs are generally more reliable than cross-race IDs. . . . It is the adversary system, after all. I think that an expert should play by the rules, but should not bend over backwards to help the other side. That's the way the game is played.

The other individual who withheld pertinent information offered a warning to other psychologists,

> In one case years ago, the lawyers talked me into presenting a watered-down version of some survey data, on the theory that the judge was too dumb to note the holes. The judge was not too dumb and the testimony went badly. I would not make that mistake again.

In contrast, a substantial number of individuals stated that they had not withheld pertinent information. They appeared strong in their belief that testifying to "the truth, the whole truth, and nothing but the truth," meant doing just that. According to one individual, "I tell lawyers that I will answer all questions that are asked. I tell them my testimony will be the same regardless of which side calls me."

Most individuals, however, offered qualified answers to this question, and suggested that they never intentionally withheld pertinent information but that the legal system was such that information they may have deemed pertinent was excluded for one reason or another. For example, one individual, "always respond[ed] fully to questions—but part of the adversarial system is knowing which questions to ask and not ask." This sentiment was echoed by others such as the individual who suggested that, in some cases, "there [was] pertinent information which was not heard because neither attorney asked. I would have given it if asked, so I didn't 'withhold' it."

Question 5: Do you feel it is the job of the opposing attorney to point out limitations or inconsistencies in an expert's testimony and/or its research basis, or should the expert point these out herself/himself?

Of the individuals responding to this question, the majority suggested that it was the expert's responsibility to point out limitations, whereas other individuals argued that it was the opposing attorney's job to point out limitations. The remaining individuals argued that it was both parties' responsibility.

Some of the individuals who believed that the expert was responsible for identifying limitations were adamant in their belief that,

> as psychologists, we must be advocates for the truth, rather than either side. Hence it is our ethical responsibility not to mislead the trier of fact by failing to point out inconsistencies and limitations. This is tantamount to lying in my view!

Others, however, agreed that although it was the expert's responsibility to point out limitations or inconsistencies, this may not always be possible given the current legal system. As one respondent explained,

> the expert has a responsibility to present a fair, unbiased picture of research findings. The expert does not have a responsibility to initially present all inconsistencies and limitations. Why not? Very impractical. [The] Judge would ask you to get to the point.

Of the individuals who argued that it was both the expert and the opposing attorney's responsibility to point out major inconsistencies or limitations, one wrote that,

> it is not that simple. We must remember that the legal system works differently and it is appropriate/necessary to play by those rules [to wait for the opposing attorney to point out limitations]. The exceptions arise when not doing so would amount to misrepresenting the basis of an opinion.

Another respondent argued that although it is the opposing attorney's job to point out limitations, "an expert should be clear and explicit with counsel concerning limitations and indicate the limits and weaknesses of his [or her] testimony."

Other respondents, however, appeared to have conformed completely with the adversarial system, and they argued that sole responsibility for identifying limitations lies with the opposing attorney. For example, one individual stated that, "[u]nless it assists [my] side of the case by forestalling anticipated problems, I will not assist the adversary in any manner."

Question 6: Are you familiar with the "Specialty Guidelines for Forensic Psychologists" (CEGFP, 1991)?

Note that although these guidelines are technically not "ethical" but rather "speciality" guidelines for forensic psychologists, they do include ethical issues and were thought to be of some importance for this survey. In addition, the fact that these guidelines "provide an aspirational model of desirable professional practice by psychologists, within any subdiscipline of psychology" (CEGFP, 1991, p. 656) indicates that they should be of interest to nonclinical as well as clinical forensic psychologists.

Of the individuals responding to this question, however, approximately one third stated that they were not acquainted with the document (CEGFP, 1991). Interestingly, of the individuals who were aware of the guidelines, a number voiced concern over their effectiveness and applicability, "like the 10 Commandments, if you don't know them by the time you're 25, reading about them won't change your behavior—similar to many pronouncements of the APA [American Psychological Association], too wordy, too preachy, and sometimes too vague."

Others, however, indicated that the guidelines (CEGFP, 1991) were a solid beginning that could become more effective with further refinements. Several respondents suggested that the effectiveness of the guidelines might be enhanced by the addition of more specific applications. One respondent said that the guidelines, "would probably be improved by the addition of a casebook containing concrete situations [problems and resolutions] that bring general principles to life." This concern may be addressed by producing manuals similar to those published by the APA (1987) and the Canadian Psychological Association (1991) which present specific ethical dilemmas and solutions regarding professional conduct in relation to therapeutic sessions, the elimination of sexual harassment, confidentiality, consumer welfare, assessment techniques, professional relationships, and other issues.

Finally, some individuals found the guidelines (CEGFP, 1991) wholly inadequate, especially in terms of their applicability to nonclinical forensic psychologists. One stated,

> They go to great lengths to discuss the peripheral aspects of expertise [e.g., preparing materials] but dodge the core issue of what it really means to be an expert. The phrase, "someone who by virtue of training, education, or practice" has something to tell the court is unsatisfactory. Clearly, the professional guild was influential in this weak definition.

DISCUSSION

As stated previously, these responses are not meant to represent a comprehensive analysis of the major ethical concerns facing psychologists today. Rather, this pilot survey was an attempt to gather preliminary information about the range and prevalence of ethical issues faced by nonclinical forensic psychologists in order to promote further rigorous empirical investigation. From the results, we argue that future research on this issue might be helpful in a number of specific areas: whether to testify (or engage in pretrial consultation), how to testify (i.e., whether to take the role of adversary or educator), and where to look for ethical guidance should you decide to engage in nonclinical forensic testimony or research. These issues are far from new. Over 80 years ago, some eminent psychologists (Freud, 1906/1959; Munsterberg, 1908) were enthusiastically endorsing the infusion of psychological knowledge into the courts. Some psychologists supported this approach, whereas others did not (Kargon, 1986); legal scholars were, in general, unimpressed (e.g., Wigmore, 1909).

The issue of whether to testify was voiced by over one third of our sample through concerns about the perceived guilt or moral culpability of a defendant. As noted, responses ranged from an unwillingness to take this factor into account ("that's the jury's decision, not mine") to an unwillingness to testify in cases wherein guilt or culpability seemed likely. Among research psychologists, Loftus was especially open in chronicling her own struggles with this issue. She wrote a guest column in *Newsweek* (Loftus, 1987) describing the factors that led her, after 2 months of indecision, to decline to testify in Israel for the defense in the trial of John Demjanjuk, alleged to have been the vicious Nazi gas-chamber operator known as "Ivan the Terrible." Later, Loftus noted that issues of apparent guilt and the educator/advocate distinction can blur together. She argued that a psychologist in a court of law may act in both roles: "If I believe a defendant is innocent, if I believe in his innocence with all my heart and soul, then I probably can't help but become an advocate of sorts" (Loftus & Ketcham, 1991, p. 238).

This issue is particularly important because, unlike attorneys, psychologists are not bound to represent their clients to the best of their ability. According to Canon 7 of the American Bar Association's (1986, p. 63, E7–1) *Model Code of Professional Responsibility and Code of Judicial Conduct,* "the duty of a lawyer . . . is to represent his client zealously within the bounds of the law." This obligation extends to all clients, regardless of whether the attorney perceives the client to be guilty or not.

In contrast to this viewpoint, many psychologists in our sample were concerned about whether they should accept a case when they perceive that a client may be guilty or morally culpable. Current ethical and specialty guidelines do not speak directly to this issue. However, one might argue that the actual guilt or moral culpability of a party in a trial does not (or should not) effect the current state of knowledge with regard to the testimony of an expert witness. For example, an expert witness who specializes in the effects of rumor transmission on perceptions of guilt should be willing to testify in a trial regardless of whether the evidence indicates that the defendant is guilty or not. Quite simply, testimony on the effects of rumor transmission should not objectively differ, regardless of how guilty an expert might perceive a defendant.

Our results indicate, however, that this is not a tenable argument for many of our respondents. A number of respondents indicated that they not only viewed the possible guilt of a defendant as an ethical dilemma but that, in some cases, they would decline to testify on behalf of an individual who they believed to be guilty. Specific ethical guidelines that speak to this issue would be helpful. For example, do forensic psychologists have the right to prejudge individuals, before trial takes place, to decide whether or not to work on their behalf? Should psychologists have an ethical duty to present research and current general psychological knowledge to the courts in all cases to which the knowledge is appropriate, not only in those cases that we deem morally correct or acceptable?

It appears that the issue of defendant guilt involves both an ethical/moral question (i.e., should one testify in favor of an apparently guilty or morally culpable defendant?) and an empirical one (i.e., if the expert wishes to use defendant guilt as a criterion of whether to become involved, with what degree of accuracy can the expert discern guilt?). As far as we know, there are no empirical data on this latter question, but research that demonstrates how difficult it is to tell when someone is lying, wherein the average perceiver does only slightly better than chance (e.g., DePaulo, Stone, & Lassiter, 1985; Ekman & O'Sullivan, 1991), suggests that an expert's pretrial judgment of a defendant's guilt or innocence may not be particularly accurate (Brigham, 1992). In addition, factors such as racial or ethnic stereotypes or the defense attorney's oratorical skill in describing the defendant's plight to the uncertain expert may play an inappropriate role in determining the decision to testify.

The issue of how to testify (i.e., the advocate/educator distinction) has also witnessed some spirited discussion through the years (e.g., Goldman, 1986; Hastie, 1986; Hollien, 1990; Lempert, 1986; Loftus, 1983; McCloskey & Egeth, 1983; McCloskey, Egeth, & McKenna, 1986b; Saks, 1990; Yarmey, 1986; Yuille, 1989). Like the issue just discussed, the question of whether one's personal values should play any role in the selection of cases or the direction of testimony has stirred intense debate. Most psychologists and ethicists appear to support the educator role and take the perspective that one should try not to let one's personal values play a substantial part, but much disagreement remains (e.g., Buckhout, 1986; Konecni & Ebbesen, 1986; Loftus, 1986; Pachella, 1986).

Like most psychologists, our respondents appear to agree in principle that psychologists have a responsibility to point out research limitations when presenting information to the courts. What is less clear, however, is how far that responsibility extends and to whom it extends. Specifically, individuals in this study were divided as to whether psychologists should make every possible attempt to point out all possible limitations of the research they are relying on as a basis for their testimony or whether some attempt should be made to report only the major limitations. A related issue concerns who should be informed. That is, does the psychologist have a responsibility to present the possible limitations of his or her work to only the attorney who has retained them, or does that responsibility extend to the judge/jury and opposing counsel?

Given these questions, it would be helpful to have more specific guidelines regarding the appropriateness of withholding pertinent information during testimony. Certainly, few would argue that psychologists should actively withhold pertinent information when testifying in court, and our results suggest that this is, in fact, not often done—only two of our respondents reported doing so. Section VII(B) of the "Specialty Guidelines for Forensic Psychologists" (CEGFP, 1991, p. 664) appears to speak directly to this issue:

> When testifying, forensic psychologists have an obligation to all parties to a legal proceeding to present their findings, conclusions, evidence, or other professional products in a fair manner. This principle does not preclude forceful representation of the data and reasoning upon which a conclusion or professional product is based. It does, however, preclude an attempt, whether active or passive, to engage in partisan distortion or misrepresentation. Forensic psychologists do not, by either commission or omission, participate in a misrepresentation of their evidence, nor do they participate in partisan attempts to avoid, deny, or subvert the presentation of evidence contrary to their own position.

What is less clear from an ethical standpoint, however, is the extent to which psychologists are responsible for ensuring that pertinent information is introduced while they are testifying. That is, although Section VII(B) of the guidelines (CEGFP, 1991) suggests that psychologists should neither actively nor passively "engage in partisan distortion or misrepresentation," (p. 664) there remains a question as to whether not volunteering data (unless asked by the opposing attorney) is an acceptable or ethical practice. Some argued that not volunteering certain pertinent information is not, in fact, an attempt to engage in partisan distortion but rather is simply answering the questions that are asked honestly and to the best of one's ability. Clarification of this issue is certainly warranted.

Finally, it is readily apparent that, should they decide to enter the legal arena, nonclinical forensic psychologists perceive that they have few formal guidelines to refer to other than the "Ethical Principles of Psychologists and Code of Conduct" issued by the APA (1992) and/or the "Specialty Guidelines for Forensic Psychologists" issued by the CEGFP (1991). Although both of these documents provide generalized standards of conduct, neither speaks directly to many of the specific questions in which individuals in our sample appeared to be interested. This absence of direction is illustrated by the varied responses of individuals regarding how they currently resolve ethical dilemmas and by the large number of respondents who suggested that other academics who may face similar issues should resolve them through personal choice or a reliance on personal beliefs/values. Note that none of the respondents stated that they resolved their current ethical dilemmas by referring to either the

APA's ethical principles or the CEGFP's specialty guidelines.

Certainly, no set of guidelines or standards will answer all possible ethical dilemmas that a psychologist may face when testifying or engaging in pretrial consultation. The current focus of attention and guidelines for the ethical behavior of forensic psychologists, however, has revolved largely around the issues that tend to face clinicians and mental health experts. Although the ethical issues that face nonclinicians overlap considerably with those faced by clinicians, responses from our survey indicate that nonclinical forensic psychologists also face a number of unique ethical dilemmas when interacting with the legal system for which there are no recognized standards or guidelines. Future research and discussion should attend to this lack of direction.

ACKNOWLEDGMENTS

Research for this article was supported in part by a Social Science and Humanities Research Council of Canada postdoctoral fellowship awarded to Jeffrey E. Pfeifer.

We thank Gloria Balius, Stephanie Croxton, Suzanne Kairalla, Christina McCarthy, and Petrina Pelletier for their invaluable assistance in the preparation of this article. We also thank Dr. Bruce Sales for his comments and suggestions on earlier drafts of this article.

REFERENCES

American Bar Association. (1986). *Model code of professional responsibility and code of judicial conduct* (EC7–1). Chicago: Author.

American Psychological Association. (1987). *Casebook on ethical principles of psychologists* (rev. ed.). Washington, DC: Author.

American Psychological Association. (1992). Ethical principles of psychologists and code of conduct. *American Psychologist, 47,* 1597–1628.

Blau, T. H. (1984). *The psychologist as expert witness.* New York: Wiley.

Brigham, J. C. (1992). A personal account of the expert in court. *Contemporary Psychology, 37,* 529–530.

Buckhout, R. (1986). Personal values and expert testimony. *Journal of Social Issues, 10*(1/2), 145–150.

Canadian Psychological Association. (1991). *Canadian code of ethics for psychologists: Companion manual.* Old Chelsea, Quebec: Author.

Committee on Ethical Guidelines for Forensic Psychologists. (1991). Specialty guidelines for forensic psychologists. *Law and Human Behavior, 15,* 655–665.

DePaulo, B. M., Stone, J. L., & Lassiter, G. D. (1985). Deceiving and detecting deceit. In B. R. Schlenker (Ed.), *The self and social life* (pp. 323–370). New York: McGraw-Hill.

Ekman, P., & O'Sullivan, M. (1991). Who can catch a liar? *American Psychologist, 46,* 913–920.

Evans, D. R. (1987). The psychologist as an expert witness in civil and criminal litigation. *Canadian Psychology, 28,* 274–279.

Faust, D., & Ziskin, J. (1988). The expert witness in psychology and psychiatry. *Science, 241,* 31–35.

Fitch, W. L., Petrella, R. C., & Wallace, J. (1987). Legal ethics and the use of mental health experts in criminal cases. *Behavioral Sciences and the Law, 5,* 105–117.

Freud, S. (1959). Psycho-analysis and the ascertaining of truth in courts of law. In J. Riviere (Ed.), *Clinical papers: Papers on technique* (Vol. 2, pp. 13–24). New York: Basic Books. (Original work published 1906)

Goldman, A. H. (1986). Cognitive psychologists as expert witnesses: A problem in professional ethics. *Journal of Social Issues, 10*(1/2), 29–46.

Hastie, R. (1986). Notes on the psychologist expert witness. *Journal of Social Issues, 10*(1/2), 79–82.

Hollien, H. (1990). The expert witness: Ethics and responsibilities. *Journal of Forensic Sciences, 35,* 1414–1423.

Howard, L. B. (1986). The dichotomy of the expert witness. *Journal of Forensic Sciences, 31,* 337–341.

Jenkins v. United States, 307 F.2d 637 (D.C. Car. 1962).

Kargon, R. (1986). Expert testimony in historical perspective. *Journal of Social Issues, 10*(1/2), 15–27.

Konecni, V. J., & Ebbesen, E. B. (1986). Courtroom testimony by psychologists on eyewitness identification issues: Critical notes and reflections. *Journal of Social Issues, 10*(1/2), 117–126.

Lempert, R. O. (1986). Social sciences in court: On "eyewitness experts" and other issues. *Journal of Social Issues, 10*(1/2), 167–182.

Loftus, E. F. (1983). Silence is not golden. *American Psychologist, 38,* 564–572.

Loftus, E. F. (1986). Experimental psychologist as advocate or impartial educator. *Journal of Social Issues, 10*(1/2), 63–78.

Loftus, E. F. (1987, June 29). Trials of an expert witness. *Newsweek,* pp. 10–11.

Loftus, E. F., & Ketcham, K. (1991). *Witness for the defense.* New York: St. Martin's Press.

McCloskey, M., & Egeth, E. (1983). Eyewitness identification: What can a psychologist tell a jury? *American Psychologist, 38,* 550–563.

McCloskey, M., Egeth, E., & McKenna, J. (Eds.). (1986a). The ethics of expert testimony [Special issue]. *Law and Human Behavior, 10*(1/2).

McCloskey, M., Egeth, E., & McKenna, J. (1986b). The experimental psychologist in court. *Journal of Social Issues, 10*(1/2), 1–13.

Munsterberg, H. (1908). *On the witness stand.* New York: Doubleday, Page.

Otto, R. K. (1989). Bias and expert testimony of mental health professionals in adversarial proceedings: A preliminary investigation. *Behavioral Sciences and the Law, 7,* 267–273.

Pachella, R. G. (1986). Personal values and the value of expert testimony. *Journal of Social Issues, 10*(1/2), 145–150.

Saks, M. J. (1990). Expert witnesses, nonexpert witnesses, and nonwitness experts. *Law and Human Behavior, 14,* 291–313.

Slovenko, R. (1987). The lawyer and the forensic expert: Boundaries of ethical practice. *Behavioral Sciences and the Law, 5,* 119–147.

Smith, S. R. (1989). Mental health expert witnesses: Of science and crystal balls. *Behavioral Science and the Law, 7,* 145–180.

Wigmore, H. H. (1909). Professor Munsterberg and the psychology of evidence. *Illinois Law Review, 3,* 339–443.

Yarmey, A. D. (1986). Ethical responsibilities governing the statements experimental psychologists made in expert testimony. *Journal of Social Issues, 10*(1/2), 101–116.

Yuille, J. C. (1989). Expert evidence by psychologists: Sometimes problematic and often premature. *Behavioral Sciences and the Law, 7,* 181–196.

The Relation Between Ethical Codes and Moral Principles

Donald N. Bersoff
Villanova Law School and Hahnemann University

Peter M. Koeppl
Hahnemann University

We describe the application of fundamental moral principles, with particular emphasis on prima facie duties, to formal codes of ethics that regulate the conduct of forensic psychologists who act as expert witnesses. Then we discuss the American Psychological Association's (1992) "Ethical Principles of Psychologists and Code of Conduct" and the Committee on Ethical Guidelines for Forensic Psychologists's "Specialty Guidelines for Forensic Psychologists" (1991) and critically appraise how these documents translate basic moral principles. We conclude that, in many ways, the documents exemplify ethical obligations such as nonmaleficence, beneficence, and justice, but they fall short in many other ways, particularly with regard to autonomy and fidelity.

Key words: expert witness, moral principles, ethics codes

One of the unavoidable and often unwelcome tasks confronting human beings is the resolution of conflict. Because "judgment and choice are pervasive activities [and] inevitable aspect[s] of living" (Hogarth, 1987, p. 1), we constantly face both mundane and complex ethical dilemmas in our personal and professional lives (Pope & Vetter, 1992). In attempting to find solutions to these dilemmas, we rarely reexamine our own system of values and beliefs. Rather, we rely on information-processing strategies that appear to be innate, automatic, and outside conscious awareness (Hollon & Kriss, 1984). Even when we seek direction, we face disappointment. Unlike "cookbooks" that help us interpret scatter on subtests of individual intelligence scales or Minnesota Multiphasic Personality Inventory (Dahlstrom, Welsh, & Dahlstrom,

---

Requests for reprints should be sent to Donald N. Bersoff, Law and Psychology Program, Hahnemann University, MS 626, Broad and Vine Streets, Philadelphia, PA 19102–1192.

1982) psychograms, there is simply no manual that prescribes a set of expected behaviors or universally acceptable solutions to moral dilemmas and ethical conflicts.

However, when ethical issues engage the core of our conscience, we become motivated to make the "correct" moral choice and search for reliable guides to help us do so. It is perhaps for this reason that scholars through the ages have striven to devise systems of rules or ethical codes that would govern our personal and professional behavior. As a prelude to the more detailed and precise analysis of ethical conflicts that confront forensic psychologists who serve as expert witnesses—the subject matter of the articles in this special issue—we focus here on the development of general moral principles and their application to formalized codes of ethical behavior relevant to the work of psychological experts.

FUNDAMENTAL FOUNDATIONS OF MORAL AND ETHICAL THOUGHT

Ethics is the study of those assumptions held by individuals, institutions, organizations, and professions they believe will assist them in making moral judgments and distinguishing between right and wrong (Delgado & McAllen, 1982). Descriptive ethicists are concerned with uncovering and delineating the moral beliefs of particular groups. They tend to reside more comfortably in the realm of empirical science than do normative ethicists, their philosophical cousins (Delgado & McAllen, 1982). Once the basic principles of morality have been identified and analyzed, normative ethicists attempt to transform these principles into concrete and behaviorally prescriptive paradigms designed to guide, if not dictate, correct behavior. Formal codes of ethics are the expressions of normative ethics.

Deontology and utilitarianism are the two most generally accepted ethical frameworks on which ethics codes can be built. Deontological theorists, beginning with Immanual Kant (1785/1969), hold that the morality of a behavior is directly related to its intrinsic or inherent nature. That is, actions are right or wrong regardless of their consequences. There are many versions of this nonconsequentialist approach to moral decision making. Proponents of deontology rely on a variety of sources such as divine revelation, hunch, and religious teaching, as well as such human traits as common sense and intuition, to arrive at moral judgments. Regardless of the diversity of deontological sources, there is a unifying imperative that is shared by all of its proponents: One's actions must strive to treat every person as an end and never as a means (Beauchamp & Walters, 1982). Thus, the categorical imperative underlying deontological ethical formulations is an unquestioning and pervasive respect for the dignity of the individual (Fine & Ulrich, 1988).

Utilitarianism, or consequentialist ethical theory (and closely akin to teleology), proposes that the results of behavior ultimately dictate its morality, an approach traditionally linked to the philosopher John Stuart Mill (1861/1957). The theory rests on the principle of utility (Beauchamp & Childress, 1989), an axiom which suggests that a behavior is most morally correct when its results are more favorable than the predicted results of its alternatives. Thus, a utilitarian ethicist is put in the position of balancing the possible costs and benefits of an action. It often means choosing among possible "evils" and searching for the least detrimental alternative.

Deontology and utilitarianism are typically portrayed as opposites. Undoubtedly, in many ways, each theory and its variants manifestly challenge the assumptions and foundations of its rival. However, as Beauchamp and Childress (1989) explained, distinguishing between these two ideologies is a relatively recent phenomenon, conceived perhaps as an attempt to meld contemporary and ancient moral theories while providing a simplified classificatory strategy. Under closer scrutiny, the border defining deonotology and utilitarianism is not always sharply drawn, especially when one looks at the subdivisions of each theory. In any event, the fact that these two divergent ideologies continue to exist suggests that neither deonotology nor utilitarianism alone provides adequate solutions for all moral conflicts.

An alternative approach to deontology and utilitarianism can be attributed to the 20th century English philosopher W. D. Ross. Ross (1930) propounded a set of prima facie duties to which the ethical person is bound. These duties include nonmaleficence, fidelity, beneficence, justice, and autonomy, each of which may be defined in the context of professional conduct. Because the concept of prima facie duties provides an array of moral choices and its principles are designed to be applied flexibly in relation to the context of a dilemma (Beauchamp & McCullough, 1984), reliance on prima facie duties has gained wider acceptance than either deontology or utilitarianism. However, only one of these principles can take precedence at any one time, and the determination of the predominating principle can be made only after examining the applicability of each to the situation in question. From this perspective, a moral principle is not absolutely binding and may be superseded by an equal or more applicable principle (Beauchamp & Childress, 1989; Kitchener, 1984).

Perhaps the bedrock ethical duty required of psychologists and other professionals is nonmaleficence, captured most felicitously in the adage, *Primum non nocere*—Above all, do no harm. Fidelity most often refers to the obligations of faithfulness and loyalty inherent in the client–clinician relationship (Kitchener, 1984). But the principle may also apply to fidelity toward the scientific roots of one's profession. Beneficence is perhaps the most intuitive, common sense principle; indeed, the very notion of psychology as a "helping profession" is its embodiment. It refers to practitioners' responsibility to benefit those they assess and treat and investigators' obligation to conduct research that will have scientific and applied value. Justice refers to the obligation of professionals to treat equitably all they serve and study and, as Kitchener (1984) suggested, the superordinate responsibility to respect the worth and dignity of each individual. Finally, but by no means least important, is the principle of autonomy, guaranteeing persons the freedom to think, choose, and act so long as one's actions do not infringe on the rights of others (Bersoff, 1992; Kitchener, 1984).

One can question whether the proper application of prima facie duties or other fundamental philosophical principles obviate the need to create codes of conduct. It is very likely that almost intuitively we consider and weigh such values as beneficence and autonomy in our attempts to resolve ethical dilemmas. This is especially true when professional codes are either in conflict with each other or fail to provide explicit direction altogether, but we often rely on philosophical values even when a predicament could be resolved by applying clearly defined rules such as legal standards (Delgado & McAllen, 1982).

In any event, every group with the pretense of presenting itself to the public as a profession has developed a formal code of ethics (Gorlin, 1986). Ideally, a code of ethics should serve as a guide to resolving moral problems that confront the members of the profession that promulgate it, with primary emphasis on protecting the public the profession serves. It should be a grand statement of overarching principles that earns the respect of that public by reflecting the profession's moral integrity.

The salient problem is that, although a profession may understand how moral reasoning develops and may subscribe to fundamental philosophical principles, a profession does not always translate these lofty duties into codes of conduct. Realistically, a code of ethics consensually validates the most recent views of a majority of professionals empowered to make decisions about ethical issues. It is, inevitably, anachronistic, conservative, protective of its members, the product of political compromise, restricted in its scope, and too often unable to provide clear-cut solutions to ambiguous professional predicaments (Bersoff, in press; Kitchener, 1984). Although we may consider fundamental principles when faced with ethical conflicts, our economic security and professional reputation are not endangered by failing to abide by them. It is the adoption and enforcement of a formal, written set of standards that dictate the behavior of professionals, not a set of soaring statements to which we pay lip service but to which we would find it burdensome to conform.

THE APPLICATION OF MORAL PRINCIPLES TO PSYCHOLOGY'S ETHICAL CODES

Now we examine the extent to which psychology has given meaning to fundamental moral principles in its ethics documents. We limit our examination to the "Ethical Principles of Psychologists and Code of Conduct" (American Psychological Association [APA], 1992) and the "Specialty Guidelines for

Forensic Psychologists" (Committee on Ethical Guidelines for Forensic Psychologists [CEGFP], 1991). Even then, the examination is meant to be illustrative, not comprehensive.

"Ethical Principles of Psychologists and Code of Conduct"

The current ethics code (APA, 1992) is a descendant of eight previous versions, the first one of which was published in 1953 (Bersoff, in press; Pope & Vetter, 1992). It was adopted by the APA's legislative and policy-making body, the Council of Representatives, in August 1992. Along with an Introduction, the code consists of three parts—a Preamble, General Principles, and Ethical Standards (which is comprised of eight major parts). "The Preamble and the General Principles are *aspirational* goals to guide psychologists toward the highest ideals of psychology" (APA, 1992, p. 1598). Only the eight parts containing provisions denominated as Ethical Standards comprise the enforceable code of conduct. Of these, the seventh part with six provisions relate directly to forensic activities. We consider those in a separate section of this article.

Each of the prima facie duties described in the prior section have been translated in some form in the code (APA, 1992). The duty of nonmaleficence is exemplifed throughout the aspirational General Principles and in the enforceable Ethical Standards. In General Principle E (Concern for Others' Welfare), psychologists are importuned to resolve "conflicts and to perform their roles in a responsible fashion that avoids or minimizes harm" (p. 1600) and, more specifically in Principle B (Integrity), to "avoid improper and potentially harmful dual relationships" (p. 1599). Similarly, psychologists are required in enforceable Provision 1.14 to "take reasonable steps to avoid harming [those] with whom they work, and to minimize harm where it is foreseeable and unavoidable" (p. 1601). The concern that psychologists' personal problems may harm clients and research participants (Provision 1.13), the highly cautionary statements about engaging in multiple relationships of any sort (Provision 1.17), and the absolute ban on sexual relations with current and recently terminated therapy clients (Provisions 4.05 and 4.07) because they "are so frequently harmful" (p. 1605) also exemplify the principle. The significant emphasis on nonmaleficence in the code may be explained by the fact that plaintiffs in malpractice actions must prove that injury has occurred as a foreseeable result of the practitioners' actions before they are awarded damages. Thus, a code that attempts to ensure that, at the very least, psychologists do not harm those they serve helps insulate them from litigation.

Fidelity, requiring that psychologists ally themselves with their clients, respect their needs and fundamental rights, and promote a relationship based on veracity and trust, is perhaps (along with nonmaleficence) the most legally salient moral principle. A duty to act in a fiduciary capacity toward those psychologists assess, treat, and study is one that should find robust expression in a code of ethical conduct. The current code (APA, 1992) does not always live up to this hope. Fidelity is best exemplified by the Preamble, which states that the "primary goal" of the code is "the welfare and protection of the individuals and groups with whom psychologists work" (p. 1599). It is represented, among others, in enforceable Provision 1.19, prohibiting the exploitation of research participants, clients, and supervisees, and in Provision 4.09, absolutely forbidding the abandonment of patients. The most obvious application of the fidelity principle, however, is in the obligation to protect the intimate disclosures we obtain in the course of evaluation, treatment, and research. As was true in the debates concerning the adoption of prior APA ethical principles (Bersoff, in press; Siegel, 1979), how assiduously psychologists are required to protect confidential communications was a source of controversy in the adoption of the current code.

In the original version of the code presented to the Council of Representatives, the central provision read: "Psychologists take reasonable precautions to respect the confidentiality rights of those with whom they work or consult, recognizing that confidentiality may be established by law, institutional rules, or professional or scientific relationships" ("APA's Ethics Code Draft," 1992). Confidentiality is a bedrock value that undergirds a sense of trust and allegiance that must necessarily exist between psychologists and their patients, clients, and research subjects. When we expect and exhort clients to disclose intimate information, they and the public at large should expect that we will protect those communications by taking more than reasonable precautions. Perhaps the greatest contribution of the late Max Siegel, president of the APA in 1983 and a warmly regarded practitioner and trainer, was his constant and compelling arguments in favor of absolute confidentiality in clinical relationships (Siegel, 1979). It would be naive to argue for absolute prohibition of unconsented disclosures given such real-world intrusions as the opinion in *Tarasoff v. Regents of the University of California* (1976), child abuse reporting statutes, and exceptions to privileged communications laws. However, such intrusions do not call for unnecessary dilution of the ethical value of confidentiality.

In an attempt to strengthen the provision, during the debate in Council on the new code I moved to amend the proposed principle to state: "Psychologists take the utmost care to respect and protect the confidentiality rights of those with whom they work or consult, and disclose confidential information only when compelled by law." The APA attorney hired to consult on this project asserted that the amendment would create undue burdens on practitioners. But the purpose of a code of ethics is to protect the public, not to protect the professionals that are bound by it. Nevertheless, the amendment failed, although some additional wording was added to the original version. Principle 5.02 now states that "Psychologists have a primary obligation and take reasonable precautions to respect . . . confidentiality rights . . ." (p. 1606). This ambivalent protection of clients' private communications does not seem to be an adequate translation of such a central prima facie duty as fidelity.

In contrast, the new code (APA, 1992) appears to endorse the principle of beneficence openly. Just as the predecessor to the current code required that psychologists use their specialized knowledge for the "promotion of human welfare" (APA, 1990, p. 390), the 1992 version encourages psychologists in the Preamble to "improve the condition of both the individual and society" (APA, 1992, p. 1599) and in Principle E to "contribute to the welfare of those with whom they interact professionally" (p. 1600). The duty to act beneficently is also carried forward in a number of the more specific, enforceable principles in the code. For example, psychologists are responsible for providing "proper training and supervision" to those they teach and oversee so they will learn to apply their services responsibly and competently (Provision 1.22, p. 1602). They are required to "consider" the "best interests" of those legally incapable of giving informed consent (Provision 4.02, p. 1605) and to terminate any professional relationship when the recipient of psychological services "is not benefiting" (Provision 4.09, p. 1606). Scientists are responsible for conducting "research competently and with due concern for the dignity and welfare of the participants" (Provision 6.07, p. 1608).

The principle of justice has also influenced the development of the new code (APA, 1992). For instance, Principle A (Competence) suggests that the competent psychologist be cognizant of the unique needs of distinct groups of people. More explicitly, Principle D (Respect for People's Rights and Dignity) encourages psychologists to "accord appropriate respect to the fundamental rights, dignity, and worth of all people" (p. 1599). Similarly, in enforceable Provision 1.10, psychologists are forbidden in their work from engaging in "unfair discrimination based on age, gender, race, ethnicity, national origin, religion, sexual orientation, disability, socioeconomic status, or any basis proscribed by law" (p. 1601). If they are not competent to work with these diverse groups, psychologists are required to "obtain the training, experience, consultation, or supervision necessary" (Provision 1.08, p. 1601) to do so. The code also prohibits harassing or demeaning behavior toward minority or underrepresented groups, students, and women (see, e.g., Provisions 1.11, 1.12, and 6.03).

Finally, the moral principle of autonomy is also directly addressed in the aspirational components of the code (APA, 1992). Several references endorse the right of users of psychological services to self-determination and free choice. Principle D reminds psychologists to "respect the rights of individuals to privacy, confidentiality, self-determination, and autonomy . . ." (p. 1599). In Principle E, psychologists are advised to be aware of the "real and ascribed differences in power between themselves and others" (p. 1600) and to avoid abusing this potential imbalance.

Whether this essential respect for the integrity and sovereignty of clients so powerfully and elegantly translated in the aspirational sections of the code

(APA, 1992) is reflected in its Ethical Standards is questionable. Certainly, there are many enforceable provisions in which choice, consent, and self-determination are valued. Provision 1.07, for example, requires psychologists to provide "appropriate information before" (p. 1600) psychologists may assess, treat, teach, or gather research data. This general principle is more explicitly reiterated in provisions ensuring that the public is accorded the rights to be sufficiently informed and to consent before one participates in therapy (Provision 4.02) or as a research subject (Provision 6.11). Although, curiously, the code has no specific provision requiring informed consent before one undergoes a psychological evaluation, the code does ensure that clients have the right to an explanation of the results of such an assessment (see Provision 2.09).

Yet, when it comes to autonomy, the code (APA, 1992) is clearly teleological and utilitarian in its approach, consistently balancing autonomy against other interests. This is particularly true when psychologists view autonomy as antagonistic to their perception of their clients' best interests; when they believe there are higher values, such as the safety of the public, that must be satisfied; or when organizational demands conflict with autonomy. For example, we have already noted that confidentiality is not fully protected in the code. But respect for private disclosures is further compromised by Provision 5.05 permitting psychologists to "disclose confidential information without the consent of the individual" (p. 1606) when psychologists consult with their colleagues, seek to protect the patient or third parties from harm, or wish to secure payment for services. Confidentiality may be limited not only by law but by "institutional rules" (Provision 5.02, p. 1606) as well. Similarly, disclosure of assessment results to test takers may be precluded by organizational concerns, by the needs of employers, and in certain forensic evaluations (Provision 2.09). When children and those adults who are not legally capable of giving informed consent receive therapy, psychologists are only required to "consider such persons' preferences" (Provision 4.02, p. 1605), not to be bound or even guided by those preferences. Despite the beneficent intent of Provision 4.07, absolutely barring sexual intimacies with former therapy patients for 2 years and after that only if several significant factors are considered, the provision can be perceived as relegating clients to the role of passive victims rather than as autonomous, self-determining consenting adults.

One can see from this exposition of a sample of relevant provisions there are very few moral absolutes in the current code (APA, 1992). Beyond unequivocally forbidding sexual intimacies with current therapy patients or those whose treatment ceased within 2 years of termination and absolutely precluding the abandonment of patients, there are few, if any other, deontological provisions in the code. It is very much a document full of moral compromise, larded with the lawyerly language of "reasonableness" and constantly balanced by the interests of professional and academic psychologists, organizations, institutions, and what are perceived to be the best interests of clients and research participants.

Standards Related to Expert Witnesses

There are two sets of standards that directly address the activities of psychologists who do forensic work and serve as expert witnesses. The first is Part 7 of the APA (1992) code, denominated Forensic Activities. The second is the "Specialty Guidelines for Forensic Psychologists" (CEGFP, 1991).[1] The Forensic Activities section of the code and the specialty guidelines do not embody as explicitly the moral principles we have found in other provisions of the code. But Provision 7.01 reminds forensic psychologists that they "must comply with all other provisions of the Ethics Code" (APA, 1992, p. 1610) and the guidelines' purpose is to "amplify" the provisions of the APA ethics code "in the context of the practice of forensic psychology" (CEGFP, 1991, p. 656). Thus, to the extent that the philosophical duties we described are represented in the other enforceable provisions of the code, they may be said to be incorporated by reference in Part 7 and in the specialty guidelines.

Although less explicit, some allusion to prima facie duties are found in Part 7 of the code (APA, 1992), particularly fidelity, justice, and to some extent autonomy. If one defines *fidelity* not only as faithfulness to one's client but as allegiance to the scientific roots of one's profession (Diener & Crandall, 1978; Kitchener, 1984), then the code's Forensic Activities provisions are particularly salutary. Provision 7.04, for example, requires that "psychologists testify truthfully, honestly, and candidly . . . (APA, 1992, p. 1610). Similarly, when necessarily compelled to testify with incomplete data, "psychologists clarify the impact of their limited information on the reliability and validity of their reports and testimony, and they appropriately limit the nature and extent of their conclusions or recommendations" (Provision 7.02, p. 1610). This emphasis on acting as a cautious, objective scientists, not as advocates for an empirically unsupported and predetermined position, also, of course, implements the obligation to act justly and equitably.

The requirements in the code (APA, 1992) that "psychologists avoid . . . potentially conflicting roles in forensic matters" (Provision 7.03, p. 1610) and "take into account ways in which . . . prior relationship[s] might affect their

---

[1] The "Specialty Guidelines for Forensic Psychologists" have been adopted by the members of APA Division 41 (Psychology and Law) and the American Psychology–Law Society and have been endorsed by the American Academy of Forensic Psychology. Although they do not yet represent official policy of the APA, they are intended to comport with and supplement the code and "to provide more specific guidance to forensic psychologists in monitoring their professional conduct" (CEGFP, 1991, p. 655) in legal settings. As with the Preamble and General Principles of the code, the specialty guidelines merely "provide an aspirational model of desirable professional practice" (p. 656) by those who regularly hold themselves out as expert witnesses.

professional objectivity" (Provision 7.05, p. 1610) translate the duty of fidelity more traditionally. In addition, these mandates and the corollary responsibilities (i.e., to clarify role expectations and the conflicts that prior relationships with one or more of the parties to a legal proceedings might produce and clarify the limits of confidentiality found in Provisions 7.03 and 7.05) foster the principles of autonomy and justice.

In like manner, the specialty guidelines (CEGFP, 1991) contain translations of the moral obligations found in the prima facie duties. For example, the responsibility to perform forensic tasks in ways that "do . . . not diminish or threaten" the civil rights of the parties (CEGFP, 1991, p. 658) and to decline to participate in activities in which one's competence as a forensic clincian would be impaired as a result of one's "personal values [or] moral beliefs" (p. 658) implement principles of nonmaleficence, justice, and fidelity. Similarly, the duty to refrain from testifying to any incriminating statements made by a criminal defendant during a forensic examination not only comports with constitutional requirements but exemplifies the principle of nonmaleficence as well (see Guideline VI[G], pp. 662–663). The guidelines ubiquitous references to fairness and accuracy in evaluations, testimony, and other public statements and the corollary obligations to avoid bias, partisanship, and misrepresentation are the most salutary translations of the duties of justice and fidelity.

The prima facie duty of autonomy is also well represented in the guidelines (CEGFP, 1991). Forensic psychologists are obligated to "inform the party of factors that might reasonably affect the decision to contract" with them (p. 658). They also have the responsibility to

> ensure that prospective clients are informed of their legal rights with respect to the anticipated forensic service, of the purposes of any evaluation, of the nature of procedures to be employed, of the intended uses of any product of their services, and of the party who has employed [them]. (p. 659)

Similarly, forensic psychologists are to "inform their clients of the limitations to the confidentiality of their services and their products . . . by providing them with an understandable statement of their rights, privileges, and the limitations of confidentiality" (p. 660). On the other hand, the suggested prohibition in the guidelines that potential experts refrain from providing forensic services to parties unrepresented by legal counsel (Guideline VI[C], p. 661), although beneficial in its intent, diminishes a party's right to self-determination. A duty to disclose the risks of such undertakings might have satisfied the dual obligations of autonomy and beneficence.

Finally, as a result of their role, expert witnesses will always be confronted with questions of loyalty and concerns about acting as double agents (Monahan, 1980), particularly if they perform court-compelled examinations. Although the code encourages psychologists to "clarify role expectations and the extent of confidentiality in advance to the extent feasible" (APA, 1992, p. 1610) and the specialty guidelines require forensic experts to "recognize potential conflicts of interest in dual relationships" (CEGFP, 1991, p. 659), they will always be faced with moral dilemmas. For instance, to whom do forensic psychologists owe ultimate loyalty, and to what extent do they abide by the duty of nonmaleficence when it is the products of their endeavors that may lead to the conviction and punishment of a defendant? Because many examinees seen by forensic psychologists are referred by a third party such as a court these referrals raise questions regarding the voluntariness of the client's participation. To which set of moral or professional principles do psychologists hold allegiance in these cases? The moral principle of autonomy assures clients that their choices will be respected. If clients do not agree to undergo a forensic evaluation, do psychologists have the prima facie duty to respect this desire? Or do they owe an overriding duty of fidelity to the referring agency? If the forensic evaluation is mandated by the court, this obligation may not be rescinded, even when the client is opposed to the procedure. As a result, a forensic psychologist may indeed be acting in accordance with the specialty guidelines but yet still be in conflict with the grander moral principles.

CONCLUSION

There is an old story that bears repeating as it is particularly apt in the context of this article. Students pursuing a masters degree in business administration at a well-known and highly respected university were asked to present an ethical dilemma they had confronted during their prior business careers. One of the older students presented the following problem: A customer walked into the small store the student once ran with another partner. The customer purchased goods worth $19.95 and handed her what he thought was a brand new $20 bill. When she went to the cash register to give the customer change, the partner noticed that the customer had actually given her two $20 bills that had stuck together. When the professor asked her to characterize the complex ethical dilemma she faced, the student replied, "Should I have told my partner?"

The point is that a code of conduct, even one that is detailed and prescriptive, can offer solutions to inappropriate problems or even raise the wrong questions. Ethical codes do not always serve as the highest expressions of moral integrity. This is particularly the case when the code serves to further the interests of the professionals compelled to abide by it rather than protecting the public the professionals serve. We hope that those who take on the Herculean task of developing codes of ethics do not lose focus of the antecedent and bedrock principles from which they arise. Unfortunately, as we demonstrated, the movement away from archetypical moral principles can lead to diminished concern over the rights and needs of the client and toward a heightened concern over the preservation of the professional.

The moral principles we described are meant to foster a responsible and respectful venue from which the professional can deliberate ethical questions. Not every reader will agree with our interpretation of these principles or balance them in the way we have, particularly our preference for autonomy over paternalistic beneficence. But a consensus should exist, acknowledging that psychology must serve the fundamental interests of those who had no voice in the development of the APA's (1992) code and the specialty guidelines (CEGFP, 1991). It is, after all, the public upon whom we depend for our status, income, and data. One means psychology has of ensuring that it earns and maintains the public's trust is through an ethics document that reflects the profession's moral integrity and its primary mission of promoting human welfare. But when such a document fails to resolves ethical dilemmas or does so inadequately, we hope that when forensic psychologists confront ethical dilemmas, they do not ignore fundamental moral principles and perhaps even agree that there may be times when these principles should supersede formal expressions of ethical conduct.

REFERENCES

American Psychological Association. (1990). Ethical principles of psychologists. *American Psychologist, 45,* 390–395.

American Psychological Association. (1992). Ethical principles of psychologists and code of conduct. *American Psychologist, 47,* 1597–1611.

American Psychological Association's ethics code draft. (1992, May). *APA Monitor,* pp. 38–42.

Beauchamp, T. L., & Childress, J. F. (1989). *Principles of biomedical ethics.* New York: Oxford University Press.

Beauchamp, T. L., & McCullough, L. B. (1984). *Medical ethics: The moral responsibilities of physicians.* Englewood Cliffs, NJ: Prentice-Hall.

Beauchamp, T., & Walters, L. (Eds.). (1982). *Contemporary issues in bioethics* (2nd ed.). Belmont, CA: Wadsworth.

Bersoff, D. N. (1992). Autonomy for vulnerable populations: The Supreme Court's reckless disregard for social science and self-determination. *Villanova Law Review, 37,* 1569–1605.

Bersoff, D. N. (in press). *Contemporary conflicts in ethics for psychology.* Washington, DC: American Psychological Association.

Committee on Ethical Guidelines for Forensic Psychologists. (1991). Specialty guidelines for forensic psychologists. *Law and Human Behavior, 15,* 655–665.

Dahlstrom, W. G., Welsh, G. S., & Dahlstrom, L. E. (1982). *An MMPI handbook* (rev. ed.). Minneapolis: University of Minnesota Press.

Delgado, R., & McAllen, P. (1982). The moralist as expert witness. *Boston University Law Review, 62,* 869–926.

Diener, E., & Crandall, R. (1978). *Ethics in social and behavioral research.* Chicago: University of Chicago.

Fine, M. A., & Ulrich, L. P. (1988). Integrating psychology and philosophy in teaching a graduate course in ethics. *Professional Psychology: Research and Practice, 19,* 542–546.

Gorlin, R. (Ed.). (1986). *Codes of professional responsibility* (2nd ed.). Washington, DC: Bureau of National Affairs.

Hogarth, R. (1987). *Judgement and choice: The psychology of decision* (2nd ed.). New York: Wiley.

Hollon, S. D., & Kriss, M. R. (1984). Cognitive factors in clinical research and practice. *Clinical Psychology Review, 4,* 35–76.

Kant, I. (1969). *Foundations of the metaphysics of morals* (L. W. Beck, Trans.). New York: Bobbs-Merrill. (Original work published 1785)

Kitchener, K. S. (1984). Intuition, critical evaluation and ethical principles: The foundation for ethical decisions in counseling psychology. *The Counseling Psychologist, 12,* 43–55.

Mill, J. S. (1957). In O. Piest (Ed.), *Utilitarianism*. Indianapolis: Bobbs-Merrill. (Original work published 1861)

Monahan, J. (Ed.). (1980). *Who is the client? The ethics of psychological intervention in the criminal justice system*. Washington, DC: American Psychological Association.

Pope, K. S., & Vetter, V. A. (1992). Ethical dilemmas encountered by members of the American Psychological Association: A national survey. *American Psychologist, 47,* 390–411.

Ross, W. D. (1930). *The right and the good*. Oxford, England: Clarendon.

Siegel, M. (1979). Privacy, ethics, and confidentiality. *Professional Psychology: Research and Practice, 10,* 249–258.

Tarasoff v. Regents of the University of California, 17 Cal.3d 425, 551 P.2d 334 (Cal. 1976).

Use and Then Prove, or Prove and Then Use? Some Thoughts on the Ethics of Mental Health Professionals' Courtroom Involvement

David Faust
University of Rhode Island

Psychologists' courtroom involvement and testimony should not be dictated solely by what the judge or court allows but also require the application of personal or professional standards. This article explores various standards that might be used to determine whether psychological evidence is ready for courtroom application, whether or which evaluative procedures should be performed prior to courtroom use, and the potential tensions between personal validation or impression and formal scientific evidence. Although determining just how tough our professional standards ought to be involves complex issues, the field should take a strong stance against testimony that is based largely on personal validation and that lacks scientific support or conflicts with research evidence. Much of current testimony violates this minimal standard.

Key words: expert witness, assessment, scientific evidence

There is far more agreement about the potential value of psychology in the courtroom then on the extent to which this promise has been realized, which accounts for much of the divergence in views on the present utility and ethics of mental health professionals' courtroom involvement. Most can agree that methods in the psychological sciences should not be applied prematurely or before they are sufficiently developed, but these same individuals often cannot agree as to whether methods have met this requirement.

The readiness of methods in psychology for courtroom use raises complex

---

Requests for reprints should be sent to David Faust, Department of Psychology, University of Rhode Island, Kingston, RI 02881.

and subtle issues, debate on which is unlikely to be progressive unless certain key premises and issues are explicated and parsed. I analyze three such elements: (a) whether standards that are internal versus external to the profession of psychology should dictate courtroom involvement; (b) whether satisfaction of such standards should be established prior to the application of methods in court; and (c) what type of evidence, assuming prior demonstration is demanded, should be required to establish utility or value. My emphasis is on standards that govern the introduction of psychological evidence or methods in court or on standards that address when evidence is ready for courtroom application, not on standards relating to other types of activities in forensic psychology.

FORMULATING STANDARDS: EXTERNAL VERSUS INTERNAL STANDARDS

The psychology–law interface obviously involves two systems or institutions in which, however, psychology and law are not equal partners. Rather, in the legal arena, psychology is subsumed under law. It is not the judge who enters the clinician's office and lies down on the couch but the psychologist who enters his or her honor's home field. The legal system dominates in determining not only whether participation occurs but, when allowing it, the rules and procedures under which it takes place.

The court's authority, however, is incomplete. Most important, the potential psychologist–expert usually is not compelled to participate but rather does so voluntarily. For example, although the judge may allow testimony on the likelihood of future violent behavior, a psychologist asked to assist in the determination can refuse the request. The choice to not participate when one could paves the way for the expression of personal or professional (i.e., internal) standards and eases or alleviates the pressure to defer to the court's external standards. Usually, one can make the choice of nonparticipation without violating the rules of the dominant authority structure or without creating legal jeopardy. In contrast, if the law required professionals to serve as expert witnesses whether they wanted to or not, and one's own standards dictated noninvolvement, this would create an immediate legal conflict and put one at risk for official sanction. Of course, one can still live by personal standards under such circumstances, but it is more difficult to do so, and the balance of pluses and minuses may shift dramatically.

Obviously, the court's standards, which are external to the psychologist, and the psychologist's internal or professional standards may clash. At opposing ends of the spectrum are psychologists who always follow external standards and those who always follow internal standards, and inbetween are various possible combinations. First, I consider extreme deference to the court's standards.

Deferring to External Standards

A number of psychologists articulate some variation of the argument, "If its good enough for the courts to admit it, it ought to be good enough for us." In this view, the court's decision to admit or not admit evidence is the deciding factor in determining its value; the decision then guides our actions and appraisals. The argument that sometimes follows is that psychological evidence is good or adequate because the courts generally admit it.

This seeming deference to external standards has some highly undesirable consequences and almost inevitably leads psychologists into logical inconsistencies. First, it does not allow for the possibility that the courts will err in either direction (i.e., not admitting what is meritorious or admitting what is not) when appraising scientific merit. And the possibility for error is great because judges may lack the technical know-how to appraise scientific products properly and may be purposely or inadvertently misled by experts (discussed later). This position, in fact, defers the ultimate evaluation of scientific products to nonscientists, or those who often are not well equipped to undertake the task.

In the infamous case of *Barefoot v. Estelle* (1983), for example, the Supreme Court ruled that psychiatric opinions on the potential for violence were admissible because they were not always wrong (thereby providing, in this particular case, a basis to uphold the death penalty). Consider that the "not always wrong" "standard" was applied to a dichotomous judgment task (i.e., the person will or will not act violently in the future), in which, in order to be wrong all the time, one would have to know the right answer in order to withhold it uniformly. (Of course, if someone were capable of always being wrong on a dichotomous judgment task, that person's conclusions would provide a perfect indicator of what not to decide.) It is hard to imagine psychology accepting such a pathetic standard in the legal or clinical context, except under the most unusual circumstances. Imagine presenting a new form of psychotherapy at a professional meeting and then arguing for its widespread deployment because it does not always lead to treatment failure.

Second, deferring to the courts, or letting the courts determine the standard for what is adequate method or practice for courtroom application, is also incompatible with the worthwhile attempts of forensic psychologists to formulate and endorse standards for the field, such as Division 41's specialty guidelines (Committee on Ethical Guidelines for Forensic Psychologists, 1991). If one argues that the court's decision to admit evidence is itself adequate to establish that evidence is good, one cannot legitimately turn about-face and assert that some other method or evidence is no good, despite the court's having admitted it. Thus, if Smith is allowed to present evidence that human figure drawings are an extraordinarily valuable method for gauging memory functioning, Jones, who defers to the court, is in no position to challenge Smith's practices, because by Jones's own standard, Smith's practices have been established as good. Instead, if the argument is that the courts make good decisions when they align with our personal standards and bad decisions when they do not, then one is really relying on one's personal judgment, and it becomes intellectually erroneous or dishonest to cite the court's acceptance of evidence as demonstration of its value.

Depending on Internal Standards

In contrast to the situation in which external standards are uniformly endorsed, one who depends on internal (personal or professional) standards can be faced with two basic dilemmas: The courts may admit evidence that does not satisfy the psychologist's own standards or may exclude evidence that does meet the psychologist's standards. I examine each of these forms of conflict and the merits of certain approaches that might be applied in attempting to resolve them.

The first form of conflict, in which the court accepts what the psychologist does not, can sometimes be resolved by substituting an acceptable alternative. For example, the Minnesota Multiphasic Personality Inventory (Hathaway & McKinley, 1983) might be used in place of some inferior method to detect malingering. If no such substitution is feasible, the psychologist can decline to enter the courtroom. There is nothing dishonorable per se about refusing to perform a clinical or forensic task, and almost any responsible professional has turned down some legal or clinical request that the practitioner feels he or she cannot or should not fulfill. For example, one would not agree to help a client who wished to feel less inhibited or guilty about impulses to commit sexual abuse. Likewise, if the client asks for something that is morally acceptable but the clinician almost surely cannot deliver it (e.g., "I want to increase my IQ by 40 points"), one does not cheerfully respond, "Well, after all, almost anything is possible," and then start depositing the checks. The choice to not participate in courtroom activities, however, is sometimes not so simple. Suppose, for example, the court asks you to perform a custody evaluation. You know the judge's belief about the accuracy of such assessments is overly favorable. But you also know that should you convey your reservations about custody evaluations, the judge would instead send the case to Jones, who, unlike you, is of doubtful character and capability.

The second type of clash, in which the courts exclude evidence that meets the psychologist's internal standards, can be very difficult to resolve and may place the clinician in direct opposition to the legal system. For example, the court may exclude some new and relatively unknown technique that has received powerful scientific support. Although the psychologist may try to persuade the court that it has erred, perhaps through a brief, the prospects for change can be dismal, and the extended time frame that may be required can preclude satisfaction of an individual's needs. For example, if someone is scheduled for execution and the psychologist believes he or she has crucial evidence that the courts will not admit, any change in courtroom policy may come about far too late.

When the cause seems right, the system nonresponsive, the delay may have irreversible consequences, and an expert believes that the court has mistakenly devalued evidence, one directed by internal values might try to circumvent the authority structure. For the psychologist, one of the most direct and accessible means for doing so is deception, most likely in the form of overrepresenting the quality or certainty of evidence so as to gain its admission into court or to increase the weight it is accorded. For example, the psychologist may believe that the For-Sure Test, which has not yet been formally published or accepted in the scientific community, is still of high quality and provides compelling evidence that the defendant meets the legal test for insanity. Were the psychologist to speak openly about the test's current status, it might be excluded. Fully believing that professional colleagues will view the instrument very favorably when they become informed, the expert overstates the test's standing so that the judge will allow its introduction.

The temptation to commit deceit of varying types and sizes can be great because it may seem that other options are limited, the chances of detection are small, and the prospects for achieving the desired outcome are good. Further, there are often no direct or concrete barriers to the action, and the mentality that is appropriate for the attorney—to put on the best case possible—can easily contaminate the expert and further encourage misrepresentation. Additionally, of course, many attorneys push psychologists in overt or covert ways to strengthen their language or conclusions or to extend their findings. When an attorney at the pretrial conference cautions the psychologist about using so many qualifiers or being so open in revealing the limits of the evaluation, counsel may be purposely or unknowingly encouraging distortion of the evidence.

Not to be overlooked is the potential for inadvertent misrepresentation, which may be far more common than intentional distortion. Experts may hold sincere, but mistaken beliefs due to factors such as unfamiliarity with the scientific literature or the overweighting of personal impressions in comparison to more rigorous forms of evidence. Some types of misappraisals seem to be common (discussed later), especially among those with courtroom involvement. To put it differently, sometimes those who will enter the courtroom to opine about a particular issue are there mainly because they hold erroneous beliefs or possess greater faith in some method than is warranted. Research showing the pervasiveness of overconfidence among professionals should make us rather nervous about unintended overrepresentations (see Lichtenstein, Fischhoff, & Phillips, 1982).

The factors that foster purposeful and inadvertent error tend to produce inflated representations of evidence, thereby creating a strange paradox. Psychological or psychiatric evidence is admitted if it meets the court's standards. At the same time, the court, in order to determine whether legal standards are met, often depends on psychologists and psychiatrists to tell them how good their methods might be. These professionals, due to normal frailties of the human mind (e.g., difficulties tracking the comparative frequency of positive and negative instances) and perhaps due to the considerable incentives involved, tend to oversell or overperceive the accuracy of their methods and judgments. Further, the subject matter may be so fuzzy, soft, and subjective that it is difficult to determine whether the information these experts provide is correct.

Restatement of the Problem

To summarize thus far, when two highly complex and heterogeneous systems interface, such as psychology and law, in which goals, methods, perspectives, domains of knowledge, and procedural rules frequently differ, conflict is almost inevitable and a complete solution difficult to achieve, if not utopian. However, in analyzing potential clashes between legal (external) and professional (internal) standards, the scope of the overall problem can be reduced considerably by identifying subdomains in which matters are relatively clear. First, as already noted, uniform deference to external (courtroom) standards is problematic and needs to be balanced against internal standards. Second, when the two conflict, the dilemma can sometimes be resolved with relative ease by deferring to internal standards that dictate nonparticipation, in particular, when the courts hold more lenient standards for admitting evidence than does the psychologist. There remains the other, potentially more difficult problem in which the courts will (or may) not admit evidence that meets the psychologist's internal standards, a dilemma that can become especially acute if a grave injustice seems imminent and there is apparently no way to work within the system. As discussed, under such circumstances, the pull to overrepresent information or to deceive may be considerable. It does seem possible, however, to make some inroads in analyzing this latter problem.

I am not endorsing dishonesty in the courtroom, although I recognize that in the world at large the issue of deception raises complexities. For example, the undercover agent does not visit the drug lord in his or her headquarters and confess: "My conscience just won't let me go on deceiving you; I must let you know I'm a cop." However, it should be possible to achieve broad consensus about at least two guides or conditionals relating to experts and deception. First, deception is not justified on the basis of self-interest. Second, in general (or more precisely, under the ceteris paribus clause), it is better not to deceive than to deceive, because, among other things, effectiveness as a healer and the privilege of performing our trade depends on public trust, and because deceptive acts in the courtroom potentially usurp the role of the trier of fact. In regards to the latter, a system in which individuals freely take the law into their own hands but disguise that fact (by secretly misrepresenting evidence so as to promote the outcome they desire) would almost certainly prove degenerative in comparison to our current justice system. Note that, in the short run at least, it may make little practical difference whether misrepresentation is purposeful or inadvertent because the outcome can be identical. In fact, inadvertent falsehood is sometimes more damaging because it can be much harder to identify, correct, and keep from propagating to other professionals. If there is at least agreement about the undesirability of these two conditions—deception stemming from self-interest and deception or misrepresentation under conditions in which viable alternatives exist—we will have effectively dealt with many of the circumstances in which the issue arises.

DETERMINING INTERNAL STANDARDS

Having now described the basic types of dilemmas that may arise when applying internal standards and having argued that sole reliance on external standards is insufficient, the problem of identifying or selecting professional (internal) standards can be considered. In this section, I cover a few possible approaches to this issue, including the adoption of clinical or therapeutic goals to courtroom work and the select incorporation of legal principles or intentions.

Therapeutic Orientation

One approach to courtroom involvement stems from the helping orientation. Many courtroom experts treat and evaluate patients in the clinic, where the primary aim is to advance the individual's interests. It is easy to carry this orientation into the legal situation and to participate in courtroom activities to the extent that it seems to help people. However, apparent parallels across the two contexts can be illusory.

In the treatment setting, helping the client usually involves such matters as promoting better adjustment, eliminating destructive symptoms, or enhancing individual potential. We may also try to aid clients with concrete life tasks or aims, for example, by facilitating their efforts to get a job or establish a significant relationship. Thus, we might help them rehearse their lines for asking Sally out on that date, role-play a job interview, or even write a letter of recommendation.

Promotion of the patient's aims or interests typically does not come at someone else's expense, and when the client's gain may be someone else's loss (as when the client triumphs in a job search), we do not aid or abet if it involves unjust harm to another person or exploitation. It might be all right to help the client prepare for a job interview but not to concoct some scheme for spreading slanderous lies about his or her competitor. We attempt to endorse and promote interests that are morally positive or at least neutral, not those that are negative or harm innocent individuals.

In contrast, the legal system is adversarial in nature, and for each winner, there is a loser. Thus, the common situation in the clinic in which what benefits one benefits another, or at least does not harm someone else, is atypical in the courtroom. Further, the outcome of many legal contests can be considered correct or incorrect in the strict, ontological sense—as a matter involving external reality—an evaluative criterion that often does not relate to the clinical context. Would one say that the client's decision to be a painter correctly mirrored reality or was right or wrong in the manner we intend it when we refer to an issue of fact or occurrence, such as, "Smith miscounted his money and really has 91, not 93, dollars," or, "Smith visited his sister Annie yesterday"? When a person who did not commit a crime is judged to have done so, the decision is plainly wrong; if punishment results on that basis, the outcome is wrong and unjust.

In legal cases, given the contest between competing interests and the possibility of a frankly erroneous outcome, the psychologist can easily end up on the wrong side or inadvertently promote an unjust cause. For example, the psychologist might testify that the evaluation results are consistent with ongoing sexual abuse when no such abuse has occurred; partly as a result, the defendant may be falsely convicted. In fact, despite noble intentions, the psychologist may have aided a parent who trumped-up malevolent accusations to win a custody battle. This does not mean that the psychologist acted in bad faith or definitely should have known better. All persons who enter the courtroom had better realize that the side of the angels is not always apparent or triumphant; consequently, they may contribute to an unjust, if not reprehensible, outcome they would have opposed mightily had they only known. Under such conditions, the psychologist has still "helped" one of the parties, but it is not the kind of aid a healer has in mind.

Further, in the clinical setting, the client usually seeks out the clinician on his or her own to obtain symptom relief, and the alliance or contract is formed between these two parties, with the understanding that the clinician will act on the patient's behalf. In the legal context, the individual is commonly referred by the attorney, who is seeking a legal advantage. Here the contract is between the psychologist and one or more third parties (the retaining attorney, the legal system), and the psychologist's duty is to try to reach accurate conclusions, not to resolve conflicts in the examinee's favor. Favoring the examinee's interests clearly violates the court's expectation that experts will remain neutral or objective. Someone who doubts this point or considers it naive should feel free to announce to the judge, "I have not tried to be objective or to reach accurate conclusions but rather to help Jones in whatever way possible, so I will be ignoring the data that oppose the opinion I'm about to express." If the expert really does act in this manner but tries to cover it up, then he or she is engaging in deception, although in less blatant cases there certainly can be grey areas. For example, the expert is not necessarily obligated to bring out every stitch of nonsupportive data that has been obtained when the material has not been raised by opposing counsel and these data do not directly or meaningfully conflict with the psychologist's findings. However, unlike the psychologist, the lawyer can legitimately try to exclude evidence that hurts his or her client's case, and if the psychologist's conclusions turn out to be of this type, this is almost surely what the lawyer will attempt to do. The courts expect lawyers to put their clients first and to employ experts in this cause, but they do not expect experts to do the same or to help examinees in whatever way they can, even if this requires distortion of data.

Finally, in the clinical context, client self-interest and honesty are usually thought to coincide. In the legal context, self-interest, as opposed to morality, may dictate deception. With forensic evaluations, examinees waive their rights to confidentiality, and particularly when they are being seen by the other side's psychologist, they can fully expect that adverse information or findings will be revealed to individuals motivated to defeat them. At the same time, the opportunity also presents itself to shape the outcome through the impressions made on the psychologist. Thus, some examines will be motivated to deceive, sometimes for base reasons, and the psychologist who is taken in may inadvertently conspire to promote an injustice. Again, this is hardly what therapists think of when they try to promote human welfare. It is the difference between ridding a client of destructive and torturous depressive ideation and helping a criminal rob a bank. Clinicians may be well intended in bringing the therapeutic orientation to their courtroom work, but it generally does not belong there because it conflicts directly with the court's expectations and presumes participants (examinees) who want to achieve just and honorable outcomes.

Selective Incorporation of Courtroom Standards

In contrast to swallowing the court's decisions wholly or taking a rule-based approach, one can evaluate whether the spirit of the court's intent, or principles underlying the admission or rejection of evidence, are worthy of adopting as professional standards or align with professional values. In contrast to the position in which one defers to whatever the courts decide or the view that the court's admission of evidence proves its worth, a psychologist who takes this approach can disagree with the court's admission or rejection of evidence in specific instances without self-contradiction because the position recognizes the court's potential for error. For example, a judge who is taken in by a psychologist may believe that some useless method is helpful to the trier of fact. One who accepts the court's standards (or certain of these standards) can still challenge the court's decision as failing to properly apply or enact its own principles.

A major problem with this principled approach is determining what the court's standards might be or how they should be interpreted. Court rulings may be inconsistent and idiosyncratic across jurisdictions and judges, and standards are in flux. For example, although prohibitions on expert testimony have been relaxed considerably in recent years, the Supreme Court is revisiting the Frye test as of this writing, and by the time this article appears major changes may have already occurred.[1] How can it be determined if the court's standards merit adoption or match professional standards if it is so hard to discern what the court intends and if the target keeps moving? Despite this noise, it is still possible to examine standards that have traditionally been applied to expert evidence. I consider two of these: (a) general acceptance within the scientific community and (b) aid to the trier of fact, with an eye toward considering their potential merit as internal standards.

General acceptance. The standard of general acceptance within the scientific community was meant to safeguard against quackery or the introduction of unreliable evidence, and it is conservative in its original intent; that is, it was meant to keep out methods until they were shown to be sound, even if this denied individuals an opportunity to put on or strengthen their cases. Although application and interpretation of this standard has changed over the years and may have undergone a major overhaul at the hands of the Supreme Court by the time this article is published, I suspect some variant of this notion will remain in effect. Assuming this, it is of interest that general acceptance is a highly fallible indicator in the soft sciences, especially within applied clinical psychology and psychiatry.

Experts testifying about the acceptance of a method frequently seem to use the community of practitioners as their primary reference point, not the scientific community. Obviously, there is only partial overlap in membership between these groups, which sometimes hold directly opposing views. Further, popularity or general acceptance within the community of practitioners may not coincide with scientific merit. For example, surveys of psychological test usage often show a low, if not negative, relation between popularity and demonstrated scientific validity (Guilmette, Faust, Hart, & Arkes, 1989; Kennedy, Faust, & Willis, in press; Wade & Baker, 1977). In fact, many

---

[1]Before this article was prepared, the Supreme Court did rule on *Daubert v. Merrell Dow*, although in a manner that seemed to necessitate no substantive changes in the text.

broadly accepted practices and beliefs conflict directly with the best available scientific evidence or lack decent scientific support. A classic example is the "debate" over clinical and actuarial judgment. Despite over 100 studies yielding remarkably consistent results, the overwhelming evidence for the superiority of actuarial judgment over clinical judgment is largely ignored in practice (see Dawes, Faust, & Meehl, 1989).

Assistance to the trier of fact. A second standard, that expert testimony assist the trier of fact to make better decisions than would otherwise be possible, seems to have much going for it. It is a variation on the psychometrician's theme of incremental validity, or the recognition that test data or evidence may be valid but still may not increase the level of accuracy that can be achieved without it, using other available information. Thus, in psychology, we do not add a wholly redundant variable to the mix because it will not increase predictive power. Likewise, in the courtroom, the footprint expert is not needed to opine that the plaster impression matches the defendant's appendage, including the webbed toes and the extra digit on the right, because the jury is perfectly capable of figuring this out on its own. Valid variables, in fact, may even decrease judgmental accuracy when they redirect attention away from superior or more powerful predictors (for a more detailed explanation see Faust, 1991).

The concept of incremental validity also encompasses another important principle of decision making—the need to examine a method's accuracy in relation to the starting point or baseline. All other things being equal, the higher the baseline (or level of accuracy possible without the method), the better the method must be to contribute something to decision making. Thus, a moderately strong method may make a substantial contribution if our predictions do not otherwise exceed chance level, but it may be worthless if strong predictors are already available. If the aim is to increase accuracy (or to continuously upgrade decision procedures), what is required partly depends on how accurate we are to begin with. To ignore the notion of incremental validity is inevitably to make mistakes of inclusion and exclusion when deciding what evidence to incorporate into clinical or legal decision making.

Incremental validity alone is often an incomplete guide because different types of errors can have widely varying costs. For example, in the criminal arena, at least in theory, we would rather let many guilty people go free than falsely convict one individual. A method that increases overall accuracy may shift the ratio of false-negative errors (i.e., calling the guilty innocent) and false-positive errors (calling the innocent guilty) in the undesirable direction. Thus, in devising decision policy, we usually must also incorporate the relative costs of different error types.

Practicality also needs to be considered. A method might produce a small increment in accuracy in a context that does not involve terribly important stakes, or collection of the needed information may require considerable time, money, or risk. Suppose some expensive psychological testing with a high morbidity rate could help determine whether motor speed will likely decrease by 10% versus 15% over the next 10 years for a person who is already far above the mean and does not make a living with his or her hands.

It would be worthwhile for social scientists to better flesh out and appraise this notion of help to the trier of fact, taking into account incremental validity, the benefits and costs of different types of errors and correct identifications, and practicality. Utility theory or some related approach would offer a formal means for evaluating these combined concerns. Despite differences in terminology, and whether one realizes it or not, the notion of incremental validity captures an area of mutual concern for psychologists and the courts, and formal study should ultimately provide important insights and guidance.

In most cases, the determination of a method's assistance to the trier of fact will ultimately come down to tests of criterion-based or predictive validity. An argument could also be made for explanation as a sometimes acceptable alternative or as an addition, and I do not exclude it, as long as it is meant in a more stringent sense—or as formally derived from a respectable theory—not as the equivalent of "seemingly plausible." Explanation of this latter type depends mainly on face validity or intuitive appeal, and it often means little because it is so easy to invent compelling but totally erroneous explanations. A hurdle that is so easily satisfied will not help much in distinguishing what is meritorious from what is worthless. (The relation between prediction and stringent explanation and whether one can be subsumed under the other is much too complex a matter to discuss here. Suffice it to say that although temporal sequence would seem irrelevant to logical analysis, most practicing scientists probably give much greater weight to prediction than explanation in appraising theories.)

If methods lack predictive or predictive/explanatory power, it is hard to see how they will really assist the trier of fact to reach judgments that are more accurate or closer to the truth, which seems to be the court's intent. (For those who believe otherwise, I again challenge them to inform the judge.) There are, of course, some methods and "knowledge" that might make decisions easier but not better. For example, a persuasive witness using a worthless method, who nonetheless confidently asserts that a criminal will kill again if released, may "help" the jury overcome their moral inhibitions about the death penalty. Therefore, I emphasize that I am not talking about making decisions easier but making them better; this being the aim, predictive validity is the most important test, for in order to reach more accurate decisions, we usually need to be able to predict (or concurrently identify) some criterion (e.g., guilt or innocence, future earnings, or capacity to care for a child).

If predictive validity is the desired goal, it is appropriate to ask, how much is enough? This seemingly simple question raises highly involved issues, such as how the particular legal context (e.g., civil vs. criminal) should be taken into account, how presented testimony ultimately impacts on the trier of fact (because truth or its approximation can repel common sense, whereas falsehood can attract it), and the rate of error deemed acceptable. The latter depends on such matters as the prior error rate; the possible shift in the ratio of false-negative and false-positive errors; and the impact of correct versus incorrect decisions on individuals, the profession, and society over time. In some situations, even a few false-negative errors can have horrific consequences, in part by altering social perceptions. For example, the release of even a single convict, who goes on to act violently, can lead to public outrage (as the 1988 loser of the presidential campaign could tell us). In any event, even if our standards are relatively loose, a method that adds nothing to predictive accuracy or formal explanatory power should not even merit serious consideration for entry into the courtroom.

USE AND THEN PROVE, OR PROVE AND THEN USE?

I discussed the need to go beyond blind adherence to external standards or decisions and described a range of professional standards that might be considered. I also argued that expert evidence should improve legal decision making, and that evaluation of this quality usually should involve tests of predictive validity or formal explanatory power. The question then arises as to whether supportive evidence should be obtained before a method is applied in the courtroom and, if so, what type, or how much, evidence for predictive or explanatory power is needed.

Standards for psychological evidence cannot be entirely separated from the issue of timing, or when validating evidence needs to be available. In some situations, we try first and test later. If the parachute does not open, and the pocketknife is lost, it is no time to await the results of a controlled study examining whether fingernails or teeth produce better outcomes. In some circumstances, action is called for, doing nothing leads to very undesirable consequences, and possible alternatives have not and cannot be tested before a decision is required. If the patient is sure to die of a certain disease, and possible treatments have not been adequately evaluated, we make the best guess and hope. There is nothing morally questionable about acting on imperfect knowledge in such situations.

There is a certain parallel here to the legal setting, absent the level of moral clarity. Some courtroom cases are very difficult to pursue without experts, but they involve controversial or experimental matters. For example, a new chemical may have caused workers to develop a previously undescribed disease, but waiting for well-corroborated, scientific evidence, which could take years, may deny them the opportunity for just (and reasonably timely or meaningful) compensation. In practice, if not in theory, the court's willingness to admit expert evidence may depend not only on its scientific status but also on the impact its exclusion has on a claimant's opportunity to pursue his or her case.

Despite complexities in determining the level of proof that should be required before we enter the courtroom, one can establish some general principles that can resolve a certain percentage of cases or issues. First, if possible or feasible, it is better to first prove and then use, rather than to use and then prove. Adequate testing helps identify poor methods before they do harm or are mistakenly substituted for superior alternatives, and it permits refinement and improvement of techniques. Even with methods that have been admitted absent formal evaluation, subsequent testing clarifies their level of accuracy and thereby provides informed guidance in deciding the weight the evidence merits.

Second, under most circumstances (or again applying the ceteris paribus clause), the burden to prove first should increase in relation to the level of negative indicators in the relevant scientific track record. For example, if many proposed methods or ideas in the area of interest eventually turn out to be fatally flawed or if the field is in an early scientific stage, we should be hesitant to accept new knowledge claims. A related predictor of success is the size of the inferential leap, or the extent to which one tries to exceed what is well established. For example, a small step beyond extremely well corroborated facts that is based on a highly developed theory and precise instrumentation has a much greater chance of success than a broad extrapolation based on a soft theory and crude measurement techniques. Taking into consideration the history and philosophy of science and the characteristics of hard sciences, it is clear that much of clinical psychology, especially in areas directly relevant to legal issues, is scientifically soft. If one reflects on both the scientific status of psychology and the general desirability of testing in advance, it seems reasonable to argue that evaluation of our methods or hypotheses should generally be required prior to their courtroom application.

Personal Validation Versus Scientific Evidence

Some psychologists and psychiatrists believe that personal validation can substitute for more rigorous scientific evidence and sometimes even treat the former as superior to the latter. To return to the example of clinical versus actuarial judgment, although there are over 100 studies demonstrating the overall superiority of the actuarial method, practitioners might argue that their personal experience provides a sufficient basis to challenge or dismiss the research. Differences in belief about the strength of personal validation or observation underlie many of the arguments about the status of methods in clinical psychology and the utility of psychologists' courtroom testimony.

Experience or clinical observation is a rich source for generating hypotheses. Some of these hypotheses are remarkably insightful and contribute much to scientific advance, but many others turn out to be wrong. Although clinical observation may be unsurpassed for generating ideas about the human mind and behavior, it is a very poor method for testing hypotheses.

In previous works, I (e.g., Faust, 1991; Ziskin & Faust, 1988) provided extended discussions of the difficulties involved in learning from experience or clinical observation in psychology, and a full exposition is not possible here. To summarize briefly, there is a considerable and consistent body of research that runs contrary to the belief that experience improves clinicians' diagnostic or predictive accuracy (see Dawes, 1989; Faust, 1991). The conditions under which clinicians practice are not conducive to experiential learning. Feedback about the accuracy of judgments is often unavailable, and the feedback that is received is usually nonrepresentative of outcomes as a whole and distorted or contaminated by various factors (e.g., self-fulfilling prophecies and intervening events between appraisal and outcome). As Dawes (1989) described it, the information we receive about our judgmental accuracy often contains a large, systematic error component that greatly impedes learning and makes it very difficult to distill from our experience that which it might teach us. Overall, given the current conditions under which we practice in the mental health field, there are strong empirical and theoretical reasons to question the stereotype that experience is the best teacher or even an effective one.

Consider the contrasts between learning through experience, or the conditions under which we treat and observe patients, and data gathering through more rigorous, scientific means. The scientific method incorporates various strategies for attenuating bias, such as blind assessment of outcome and formal, numerical (vs. subjective) examination of co-relations among variables. In addition, in comparison to the skewed sample of humanity seen in the clinic and the limited, nonsystematic feedback received about outcome, the researcher often can obtain a representative sample of cases and can study outcomes across these cases. Further, unlike the clinical situation, in which we do not know what would have happened had we done otherwise, the researcher can manipulate variables and set up counterfactuals; that is, it is possible to find out what does happen when variables are altered systematically. For example, a therapist treating individuals with mild anxiety disorders may consistently apply Jones's Eclectic Mix because it usually produces a good outcome, and thus cannot know or determine whether Smith's Homemade Mash would prove as effective or more effective with comparable individuals.

One need not blindly worship science or believe that the method has approached perfection to recognize the numerous advantages it provides over uncontrolled observations made in the course of treating patients. As Meehl (1993) stated:

> It will not do to say "I don't care what the research shows, I am a clinician so I rely on my clinical experience." Clinical experience may be invoked when it is all we have, when scientific evidence is insufficient (in quantity or quality) to

tell us the answer. It is *not* a valid rebuttal when the research answer is negative. One who considers "My experience shows . . ." a valid reply to research studies is self-deceived and must never have read the history of medicine, not to mention the psychology of superstitions. . . . It is absurd, as well as arrogant, to pretend that acquiring a Ph.D. somehow immunizes me from the errors in sampling, perception, recording, retention, retrieval, and inference to which the human mind is subject. (p. 728)

Types and Levels of Support

Moving back to the courtroom, we would prefer to base our expert opinions on a strong and consistent body of scientific evidence, which establishes the effectiveness of a method for the particular question(s) and population(s) of interest. Effectiveness can be established by showing that the method surpasses three hurdles: It provides valid information, beats the base rates, and produces incremental validity (i.e., it adds to the level of accuracy that can be achieved without its use, based on what are otherwise the best available methods). There is little practical benefit if increased accuracy is limited to the psychologist's judgments; ideally, we would like scientific verification that introduction of the evidence also helps the trier of fact reach better decisions. When psychological evidence or techniques meet these types of standards, a strong argument can usually be made for their potential value and appropriateness in the courtroom. However, within psychology, particularly when it comes to clinical evaluation for courtroom purposes, there are few areas in which satisfaction of such standards has been formally demonstrated.

Consider now the circumstance in which formal scientific evidence is lacking and support is mainly limited to personal validation. In the mental health field, subjective belief or impression alone is just not sufficient, and I doubt whether those experts who suggest it is sufficient would accept the exact same argument were the roles reversed and were they faced with an expert's adverse testimony on a matter of great personal importance. Would they agree that Astrologer, Aquarius-the-Great, who really believes in himself, should be free to "inform" the judge confidently that "Smith has made and is sure to continue to make a lousy parent"? Yet, if personal validation is presented as a sufficient test for us, can we legitimately maintain that it is too lenient for other potential experts?

Suppose the clinician argues that he or she is not a palm reader or a crystal ball gazer and that the combination of scientific training, education, and professional skills have produced special capacities for observation and for separating truth from falsehood? The track record in psychology, however, should make us very leery about placing faith in these types of claims or in the value of personal validation. Such faith is challenged, for example, by repeated instances of mistaken beliefs in the history of psychology and, as already noted, by the extensive literature documenting problems with subjective clinical judgment and the comparative success of clinical versus actuarial methods (see Dawes et al., 1989; Faust, 1984).

Someone well trained in science should recognize the grave shortcomings of unchecked and uncontrolled personal observation. In contrast, if it could be shown that representative sampling of the historical track record, which entailed a related family of personal impressions or hypotheses, demonstrated a respectable accuracy rate, there would at least be a preliminary basis for placing some faith in a current impressionistic belief. Alternatively, perhaps as part of a qualifying examination for forensic work, we could evaluate a particular clinician's hit rate with comparable judgments, thereby calibrating a personal "accuracy quotient." Absent such forms of support and given the history of psychology, the general state of theory in applied clinical psychology, and the serious methodological limits of the case study method, personal faith or belief based on experience is a very deficient form of evidence and does little to set the psychologist and the nonscientist apart.

Unfortunately, much of what psychologists and psychiatrists present in court is supported by little more than personal validation. For example, surveys show that many neuropsychologists use flexible (i.e., unstructured) or related assessment approaches (e.g., Guilmette et al., 1989; McCaffrey, Malloy, & Brief, 1985). Very little research has examined clinicians' accuracy using these strategies, and arguments for their effectiveness rest mainly on personal experience or impression.

How could such a weak form of evidence be so overvalued, or how is it that practitioners, many of whom are informed about scientific method, develop such unshakeable faith in their personal impressions? Indeed, research shows that individuals (professionals included) are often more confident or far more confident in their judgments than is warranted by their actual level of accuracy (Lichtenstein et al., 1982). In the practice setting, overconfidence likely results because the frequency with which the clinician's judgments seem to be confirmed typically exceeds the true rate of confirmation or accuracy (for materials on this phenomenon, see Chapman & Chapman, 1967, 1969; Hyman, 1977; Snyder, Handelsman, & Endelman, 1978). For example, clients are overly inclined to endorse the psychologist's interpretations or conclusions. Consequently, whether a patient with minor memory complaints is told that his or her slips are unremarkable or pathological, the patient will often accept either interpretation. Obviously, both conclusions cannot be correct, but if the examinee tends to agree no matter which of opposing possibilities is presented, the frequency of patient agreement will exceed the frequency of correct judgments. For these and other reasons, subjective confidence is often a flawed indicator of accuracy, and thus a clinician's sense of confidence, by itself, is worth little, unless that clinician has formally proven that he or she is an exception.

In comparison to a research vacuum, there is the more extreme situation in which personal observations or impressions directly conflict with a body of consistent, well-conducted scientific research. Although the research will not always be right and the clinician will not always be wrong, the research will usually be correct and the exceptions difficult to identify in advance. The effective identification of exceptions would seem to require an approach that is superior to the scientific method, something we have not hit on yet. For example, if scientific findings are more accurate than unvalidated subjective impression in, say, 95% of the cases, then one could identify the winner 95% of the time by always deferring to the research. Therefore, judgments or impressions about exceptions would have to be right more than 95% of the time to improve on the accuracy that could be achieved by playing the base rates, or always guessing that the more frequent outcome applies (Meehl & Rosen, 1955).

Clinicians who generally defer to their personal impressions over solid research evidence and who present in the courtroom accordingly, for example, by expressing positive sentiment toward a scientifically discredited method, have abandoned their scientific foundations. As such, these clinicians are not testifying to a branch of science, and they should not pretend (or think) that they are scientific and should not cite scientific evidence to support their positions. The latter is a sham or a potential act of deception because the expert's view is not based on scientific evidence, which is ignored when it is not supportive. It is like citing the favorable lines in an otherwise negative movie review in order to convey endorsement of the product, an attempt to inflate impressions on false or misleading grounds, or what is usually called propaganda.

Not uncommonly, mental health professionals' testimony is based largely on personal impression and, intentionally or not, directly conflicts with scientific evidence. For example, testimony on clinical versus actuarial judgment and on experience and accuracy often conflicts with a large and consistent body of scientific research. Clashes between personal impressions and well-supported scientific findings provide important test cases because if a psychologist will knowingly testify to personal views under these circumstances, that professional's actions show that scientific evidence is no barrier to courtroom work or is really of no concern. Obviously, if experts will testify even when a large body of well-conducted research directly contradicts their opinions or discredits their methods, they are unlikely to be bothered when there is less conflicting research, mixed research outcomes, or no research at all. This position is not one of prove and then use or even use and then prove, it is one of use no matter what the evidence shows. We would never tolerate such an attitude in persons treating our pets, much less our family members.

The field should not endorse or permit this type of disregard for scientific evidence or these types of (non)standards. They fall far short of the profession's stated ethical and practice guidelines (see, e.g., Standards 1.1, 1.2, 3.1, 6.3, and 7.1 of the American Psychological Association's [APA], 1985, *Standards for Educational and Psychological Testing;* the Preamble, and Principles 1.05, 1.06, and 2.04 of the APA's, 1992, "Ethical Principles of Psychologists and Code of Conduct;" and Guideline VI.A. of the Committee on Ethical Guidelines for Forensic Psychologists's, 1991, "Specialty Guidelines for Forensic Psychologists"). And if, de facto, we foster such laxity, mainly by doing nothing about it, we should have the courage and integrity to make our policy explicit and not invoke the name of science to manipulate impressions while violating its spirit.

Beyond demanding some accountability to scientific evidence, it is no easy matter to decide just how tough our standards ought to be, given the complexities just outlined, such as the need to consider legal context. There seems to be considerable danger, however, in being too nonrestrictive. For example, given its very tenuous nature, I would contend that personal validation without scientific backing should generally be considered insufficient evidence for the value of a method. Suppose instead, under most circumstances, we set the following standard: Effectiveness should be demonstrated prior to courtroom application through formal scientific study, the minimal requirement being a modest body of consistent or converging evidence gathered from well-conducted studies across at least a few independent settings, which shows that the method contributes meaningfully to the incremental validity of clinical evaluations directed specifically at the matter of courtroom interest. Each of these stated elements would seem to be essential. For example, replication is a very basic requirement in science. Direct relevance to the matter of legal interest is also important because a method may be excellent in answering a question that has nothing to do with a courtroom issue. Scientifically modest standards of the type stated here, if enforced, would eliminate much of mental health professionals' current courtroom activities and would substantially reduce the risk that our profession will experience major grief through its courtroom involvement.

SUMMARY AND CONCLUSIONS

Psychologists' courtroom involvement and testimony should not be solely determined by what the judge or court allows (external standards) but also by professional (internal) standards. In formulating internal standards, a key concern is predictive validity, or predictive validity and explanatory power, if the latter is intended in its stricter form—as formal scientific explanation as opposed to the appearance of plausibility. In contrast to formal scientific evidence, personal validation is a weak form of support and has serious shortcomings. Most important, although personal experience or clinical impression is an excellent basis for formulating hypotheses, it is a very poor means for testing them, and the historical track record in such areas as psychology and medicine suggests that these hypotheses are frequently wrong. In fact, as much as anything, it was the recognition of such human cognitive shortcomings centuries ago that motivated and necessitated the development of scientific method. Although personal beliefs may sometimes prove correct and scientific findings wrong, it is usually the other way around, particularly when there is a large and consistent body of well-conducted, contradictory research. Further, we generally have no trustworthy means for identifying exceptions; thus, one who usually or always defers to the scientific evidence will achieve greater or much greater overall accuracy than one who freely relies on personal impressions.

Situations in which personal validation directly clashes with a large and consistent body of research provide test cases because psychologists who will nevertheless testify on the basis of their personal beliefs have rejected the scientific commitments of the field. Such psychologists should at least be forthright about their position, and they should not cite scientific evidence or pretend to be scientific in order to bolster their opinions because it is misleading and inadvertently deceptive at best. Further, the profession should make it very clear, through both word and action, that such psychologists are practicing outside of the field's ethical guidelines.

Most courtroom activities in psychology are voluntary, thereby providing free opportunity to exercise personal or professional standards. Psychologists can adopt the policy of not entering the courtroom, even if their testimony could be admitted, unless methods are first shown to meet some type of scientific standards. If we were to adopt even modest standards for the quality and quantity of evidence and the specific types of research outcomes that were necessary (e.g., appropriate forms of incremental validity), by adhering, for example, to the professional guides we have already articulated in such documents as the *Standards for Educational and Psychological Testing* (APA, 1985), we would eliminate much of psychologists' current courtroom activities.

The question of how tough our internal standards should be will not be easily solved. The field, however, needs to guard against becoming (or remaining) too lax, and psychologists should at least strongly discourage testimony that directly conflicts with a large and consistent body of well-conducted research or that is based mainly or solely on personal validation. Further, determining how strict we ought to be can be partly resolved by adequate study of incremental validity in courtroom situations, some suggestions for which have been provided. Ultimately, as the field advances, one would hope that, in many areas, support for our methods will be such that debate about whether lenient standards are good enough will be rendered moot. I suspect that, over time, our tolerance for standards of evidence that are weak will decrease proportionately to the number of areas in which our scientific knowledge becomes strong.

ACKNOWLEDGMENTS

I express sincere appreciation to Robyn M. Dawes, Paul E. Meehl, Leslie J. Yonce, and Jay Ziskin, who reviewed earlier drafts of this article and made many helpful suggestions.

REFERENCES

American Psychological Association. (1985). *Standards for educational and psychological testing.* Washington, DC: Author.
American Psychological Association. (1992). Ethical principles of psychologists and code of conduct. *American Psychologist, 47,* 1597–1611.
Barefoot v. Estelle, 463 U.S. 880, 77 L.Ed.2d 1090, 103 S.Ct. 3383 (1983).
Chapman, L. J., & Chapman, J. P. (1967). Genesis of popular but erroneous psychodiagnostic observations. *Journal of Abnormal Psychology, 72,* 193–204.
Chapman, L. J., & Chapman, J. P. (1969). Illusory correlation as an obstacle to the use of valid diagnostic signs. *Journal of Abnormal Psychology, 74,* 271–280.
Committee on Ethical Guidelines for Forensic Psychologists. (1991). Specialty guidelines for forensic psychologists. *Law and Human Behavior, 15,* 655–666.
Daubert v. Merrell Dow Pharmaceuticals, Inc., 113 S.Ct. 2786 (1993).
Dawes, R. M. (1989). Experience and validity of clinical judgment: The illusory correlation. *Behavioral Sciences & the Law, 7,* 457–467.
Dawes, R. M., Faust, D., & Meehl, P. E. (1989). Clinical versus actuarial judgment. *Science, 243,* 1668–1674.
Faust, D. (1984). *The limits of scientific reasoning.* Minneapolis: University of Minnesota Press.
Faust, D. (1991). What if we had really listened? Present reflections on altered pasts. In D. Cicchetti & W. M. Grove (Eds.), *Thinking clearly about psychology: Vol. 1. Matters of public interest* (pp. 185–216). Minneapolis: University of Minnesota Press.
Guilmette, T. J., Faust, D., Hart, K., & Arkes, H. R. (1989). A national survey of psychologists who offer neuropsychological services. *Archives of Clinical Neuropsychology, 5,* 373–392.
Hathaway, S. R., & McKinley, J. C. (1983). *Minnesota Multiphasic Personality Inventory.* New York: Psychological Corporation.
Hyman, R. (1977). "Cold reading": How to convince strangers that you know all about them. *The Zetetic, 1,* 18–37.
Kennedy, M. L., Faust, D., & Willis, G. W. (in press). Social-emotional assessment practices in school psychology. *Journal of Psychoeducational Assessment.*
Lichtenstein, S., Fischhoff, B., & Phillips, L. D. (1982). Calibration of probabilities: The state of the art to 1980. In D. Kahneman, P. Slovic, & A. Tversky (Eds.), *Judgment under uncertainty: Heuristics and biases* (pp. 306–334). New York: Cambridge University Press.
McCaffrey, R. J., Malloy, P. F., & Brief, D. J. (1985). Internship opportunities in clinical neuropsychology emphasizing recent INS training certificate. *Professional Psychology: Research and Practice, 16,* 236–252.

Meehl, P. E. (1993). Philosophy of science: Help or hindrance? *Psychological Reports, 72,* 707–733.

Meehl, P. E., & Rosen, A. (1955). Antecedent probability and the efficiency of psychometric signs, patterns, or cutting scores. *Psychological Bulletin, 52,* 194–216.

Snyder, C. R., Handelsman, M. M., & Endelman, J. R. (1978). Can clients provide valuable feedback to clinicians about their personality interpretations? A reply to Greene. *Journal of Consulting and Clinical Psychology, 46,* 1493–1495.

Wade, T. C., & Baker, T. B. (1977). Opinions and use of psychological tests: A survey of clinical psychologists. *American Psychologist, 32,* 874–882.

Ziskin, J., & Faust, D. (1988). *Coping with psychiatric and psychological testimony* (Vols. 1–3). Los Angeles: Law and Psychology Press.

THE FORUM

Case Vignette: Expertise for Sale. Zack and Martha Prophet are behavioral scientists with more than 20 years experience in studying the behavior of jurors. They have set up a consulting firm, Jury Dynamics Inc., to work with lawyers in two major arenas. The first consulting activity is jury selection. They advise lawyers on which questions to ask and how to exercise challenges in order to empanel a jury most sympathetic to the case the attorney plans to present. The second major consulting activity involves empaneling shadow juries, comprised of demographically similar individuals to the actual juries. These shadow juries are used to test lawyer's tactics for effectiveness and to listen to tapes of trials in progress. In the latter instance, the shadow juries can provide advance data on potential outcomes, thereby indicating when settlement options should be considered.

Last week Jury Dynamics Inc. received calls seeking to retain their services as consultants in a major civil litigation case filed by the Sky Blue Waters Environmental Trust against International Solvent Corporation. The lawyers for International Solvent Corporation got Zack on the phone at 10:15 A.M., and counsel for the Sky Blue Waters Environmental Trust reached Martha at 10:30 A.M., while Zack was on the other line. International Solvent Corporation wants to purchase a broad array of services from Jury Dynamics Inc. in this case, and they would most likely generate a substantial number of billable hours. The Sky Blue Waters Environmental Trust has much less cash to spend on consultants, but they noted that Martha subscribes to their newsletter and hope the firm will give them a price break in consulting on jury selection services.

What are the ethics that bind (or ought to bind) Jury Dynamics Inc.? On what basis should Zack and Martha make their services available to the parties in *Blue Sky Waters Environmental Trust v. International Solvent Corporation?* Should the personal or political views of Zack and Marsha be considerations in the case?

Discussants. Jonathan Brant is associate justice of the Cambridge District Court in Cambridge, Massachusetts. He is a graduate of Brandeis University and Harvard Law School. He is also the author of *Law and Mental Health Professionals: Massachusetts,* published by the American Psychological Association. Prior to his appointment to the bench, he litigated many issues involving the right to refuse treatment and other bioethical issues. Thomas Grisso chaired a committee of the American Psychology–Law Society (Division 41, American

Psychological Association) which developed "Specialty Guidelines for Forensic Psychologists" (see the reference in his commentary). He directs the postdoctoral training program in forensic psychology at the University of Massachusetts Medical School. His co-authors, Randy Borum and William Warnken, were the program's two fellows for 1992-1993. The commentary reflects an analysis of the case conducted as part of their weekly seminar. Dorothy Keiko Kagehiro received her PhD in psychology from the University of Utah and took a postdoctoral fellowship in the Law–Psychology Program at the University of Nebraska. Her interests include juror decision making and the application of environmental psychological theories to privacy rights and regulation. She is currently a senior research associate in the New York regional office of a national trial consulting firm. Her opinions expressed here are not necessarily those of her employer. Michael J. Saks is professor of law and psychology at the University of Iowa. He holds both a PhD (social psychology, Ohio State University) and an MSL degree (Yale University). His work focuses on empirical studies of behavior of the legal system, although his early work included research on jury decision making. He reports that he was once offered a vice presidency in an organization providing services of the type rendered by the Zack and Martha Prophet, and he was more than a little tempted to take the position.

Ethics in Trial Advocacy: The Prophets' Dilemma

Thomas Grisso, Randy Borum, and William Warnken

The case of Zack and Martha Prophet presents a challenge partly because it discourages a straightforward application of existing ethical guidelines with which most readers of this journal will be familiar. Zack and Martha are not engaged in clinical psychological or psychiatric evaluations, treatment, or expert testimony, which form so much of the context for existing ethical codes for these professions. They function as trial consultants, but we are not sure of their profession or of their membership in professional associations that may have ethical standards to which they would be bound.

Even if they are not bound formally by existing professional codes of ethics, they would be well advised to adopt established ethical standards as a guide for conducting their business affairs. Ethics codes can assist professionals to modulate their behavior in ways that promote fairness in their relations with other professionals and lay clients. This may help one to avoid certain unfair business practices that have legal sanctions and to establish one's reputation as a trustworthy business associate. Ethical practice is right, whether or not one is "bound" by a profession's code. It is also good business.

The Prophets might consider three sets of aspirational codes worthy of study: (a) the American Psychological Association's "Ethical Principles for Psychologists and Codes of Conduct" (APA, 1992); (b) the "Specialty Guidelines for Forensic Psychologists" (Committee on Ethical Guidelines for Forensic Psychologists [CEGFP], 1991), promulgated by Division 41 (American Psychology–Law Society) and the American Academy of Forensic Psychology; and (c) the American Bar Association's *Model Rules of Professional Conduct* (ABA, 1989).

The first two choices are obvious enough, but the third requires explanation. In brief, the trial consultant's role is like the lawyer's in many ways. Upon accepting a request for services, the trial consultant becomes an ally of the attorney, bound by the same responsibilities to advocate the interests of the attorney's client. The trial consultant's primary obligation is to apply scientific methods to assist the attorney in winning. Client privilege regarding any information obtained by the trial consultant flows from the attorney–client relationship. Therefore, the Prophets might find more specific guidance for fulfilling their role in the lawyer's code of ethics than in other professional standards intended primarily to deal with relationships between clinical professionals and their clients or to guide expert witnesses.

Turning to the problem, let us presume that neither Zack nor Martha accepted the initial telephone requests of International Solvent Corporation (ISC) or Sky Blue Waters Environmental Trust (SBWET). What should they consider while deciding how to respond?

First, they should determine whether either of them may have learned anything about the strategies or positions of either ISC or SBWET that might compromise the interests of one party in the event that they chose to work with the other. Neither ISC nor SBWET is yet their client, but both parties reasonably may expect that anything they told Zack and Martha would be held in confidence (APA, 1992, Principle D). In addition, once they chose a client, it would be difficult for them to avoid taking the opposing party's strategy into consideration while working with their client. Unfortunately, the Prophets might find that they cannot accept either offer without risking breach of these confidences.

Second, the Prophets should consider whether they hold any personal or political views that would make it difficult for them to advocate fully the interests of either party (APA, 1992, Principle B; (EGFP, 1991, IV–A–2 and IV–D). For example, Martha's subscription to SBWET's newsletter suggests that she personally might support environmental causes. This would not necessarily prevent the Prophets from taking ISC as a client. The *Model Rules of Professional Conduct* (ABA, 1989) for client–lawyer relationships, for example, state that lawyers often will accept clients whose causes are controversial or unpopular. "A lawyer's representation of a client . . . does not constitute an endorsement of the client's political, economic, social or moral views or activities" (Rule 1.2–b, p. 26), and it does not necessarily represent the professional's own personal views. But the Prophets should not take ISC as a client if, on reflection, Martha believes that she would find it difficult to work zealously against SBWET.

When making this judgment, Martha should be aware that if the Prophets take ISC as a client, they might discover later that ISC is defending itself against substantial evidence that it has been engaging in harmful or illegal practices (e.g., dumping toxic wastes in riverways). Moreover, ISC might seek to conceal damaging information that has not been discovered by SBWET. Therefore, Martha must determine whether she could work zealously to defend ISC under worst scenarios. The Prophets cannot inquire further about the merits of SBWET's claim or the substance of ISC's activities because, as noted earlier, their further knowledge of one party's position probably will rule out their ability to work with the other party, in light of information acquired in confidence.

Having considered these matters, the Prophets might decide that the safest decision is to follow their own personal or political values in selecting a client. If they decide otherwise (taking the client whose objectives they personally would not favor), there are several things that they should consider doing. The *Model Rules of Professional Conduct* (ABA, 1989) for client–lawyer relationships notes that the objectives and scope of services to be provided by a lawyer "may be limited by agreement with the client or by the terms under which the lawyer's services are made available to the client. . . . Such limitations may exclude objectives or means that the lawyer regards as repugnant or imprudent" (Rule 1.2–Comment, p. 27). The Prophets could consider drawing up a contractual agreement that clearly limits their proposed services. For example, they might feel comfortable assisting ISC to select jurors that are not resistant to ISC's proposed presentation, but they might find it objectionable to assist ISC by researching the literature on some scientific topic (e.g., behavioral and neuropsychological effects of water-borne toxins on children) and critiquing the research in a way that would minimize the strength of SBWET's claim. If this is stated in a prior agreement, ISC will be informed adequately of the limits, thus avoiding later misunderstanding. Moreover, Martha should make

ISC aware of her past support (if, indeed, her subscription was so motivated) for SBWET's work; ISC might take issue with hiring a consultant who personally supports its opponent.

SBWET's financial circumstances might make it an appropriate candidate for pro bono services. The Prophets probably should consider this in selecting their client or in establishing their fees if they select SBWET (APA, 1992, Principle F; (EGFP, 1991, IV-C). But they are under no obligation to offer any particular client pro bono services. Indeed, they could as easily select ISC on humanitarian grounds, in that the financial gain will increase their capacity to offer other clients pro bono services in the future. The important thing is to provide pro bono services to someone from time to time.

Imagine that the Prophets assist ISC in successfully defending the case, despite compelling evidence that ISC engaged in harmful acts. Have the Prophets violated the admonition of Principle F (APA, 1992) that professionals should "apply . . . their knowledge of psychology in order to contribute to human welfare?" (p. 1600). Attorneys are more accustomed to dealing with this conflict than are behavioral scientists or mental health professionals. The legal defense of a client operates not only to advocate for the interests of the client but also to contribute to the integrity of society's legal system and legal process. Our system of justice cannot function to protect society or the rights of the accused without strong advocacy for both parties. In this sense, the defense of a guilty party is a contribution to the integrity of the legal system (human welfare), and the contributor does nothing unethical by assisting the defense. Certainly some professionals might find the concrete outcome of such cases too repugnant to justify the more abstract objective. If so, they would be ethically obliged to avoid becoming involved in assistance to attorneys in cases that run this risk.

What has been the value of considering the Prophets' dilemma? It poses interesting challenges because the Prophets apply their scientific knowledge in a role that fits more closely that of the lawyer than the behavioral scientist. For this reason, lawyers' ethics codes sometimes may assist the behavioral scientist in this nontraditional territory. It is encouraging, nevertheless, to note that psychologists' principles for ethical conduct provide guidance and can be fulfilled, even in this difficult context, provided that the effort is made.

REFERENCES

American Bar Association. (1989). *Model rules of professional conduct*. Chicago: Author.
American Psychological Association. (1992). Ethical principles of psychologists and code of conduct. *American Psychologist, 47*, 1597–1611.
American Psychology–Law Society, Committee on Ethical Guidelines for Forensic Psychologists. (1991). Specialty guidelines for forensic psychologists. *Law and Human Behavior, 15*, 655–665.

386 THE FORUM

The Consultant's Conundrum

Dorothy Keiko Kagehiro

GENERAL ETHICAL PRINCIPLES (APA, 1992)

Integrity

The personal or political views of trial consultants should no more be a consideration in professional services rendered than therapists providing counseling services to clients or for faculty members providing instructional services to students. If Zack and Martha Prophet have spent more than 20 years in private sector consulting, they have long ago resolved possible conflicts between their own values and those of their clients.

The servicing goal of trial consultants is to assist clients in preparing the most effective presentation of case facts and arguments. This goal in no way trespasses on the prerogatives of a jury anymore than does the advocacy by the attorneys for each side. The jury, as always, makes its own judgment about the merits of each side's arguments. Clarity of presentation merely reveals more effectively what is—or is not—there. Neither the expertise nor the political sympathies of trial consultants will salvage a case without merit. This truism may provide perspective to consultants (and commentators) when weighing their contributions to case preparation.

Competence

The Prophets are described as specializing in two services, jury selection and shadow juries. These services do not come into play until very late in the trial preparation process—at voir dire and during trial. More effective consultation services can be provided at earlier stages of the trial process (e.g., during discovery phase) by conducting empirical research to: (a) determine mock jurors' perceptions and misperceptions of case issues and possible arguments, in other words, by assisting attorney clients with case preparation; (b) develop and refine case arguments identified in previous research as most persuasive to mock jurors; and (c) identify characteristics of plaintiff-oriented and defense-oriented jurors to be used during jury selection.

These research projects typically involve sample sizes of 60–200 "jury-qualified" respondents recruited from the trial venue through random-digit dialing of home telephone numbers. These research activities may be the "broad array of services" that International Solvent Corporation (ISC) has in mind. There is no mention in the vignette of a support staff or of other research-trained personnel within Jury Dynamics Inc. Presumably, Zack and Martha are the firm's only consultants. Thus, Jury Dynamics Inc. may not have the resources to provide the consulting services desired by ISC. Zack and Martha may choose to decline ISC as a client or to refer it to a larger consulting firm. Such referrals are done on occasion.

Professional and Scientific Responsibility

The more common ethical quandaries are created by clients' budget limits for consulting services and by clients' lack of empirical research training.

Sky Blue Waters Environmental Trust is described as having "much less cash to spend." This budget limitation may affect the type and quality of research that is conducted on behalf of the client. To keep within a project's budget, the trial consultant may be tempted to cut corners in ways that jeopardize the generalizability and, hence, the validity of the research findings (e.g., smaller sample sizes and recruitment of mock jurors from market research facilities' databank lists of respondents rather than through a random-digit dialing method).

The temptation is made all the harder to resist because the cutting of methodological corners is highly likely to go undetected by clients. Corporate and attorney clients typically lack training in empirical research design and methods. In the absence of initial explanation and education by consultants, they will neither understand nor appreciate the significance of sample size, random sampling, and so on. To the extent that clients are unable to distinguish among quality of research services offered, they are more likely to engage consultants solely on the basis of price.

In the short term, the trial consultant that offers to provide a methodologically sound but costlier research design may be at a disadvantage in the marketplace. However, trial consultants and commentators can take comfort from the growing exposure of legal practitioners in complex civil litigation to trial consultants and attorney colleagues who possess psycholegal training backgrounds. As these law–psychology programs continue to produce graduates, more and more of them may migrate into the civil law. Clients of trial consultants will become more sophisticated and discerning consumers of research services. In competitive bidding or fee negotiation situations, trial consultants should take care that their expertise—and not their ethics—is the only thing for sale. Maintaining ethical standards will pay off in the end.

REFERENCE

American Psychological Association. (1992). Ethical principles of psychologists and code of conduct. *American Psychologist, 47,* 1597–1611.

The Professor's Perspective

Michael J. Saks

Let's proceed by carefully trying to identify the ethical issues in this case and the considerations that might nudge us in one direction or the other, and only then try to decide what the "correct" answer is. Articulating the ethical issues may be the more important thing to do here, so I emphasize that.

1. Does temporal priority of agreement make a difference?

Does it matter whose business was accepted first? If one party is accepted as a client, can they be thrown aside when a more desirable client comes knocking? Suppose Zack accepted International Solvent Corporation's (ISC) business a few minutes before Martha accepted Sky Blue Waters Environmental Trust's (SBWET)? Are they bound by whichever agreement was made first? Can there be a justification for breaking an agreement that was made when no conflict existed but came into being only because the Prophets wanted to take on a conflicting case? Suppose the emergency room physician begins to treat you, but then a movie star is wheeled in. Can the doctor ethically abandon your care in favor of a more attractive patient? But litigation is no emergency. Either litigant can find another consulting firm to do what the Prophets reneged, for whatever reason, on doing. The justifiability of the breach would depend on why it was being done.

Breaching an agreement to make more money or to work for a client of more pleasing aroma are reasons that would be well within the contemplation of a firm at the time of taking on a client. Therefore, in agreeing to take the case, the Prophets were well aware that more attractive clients might come along later whom they might have to forego as a result of their prior agreement with someone else. So these are quite routine circumstances for a business and ideal circumstances under which to be bound by a prior agreement to work with someone (not to mention the lawsuit for breach of contract that could greet their decision).

I gather from the problem that the two potential clients were approached at essentially the same time. I presume that the companies were not accepted as clients right then and there on the phone; this would enable Jury Dynamics Inc. to check if any conflicts of interest existed between a prospective client and existing clients. If that is correct, then there is no prior-order problem, and the issue is which client to choose.

2. Can a client be refused because of existing clients who present conflicts of interest?

This is a familiar reason for not taking a case. If a later client's relationship to an earlier client would produce a motivational tug-of-war so that either or both would get less than the faithful and vigorous service they have a right to expect, then the conflict should be avoided by not accepting the new client.

Suppose there would not be a conflict of interest, but the appearance of one would be unavoidable: Zack and some of the staff could work on ISC's case, Martha and some other staff could work on SBWET's, they could each do a highly competent job for their respective clients, and they could keep each group so insulated from the other that no information about one passed to the other. The question here is whether only reality (not appearance) matters. Or is appearance part of the reality? If the clients, the profession, or the public would view the two-client arrangement as problematic, maybe that in itself makes it a problem to be avoided. Or perhaps the mere risk of compromising either client's interests is enough to counsel against taking on both.

Clearly, the safe and conventional thing to do is to take only one of the prospective clients.

3. May one choose to work only for those clients whose values comport with one's own?

Martha and Zack sit down to decide between the two clients who seek their services. They have to choose one over the other. Is it ethically permissible to make that choice on the basis of whose values and politics they prefer?

If they choose the one they like better, they can feel especially good about their work, can really put their hearts into it, and so on. It is better for them, and better for the client.

On the other hand, what would happen if all trial consulting firms were on one or the other side of the political fence and all refused to work for people from the "other" side? This would introduce a distortion into the litigation process that would systematically disadvantage one kind of person or organization. In the face of such a happening, the legal system might sensibly outlaw trial consultation services. But maybe it depends on which side the consultants lean toward. If they all lean toward corporate interests, the less well endowed (who may be more likely to represent the less well organized public interest) may have little hope of gaining the same help. If the situation were reversed, the better endowed business interests stand a far better chance of finding someone to take their money in exchange for trial consultation services. (This is exactly what has happened: Many of the people who began the jury consultation business to help politically antiestablishment causes, often for no remuneration, did not take long to make their services available to corporations that wanted to pay for them.)

Would the services of professionals be more honorably offered if the professionals remained neutral on the question of the client's worthiness as a person or organization or the political values reflected in the client's cause? Or would professionals be more honorable if they refused to be a hired gun for just anybody, and instead they worked only for people of whom they approved?

Lawyers and physicians, for example, have confronted this problem. To become a professional is to give up some of the freedom to pick and choose to whom you want to offer your services. Society as a whole makes it possible for you to be what you are; all members of society have a fair claim on your services without you judging them. Should a doctor ask about your politics before deciding whether to treat you? One of the admirable things about their profession that they refrain from conditioning their services on such judgments. Lawyers have a tougher time. They generally subscribe to the same neutrality about clients, and yet they are criticized for a willingness to serve as hired guns for anybody. Perhaps that is because lawyers become more visible agents in advancing the interests of the persons they represent. (But don't doctors do the same, though less directly? The doctor who kept Hitler well allowed him to kill another day.) Trial consultants may be in a similar situation as the lawyer: They will be seen as more immediate agents advancing the cause of a client.

Perhaps for the same reason that lawyers have an ethic of representing anyone and everyone, trial consultants need to do the same. But to do so safely and effectively that ethic has to become an explicit norm of the field, something trial consultants can point to and be able to say it would be unethical to refuse to serve. The risk of not taking this course is that politically unpopular people, causes, and organizations would find themselves treated unfairly in the legal process, with trial consultants exacerbating that risk.

4. May one prefer clients who pay more over clients who pay less?

This issue looks much like the preceding one, except that now the criterion is money. Martha and Zack sit down to decide between the two clients who seek their services. They have to choose one over the other. Is it ethically permissible to make that choice on the basis that one seeks a discount, whereas the other is likely to provide considerable future business at top rates?

Well, what are Martha and Zack in business for, to go broke? They owe it to themselves and their employees, and they have a duty to their shareholders (if they have any) to make a handsome profit.

But much like the preceding problem, the difficulty is that if the best consultants or all consultants work only for those who can pay the most, then those who can pay the least (or nothing at all) will find themselves systematically disadvantaged.

Again, the problem has been confronted by lawyers and physicians. The practical answer is that a majority of them work mostly and hardest for those who will pay the most. But both professions and society have recognized this as a problem and have taken steps to mitigate its most unfair effects. Trial consultants are unlikely to be able to follow the lead of physicians and make their services more widely available through private insurance or social welfare funds. Lawyers are made available to those with limited or no resources through assigned counsel and public defenders or the legal services corporation (for civil matters). Lawyers also have imposed on themselves the ethical obligation of providing services free pro bono publico (for the public interest or welfare).

Trial consultants face a similar situation, but they are unlikely to be made a part of the nation's social welfare system any time soon. However, they do create a social problem that they have some responsibility to solve. As individuals and as a profession, trial consultants should seriously consider following the law's lead with an obligation to accept some portion of their clients each year on a pro bono publico basis.

If Martha and Zack have not served a poor or unpopular client in a while, they should seriously consider taking on **SBWET** as a client.

View From the Bench

Jonathan Brant

This problems is less a question of ethics than one of practical business decisions. Zack and Martha Prophet have established a corporation to offer their consulting services about jury selection and jury behavior. In a legal sense, the corporate entity Jury Dynamics Inc. is a person. As such, the corporation may not be involved on both sides of a legal issue. It would be unethical behavior because the principals in the corporation would have access to the thinking of the opponent.

Zack and Martha must decide which side to take on as a client. If Zack made a commitment to represent International Solvent Corporation (ISC), there is at least a moral obligation to take on that side. However, there would be no legal commitment until a retainer is paid. As a practical matter, if Zack and Martha decide to work for Sky Blue Waters Environmental Trust (SBWET), I rather suspect that ICS would gladly take their business elsewhere, even had a retainer been wired in the few minutes that passed before SBWET called Martha. Therefore, the fact that ISC made the earlier contact is not determinative.

Zack and Martha must make their determination based on all of the factors that are significant to them in operation of their business. These may include cash flow, political views, and any other factors that motivate them. This decision is likely to have long-term repercussions. More than likely, in as contested an areas as environmental litigation, the side they scorn in this litigation will not return as a client. Thus, they must elect whether they prefer to be industry or environmental advocates. In addition, because ISC offers the probability of a greater amount of billings, Zack and Martha must consider the practical issue of their financial goals and needs.

Any decision that Zack and Martha make is appropriate. It is ethical for them to represent ISC as long as they can provide their services in a professional manner. They do not have to endorse all of the activities of ISC in order to serve as consultants to it. Similarly, it is ethical for Zack and Martha to elect to represent SBWET. Zack and Martha may have strong views about the environment and apply those views to their work. It is ethical to elect favored work over more remunerative work.

As long as Zack and Martha are comfortable with their election, they have made the right decision.

NOTES

This section of the journal features a fictionalized case vignette that embodies one or more important and complex ethical dilemmas with professional or public policy overtones. Each case is accompanied by two or more independently crafted commentaries of approximately 1,000 words by experts with diverse backgrounds and perspectives. Readers are invited to submit cases and brief follow-up commentaries that raise new and important issues.

Requests for reprints of the Forum section should be sent to the Editor, Gerald P. Koocher, Department of Psychiatry, Children's Hospital, 300 Longwood Avenue, Boston, MA 02115.

DYNAMICS OF AGGRESSION
Biological and Social Processes in Dyads and Groups
Edited by
Michael Potegal
Department of Medical Neuroscience, WRAIR/WRAMC Division of Neuropsychiatry, Washington, D.C.
John Knutson
University of Iowa

This book emerged from a symposium on the temporal aspects of aggression focusing on this common denominator: When aggression is analyzed over time, escalations in the form or intensity of aggression often appear. The editors felt that a focus on such escalations, and the dynamics of aggression in general could provide a context in which social or biological research on the aggressive behaviors of human and nonhuman subjects — interacting in dyads or groups — could be compared and integrated.

A diversity of chapters on aggression and its vicissitudes has been assembled — describing aggressive behavior at different levels of analysis in a variety of animal species including Siamese fighting fish, laboratory strains of the house mouse, Syrian golden hamsters as well as human beings. A major question being addressed by this juxtaposition is whether it is possible to discern general principles controlling the dynamics of aggression.

Three basic interpretations of escalation are delineated by the book's contributors:
- aggression will be escalated when it pays one of the combatants to do so or more generally, when the potential benefits outweigh the risks
- emphasis is on processes within the individual
- the interaction between antagonists — an emerging event

Contents: Part I:*Differing Perspectives on Aggression Dynamics: Introduction to Game Theoretical Analyses and Arousal Hypotheses.* **J. Archer, F. Huntingford,** Game Theory Models and Escalation of Animal Fights. **L. Berkowitz,** On the Escalation of Aggression. **Part II:***Aggressive State and Trait: Behavioral and Physiological Processes Within Individuals.* **D. Zillmann,** Cognition-Excitation Interdependencies in the Escalation of Aggression. **M. Potegal,** Aggressive Arousal: The Amygdala Connection. **P.M. Bronstein,** Aggression Waxing (Sometimes Waning): Siamese Fighting Fish. **G.V. Caprara, M. Perugini, C. Barbaranelli,** Studies of Individual Differences in Aggression. **Part III:***Aggression Dynamics in Development: Interaction Within and Outside the Family.* **D. Einon, M. Potegal,** Temper Tantrums in Young Children. **J. Knutson, M. Bower,** Physically Abusive Parenting as an Escalated Aggressive Response. **R.B. Cairns, C. Santoyo, K.A. Holly,** Aggressive Escalation: Toward a Developmental Analysis. **Part IV:***Aggression Dynamics in Larger Social and Political Contexts: Game Theory Revisited.* **J. Bohstedt,** The Dynamics of Riots: Escalation and Diffusion/Contagion. **R.J. Leng,** Interstate Crisis Escalation and War.
0-8058-0729-2 [cloth] / July 1994 / approx. 352pp. / $69.95
Special Prepaid Offer! $34.50
No further discounts apply.

Prices subject to change without notice.

Lawrence Erlbaum Associates, Inc.
365 Broadway, Hillsdale, NJ 07642
201/666-4110   FAX 201/666-2394

LEA

Call toll-free to order: **1-800-9-BOOKS-9**...9am to 5pm EST only.
e-mail to: orders@leahq.mhs.compuserve.com

Subscription Order Form

Please ❏ enter ❏ renew my subscription to

ETHICS & BEHAVIOR
Volume 4, 1994, Quarterly

Subscription prices per volume:

Individual: ❏ $27.50 (US/Canada)   ❏ $52.50 (All Other Countries)
Institution: ❏ $150.00 (US/Canada) ❏ $175.00 (All Other Countries)

Subscriptions are entered on a calendar-year basis only and must be prepaid in US currency -- check, money order, or credit card. Institutional checks for individual orders will not be accepted. **Offer expires 12/31/94.**

❏ Payment Enclosed
   Total Amount Enclosed $_____

❏ Charge My Credit Card
   ❏ VISA   ❏ MasterCard   ❏ AMEX   ❏ Discover

   Exp. Date_____

   Card Number _____

   Signature _____
           (Credit card orders cannot be processed without your signature.)

Please print clearly to ensure proper delivery.

Name _____

Address _____

_____

City _____ State _____ Zip+4 _____
           Prices are subject to change without notice.

Lawrence Erlbaum Associates, Inc.
Journal Subscription Department
365 Broadway, Hillsdale, New Jersey 07642
(201) 666-4110   FAX (201) 666-2394

JUSTICE IN THE WORKPLACE
Approaching Fairness in Human Resource Management

edited by
Russell Cropanzano
Colorado State University
A VOLUME IN THE APPLIED PSYCHOLOGY SERIES

In recent years the administrative sciences have provided a variety of techniques for allocating pay, resolving grievances, evaluating performance, testing for illicit substances, providing feedback, and just about any other activity that an organization must perform. However, what is often missing from these systems is an understanding and appreciation of human consequences. In a very real sense, every one of these techniques is about people. These systems stand or fall largely on how individuals react to them.

Borrowing from the work of social psychologists, sociologists, and legal scholars, this book addresses how people respond to organizational interventions. A diverse set of organizational policies is discussed, including techniques for maintaining customer satisfaction, managing layoffs, providing effective performance feedback, administering compensation systems, conducting drug tests, and resolving conflicts. Psychological and sociological research is applied in an effort to understand the ways in which individuals respond to organizational policies and procedures. The research shows not only that the human side of management is important, but also contains suggestions for more effective organizational interventions. The anticipated result: application of these techniques to make organizations better and more productive places to work.

Contents: E.A. Fleishman, Series Forward. **Part I:** *Introducing Justice to the Workplace.* **R.C. Cropanzano, M. Randall,** Injustice and Work Behavior: An Historical Review. **K. James,** The Social Context of Organizational Justice: Cultural, Intergroup, and Structural Effects on Justice Behaviors and Perceptions. **D. Shapiro,** Reconciling Theoretical Differences Among Procedural Justice Researchers by Re-evaluating What it Means to Have One's Views "Considered": Implications for Third-Party Managers. **J. Greenberg,** The Social Side of Fairness: Interpersonal and Informational Classes of Organizational Justice. **Part II:** *Hiring, Firing, and Evaluations.* **R. Folger, D. Lewis,** Self-Appraisal and Fairness in Evaluations. **M.A. Konovsky, J. Brockner,** Managing Victim and Survivor Layoff Reactions. **R.A. Baron,** Criticism (Informal Negative Feedback) as a Source of Perceived Unfairness in Organizations: Effects, Mechanisms, and Countermeasures. **M.A. Konovsky, R. Cropanzano,** Justice Considerations in Employee Drug Testing. **E.C. Clemmer,** An Investigation of the Relationship Between Fairness and Customer Satisfaction. **Part III:** *Justice at the Organizational and Interorganizational Level.* **M. Citera, J.R. Rentsch,** Is There Justice in Organizational Acquisitions? The Role of Distributive and Procedural Fairness in Corporate Acquisitions. **M.E. Gordon, G.E. Fryxell,** The Role of Interpersonal Justice in Organizational Grievance Systems. **M.P. Miceli,** Justice and Pay System Satisfaction.
0-8058-1055-2 / 1993 / 304pp. /$59.95
**Special Prepaid Offer! $34.50
No further discounts apply.**

Prices are subject to
change without notice.

Lawrence Erlbaum Associates, Inc.
365 Broadway, NJ 07642
201/666-4110   FAX 201/666-2394

Call toll-free to order: 1-800-9-BOOKS-9...9am to 5pm EST only
e-mail to: orders@leahq.mhs.compuserve.com

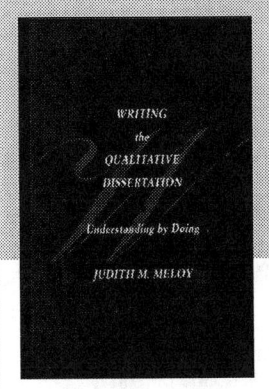

WRITING THE QUALITATIVE DISSERTATION
Understanding by Doing
Judith Meloy
CASTLETON STATE COLLEGE

Doing qualitative research for one's thesis requires a conscious, internal awareness within the external structural, political, and human context of higher education. This book is the result of a desire to fill a void that had not yet been addressed in a text format -- the needs and confusions of the doctoral student selecting qualitative methodologies for his/her dissertation research. That desire, emerging from a noticeable lack of resources during the author's studies, finally led to an exhaustive research project. 20 individuals -- from a range of disciplines including communication, sociology, nursing, and education -- corresponded with the author about the structure and format of their "qualitative" dissertations. Their reflections describe some of the interactions and sources of ambiguity that are a part of the process of qualitative research and hence of concern to doctoral students choosing such methodologies for their thesis research. Their questions, concerns, and ideas highlight the complexity of the concept of the researcher as the human instrument. Although many "how to" books already exist, this is the first one that explicates the feelings, meanings, and concerns of those who have been through it. Conceptions about the "whole" of a research project, committee-student interaction, and learning by doing are foundational to this volume.

Different from other texts about qualitative research in many ways, this volume's
- style is informal, reflecting the personal and personable nature of the research
- data are letters
- organization begins with a chapter about "the end," where an amount of certainty and confidence finally emerge for the novice qualitative researcher
- chapters feature one or more sets of "questions" meant to serve as a possible guide to decision making and subsequent action for those to whom they may not have occurred.

Contents: Foreword. Introduction. Understanding by Finishing: The End Is the Beginning. Understanding at the Beginning: Selecting and Working with a Committee. Understanding by Proposing: Preparing and Defending the Proposal/Prospectus. Supporting Understanding: Maximizing Resources. Understanding by Focusing: Connecting Focus, Literature and Ownership. Understanding by Writing: Keeping a Journal. Understanding by Doing: Methodology, Analysis, Etc. Understanding by Finishing: Defining "the End." Beginning with Endings. **Appendices:** Original Letter to Correspondents. Tables of Contents. **Indices:** Topic. Questions. Correspondents.
0-8058-1416-7 [cloth] / 1994 / 128pp. / $29.95
0-8058-1417-5 [paper] / $14.95

LAWRENCE ERLBAUM ASSOCIATES, INC.
365 Broadway, Hillsdale, NJ 07642
201/666-4110   FAX 201/666-2394

Prices subject to change without notice.

Call toll-free to order: 1-800-9-BOOKS-9...9am to 5pm EST only.
e-mail to: orders@leahq.mhs.compuserve.com

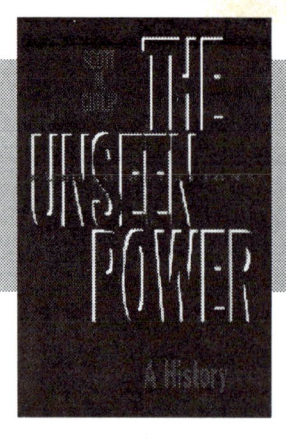

THE UNSEEN POWER PUBLIC RELATIONS
A History
Scott M. Cutlip
Dean Emeritus, The University of Georgia

Based largely on primary sources, this book presents the first detailed history of public relations from 1900 through the 1960s. The author utilized the personal papers of John Price Jones, Ivy L. Lee, Harry Bruno, William Baldwin III, John W. Hill, Earl Newsom as well as extensive interviews -- conducted by the author himself -- with Pendleton Dudley, T.J. Ross, Edward Bernays, Harry Bruno, William Baldwin, and more. Consequently, the book provides practitioners, scholars, and students with a realistic inside view of the way public relations has developed and been practiced in the United States since its beginnings in mid-1900. For example, the book tells how:

- President Roosevelt's reforms of the Square Deal brought the first publicity agencies to the nation's capital.
- Edward L. Bernays, Ivy Lee, and Albert Lasker made it socially acceptable for women to smoke in the 1920s.
- William Baldwin III saved the now traditional Macy's Thanksgiving Day parade.
- Ben Sonnenberg took Pepperidge Farm bread from a small town Connecticut bakery to the nation's supermarket shelves -- and made millions doing it.
- Two Atlanta publicists, Edward Clark and Bessie Tyler, took a defunct Atlanta bottle club, the Ku Klux Klan, in 1920 and boomed it into a hate organization of three million members in three years, and made themselves rich in the process.
- Earl Newsom failed to turn mighty General Motors around when it was besieged by Ralph Nader and Congressional advocates of auto safety.

This book documents the tremendous role public relations practitioners play in our nation's economic, social, and political affairs -- a role that goes generally unseen and unobserved by the average citizen whose life is affected in so many ways by the some 150,000 public relations practitioners.

Contents: Prologue: The Unseen Power. **Part I:** *The Early Years of Public Relations, 1900-1919.* Introduction. Number One: The Publicity Bureau. The First Two Washington Agencies. Parker & Lee, Then Lee Harris Lee. Hamilton Wright Organization Pioneers International Public Relations. Pendleton Dudley Starts Fifth Agency in 1909. **Part II:** *The Booming Twenties, 1919-1930.* Introduction. Ivy Lee Returns to New York, Is Joined by T.J. Ross. Edward L. Bernays: Pioneer, Philosopher, Centurion. Bernays: The Counselor, His Genius, His Role in the Profession. John Price Jones Tries to Ride Two Horses. Steve Hannagan: America's Super Press Agent. Harry Bruno: Aviation and Public Relations Pioneer. William Baldwin: Citizen and Counselor. Ben Sonnenberg: Sui Generis. Clarke and Tyler: Builders of the Ku Klux Klan. John W. Hill Starts in Cleveland, Moves to New York. John W. Hill: Steel, Tobacco, and the Person. **Part III:** *The Depression Years and Beyond.* Introduction. Carl Byoir: The Little Giant of Public Relations. Carl Byoir: Years of Success and Storm. Whitaker & Baxter: Architects of the New Politics. Earl Newsom: Counselor to Corporate Giants. Earl Newsom: Counselor to Ford, then GM. Earl Newsom and the Ford Foundation. Epilogue: A Perspective on Today's Practice.

0-8058-1464-7 [cloth] / 1994 / 808pp. / $125.00
0-8058-1465-5 [paper] / $39.95

Prices subject to change without notice.

Lawrence Erlbaum Associates, Inc.
365 Broadway, Hillsdale, NJ 07642
201/666-4110   FAX 201/666-2394

Call toll-free to order: 1-800-9-BOOKS-9...9am to 5pm EST only.
e-mail to: orders@leahq.mhs.compuserve.com